Eriugena

Medieval Irish Philosopher, Poet, and Translator

Eriugena

Medieval Irish Philosopher, Poet, and Translator

Eoghan Mac Aogáin

evertype
2017

Published by Evertype, 73 Woodgrove, Portlaoise, R32 ENP6, Ireland. *www.evertype.com*.

Second, revised edition 2017. First edition published in 2015 with the title *Eriugena: An Introduction* by Original Writing, Dublin, ISBN 978-1-78237-857-0

A catalogue record for this book is available from the British Library.

ISBN-10 1-78201-191-9
ISBN-13 978-1-78201-191-0

Typeset in Baskerville by Michael Everson.

Cover design by Michael Everson. The image is of St John the Evangelist, from the Irish Evangelary (8th–9th century), St. Gallen Stiftsbibliothek.

Printed and bound by LightningSource.

Contents

For my sister, Annette

Preface

This book is an introduction to the life and work of the Irish philosopher Johannes Scottus Eriugena (c. 800–870). Like many Irish scholars of his time he emigrated to the Continent where he had the good fortune to become a close friend of the Emperor, Charles the Bald (823–877), serving him as Court Poet and Master of the Palace School somewhere in the vicinity of the modern city of Laon, north-east of Paris. Since the publication of the first full-length biography of Eriugena by the Belgian scholar Dom Maïeul Cappuyns in 1933, he has become one of the most studied of all medieval intellectuals in recent times. But the extensive literature that now exists on him has been written mostly for students of philosophy and medieval history, and so I wrote this short book in the hope of bringing his work to a more general readership.

When I gave talks on Eriugena here in Dublin, listeners constantly asked where they might find the passages from his work that I had read to them. Evidently they wanted to read him for themselves. This is exactly what I wanted to hear, but it also poses a problem: the English translations, if they exist at all, lie scattered in books that can be difficult to come by. So, having selected the short passages that I would like newcomers to read first, I translated them again, and around them I have written the story of Eriugena's life and his extraordinary account of "all the things that are and those that are not."

Having done that much, however, I found that I was obliged to do the same again for the three Byzantine scholars whose work he translated into Latin, Gregory of Nyssa, Dionysius the Areopagite, and Maximus the Confessor; and likewise for the Graeco-Roman poet and educationalist Martianus Capella whose famous Latin textbook for the teaching of the Liberal Arts was richly annotated by Eriugena for his students. He was greatly indebted to all four, in both the content and presentation of his work, and I felt that they too needed to be heard in their own words.

There was another reason for the text-based approach: Eriugena was a poet, and even in his most abstract work he writes in a style that lies somewhere between prose and poetry. I have tried to acknowledge this in my selections and translations, partly just to complete the picture and also because Eriugena's poetry is an important part of the aesthetic that pervades his work.

He was also a naturalist and a scientist, and this is another perspective I have retained. Not only was he enthralled by the beauty of nature, he also wanted to understand its origins and composition. Above all else, he sought a more adequate account of the functioning of the human mind, in both anatomical and psychological terms, and a fuller account of where it stands in relation to the rest of Creation.

Finally, I present Eriugena as a thinker who was affected deeply by the division of Christianity into its Greek and Latin traditions. The schism was already a bitter reality in the scholarly environment in which he worked, and it soon brought him into open conflict with Church authorities since his sympathies were with the Greeks.

The book has separate chapters on Martianus, Gregory, Dionysius, and Maximus and what Eriugena had to say about them, and seven chapters on his own work, one for the *Book on Predestination*, one for the homily and commentary on John's Gospel, one each for the five books of *Periphyseon* (Concerning Natures), and a concluding chapter, followed by chapter summaries. Martianus is placed first because Eriugena began his career as a teacher of the humanities and sciences, and the influence of Martianus is evident from his earliest writings. The chapter on Gregory has been placed before *The Book on Predestination* because this is where I think it belongs in the development of Eriugena's thinking. And while *Periphyseon* was not Eriugena's last work, it is kept until last because it gives the best overview.

My thanks to Coiscéim for permission to use some materials on Eriugena here that were previously published in Irish (Mac Aogáin, 2009), to the staff of Trinity College Library, where most of the research was done, to Breandán Ó Cíobháin for our discussions of Eriugena, and to Paddy Sammon and Seán McCrum for reading the manuscript and making many useful comments on it.

Eoghan Mac Aogáin
Dublin, February 2017

Abbreviations

CCCM	Corpus Christianorum Continuatio Mediaevalis
CCSG	Corpus Christianorum Series Graeca
CCSL	Corpus Christianorum Series Latina
PG	Patrologia Graeca
PL	Patrologia Latina

AdIo	Ad Iohannem (Maximus). *PG* 91, 1061–1418
AdTh	Ad Thalassium (Maximus). Laga & Steele (1980, 1990)
AM	Annotationes in Martianum (Eriugena). Lutz (1939)
AM2	Annotationes in Martianum 2 (Eriugena). Jeauneau (1978a)
Carm	Carmina (Eriugena). Herren (1993)
ComJ	Commentary on John (Eriugena). Jeauneau (2008)
DeIm	De Imagine (Gregory of Nyssa). *PG* 44, 123C–256C
DeNupt	De Nuptiis (Martianus Capella). Willis (1983)
DePr	De Praedestinatione Liber (Eriugena). Mainoldi (2003)
DN	De Divina Nomina (Dionysius). *PG* 3, 585A–984A
ExpIC	Expositiones in Ierarchiam Coelestem (Eriugena). Barbet (1975)
HC	Hiérarchie Céleste (Dionysius). Heil (1970)
HomJ	Homily on Prologue to John (Eriugena). Jeauneau (2008)
MT	De Mystica Theologia (Dionysius). *PG* 3, 997A–1064A
PP1–5	*Periphyseon 1–5.* (Eriugena). Jeauneau (1996, 1997, 1999a, 2000, 2003)

Chapter 1

Martianus Capella

Martianus Capella was a Roman writer of Greek stock who lived in the fifth century CE. He is thought to have been from North Africa but little is known for sure about him except that he was the author of *De Nuptiis Mercurii et Philologiae* (*The Wedding of Mercury and Philologia*), a textbook for the seven liberal arts, namely Grammar, Dialectic (i.e. logic), Rhetoric, Geometry, Mathematics, Astronomy, and Music. *De Nuptiis* is a wonderful book, crammed with information about the life and culture of the educated classes in the last days of pre-Christian Europe, and also an excellent school book. Written partly in verse and partly in prose, the teaching material is enclosed in an amusing frame-story set among the planets and stars of the night sky, symbols of the Gods, Goddesses, and Muses of the Greek Pantheon. Mercury has come of age and begins his search for a suitable bride, eventually choosing the Muse Philologia on the advice of Apollo (the sun, and also Mercury's brother). Apollo then calls the Gods and Goddesses to a meeting in his celestial palace, first to agree to the marriage, then to celebrate it, and finally, to learn all about the liberal arts. For Mercury's wedding gift to his bride Philologia consists of the seven Muses of the liberal arts, members of his own household who are henceforth to be her personal servants, and once the wedding is over they are called upon, one by one, to tell their stories to the assembled Pantheon.

Eriugena admired Martianus's work greatly and wrote a line by line commentary on it, probably for students of his at the palace school of Charles the Bald where he is known to have been a teacher of the liberal arts in the 840s. The rest of this chapter will consist of some extracts from *Book 1* of Martianus's text and the comments that Eriugena had to make on them. I selected the passages with two purposes in mind, firstly to give the reader an idea of the Neoplatonic world-view that Eriugena shared with Martianus, and secondly, to show him at work as a humanities teacher using a pre-Christian text to discuss some of the same moral and philosophical themes that will occupy him later in his work as a Christian philosopher.

Martianus and *De Nuptiis*

Here is how Eriugena introduces Martianus to his students:

> I discovered that Martianus, the author of this story, was a Carthaginian and also a Roman citizen and hence, in accordance with Latin tradition, a *tetranomos*, i.e. he had four names, *Martianus*, *Minneus*, *Felix* and *Capella*. *Martianus* was his personal name, *Minneus* is from the colour for he is said to have been red-headed, *Felix* for happy, although we don't know whether he lived happily or otherwise, and he was called *Capella* [she-goat] as if a Satyress[1] had reared him or been his mentor—it is not entirely clear from his writings. He was mischievous because he had the wantonness of a poet, and when he ought to have been a philosopher instead he changes his mind, not I suspect because he actually changed it but because he pretended to do so, for he had the name of being something of an actor who mixed pretence with true philosophical reasoning in the manner of a poet. The way his work is written clearly shows Martianus to have been highly skilled in both languages, Greek and Latin, and anybody who has examined his writings will not deny that he was a disciple of Marcus Tullius Cicero, whether he worked during the latter's life-time or after his death, for the examples and arguments he uses in the chapter *De Rhetorica* come exclusively from him. Wishing to write about the disciplines of the seven liberal arts, he made up a story about the marriage of Philologia and Mercury, an impossible task without great reserves of talent. Philologia actually stands for the study of reason, and Mercury for fluency of speech, as if they had come together in a kind of marriage in the minds of those engaged in the study of wisdom—a very obvious

---

1   A mythical creature, half woman half goat.

and self-evident reference to the knowledge and practice of the liberal arts. (*AM*, p. 3)

Eriugena was not the only one to write notes on Martianus.[2] Even in his time the book would have been difficult for Christian readers, partly because it assumes a good knowledge of the Greek Pantheon and also because of sudden twists in its complex story-line, while in the later books on Geometry, Mathematics, Astronomy and Music, the text is often difficult because Martianus does not have a good grasp of the fragments of Greek learning he is trying to revive. Eriugena tries to keep his distance from the pagan writer, accusing him of mixing "true philosophical reasoning" with the fictions of poetry and drama. But he was accused of doing exactly the same thing himself.

Eriugena knew *De Nuptiis* well, and indeed his notes are still a great help to a modern reader of Martianus. He intervenes where necessary to explain who is speaking to whom, he paraphrases difficult sentences, or else puts Martianus's words in a different order that will be easier for the learner. He is aware of alternative readings that are to be found in other manuscripts, and draws attention to sentences that may have been transcribed incorrectly. He queries some of the information provided by Martianus, and at other times dismisses it out of hand, and he is not slow to give his own views on topics of special interest to him, even when their relevance to Martianus's text is slight. Above all else, he is at pains to translate and explain the many Greek words that are to be found in *De Nuptiis* and everything else to do with the world of Greek learning and mythology, since he shared Martianus's primary objective of reviving Greek culture in the Latin West. *De Nuptiis* was therefore an ideal manual for the Carolingian renaissance then being promoted by the Emperor in the palace school. This "breviary of the middle ages," as Jeauneau calls it, "studded with Greek words, could not fail to revive among Carolingian scholars the desire to learn the language of the Gods and the Muses" (1979, p. 16).

2   Ramelli (2006) contains the notes of six commentators on Martianus, beginning with Eriugena.

The world-view of *De Nuptiis* is a pre-Christian variety of Neoplatonism, a philosophy in the idealist tradition in which the universe and the human mind are taken to be aspects of the same reality. The sun and the invisible ether around it are identified with divine intellect, the stars and planets stand for various cultural domains, while human thought and feeling are represented by the earth and its changeable atmosphere. And the mind itself— "consciousness" as we would call it—is taken to be to be part of the immaterial "fire" of the divinity that has somehow made its way to earth, where it now finds itself embedded in the natural world, most notably (but not exclusively) in the mind of the human, with a mission to return Creation to the realm of the supernatural.

The Hymn to Hymen

De Nuptiis contains a good many poems, one to open each of the nine books, and many more scattered throughout the text—a common practice in scholarly writing of Martianus's time. Here is the first poem, in which he calls for the assistance of Hymen, Goddess of weddings, to whom *De Nuptiis* is dedicated.

You sing at weddings, they say, to the sound of your lyre,
born of a Muse, a sacred bond between the Gods,
binding together the warring seeds with secret chains
inspiring opposites to combine in holy embrace,
for you link the elements and bring the world to fruition
merging the breath of mind with inanimate things,
through the law of delight that holds nature together
reconciling the sexes in the pledge of love;
O beauteous Hymen, protected child of Venus,
your face alight with love inspired by Cupid,
your fondness for the dance perhaps, child of Bacchus,
or the wedding songstress, on your mother's side,
or because the three Graces asked you, one of their own,
to garland the thresholds with flowers in spring—
whatever the reason, it is you who are chosen to bless the opening
of Calliope's song about the wedding of a God. (*DeNupt*, pp. 1–2)

This is the Neoplatonic ideal of universal harmony, the music of the heavens bringing opposites of all kinds together in accordance with "the law of delight." The world that seems at first to be fixed is in fact an invisible balance of opposites that is in a constant state of renewal. Nothing can endure without interacting with its opposite. The warring elements of the physical world must bind together to assure its continued existence, likewise the sexes of the living world, and even the brute material world continues to survive only because immaterial mind has also been breathed into it.

Eriugena begins his notes by explaining the term "Muse" and then turns to Hymen's name:

> To understand the etymology of the name "Hymen" you need to know that medical science shows there to be three *membranulae*[3] in the bodies of animals, two of which are found in the male sex, and all three in the female. There is the *membranula* of the cerebrum which the Greeks call the μήνιγγα [*ménigga*][4] that is common to all animals, rational and irrational, from which the five-fold tubes of the senses emanate. Also found in both sexes is the *membranula* that separates the innards, that is, the lower organs of the abdomen, from the higher organs of the chest, namely the liver, heart and arteries, which the Greeks call φρήν [*phrén*] (from which we get the word "frenetics"). The *membranula* of the womb, on the other hand, in which new-born children are conceived, is specific to the female gender and called ὑμήν [*hymén*] by the Greeks, from which we get "Hymenaeus," the defender of earthly new-borns in the stories of the poets. (*AM*, pp. 3–4)

The *ménigga* or meninges, the three internal linings of the skull that enclose the brain and the spinal cord, will be mentioned again in Eriugena's work.[5] Greek anatomists believed that this was the organ

---

3   *Membranula* i.e. "a little membrane," i.e. one that is thin and film-like.

4   Greek words are given in Greek script, followed by a Latin transliteration in [square brackets].

5   Below, p. 160.

in which vision, hearing, touch, taste, and smell were brought together, since it appeared to them to be the only part of the brain that was in physical contact with all five organs of sensation. This was of special interest since they held that the beauty of the natural world—which for many of them was the presence of God in Creation—was based on the merging of the five senses into a harmonious totality.

The phrase "for you link the elements," in the fifth line of the poem, gives Eriugena the opportunity to teach a little physics, pointing out that the world as it appears to us is held together by combinations of its four invisible elements, fire, air, water and earth:

> The universal structure of this visible world is woven together from four elements, fire, air, water and earth, and each of the elements I refer to has its own special quality, the quality of fire being heat, of air humidity, of water frigidity, and of earth dryness. From these four qualities physics shows that six συζυγία [*syzygía*], namely compounds, can be constructed through natural linkage … (*AM*, p. 4)

This is a long note (only the beginning is shown here) in which Eriugena gives a summary of the medieval table of elements. Although it could be justified on the grounds that the words *nexus* and *elementum*, i.e. "bond" and "element," in Martianus's poem were technical terms in the physics of the time, it is also the first of many examples of Eriugena's eagerness to place Martianus's account of the seven liberal arts in a broader setting that also includes biology, anatomy, and physics.

Jupiter and Juno

Developing the theme of universal love, Martianus takes the case of Jupiter, father of the Gods, and his wife Juno. "For all the joys of heaven," he says, "nothing is sweeter to Jupiter than his own wife" (*DeNupt*, pp. 2–3) which is the reason experienced priests advise people to switch their offerings to Juno if they are not getting the desired response from Jupiter.

Eriugena paraphrases what Martianus has to say on the matter:

> So if it should happen that people are in doubt about their affairs, having burned many offerings in the hope of obtaining a definite response from Jupiter while he, unwilling to be swayed by the multitude of sacrificed animals and spurning the offerings of mortals—because he is harsh in some ways—should refuse to give a definite answer, then, as soon as these people take wiser counsel, realizing the futility of their sacrifices to Jupiter and turning to Juno instead and placating her with sacrifices, there is no doubt that everything Jupiter previously refused them will come to pass without delay through the intercession of Juno's humanity (so to speak) and her feminine quality. (*AM*, p. 6)

And as he often does, Eriugena now moves from matters of psychology to their physical foundations in the elemental properties of fire, air, earth and water:

> There is a physical aspect to this. When the earth is dry and barren and its seeds are not just withering but actually dying because of excessive drought, then, following a natural impulse it looks for the assistance of the fiery element (from which comes everything that originates from earth and water) so that they can be born and begin to move. But if the humidity of the air, symbolized here by Juno, is not present, the heat of the fiery element is of no help at all to the barren earth since it is through the humidity of the air and the coldness of water that the power of fire develops and nourishes everything born of earth. (*AM*, pp. 6-7)

And finally, having linked the mental and physical domains, Eriugena relates them both to the structure of the cosmos. Jupiter is the fiery sun at the pinnacle of the universe, pure and unchanging, a symbol of divine intellect, while the turbulent air around the earth, identified with Juno, stands for the human mind, bereft of intuitive or angelic intellect, as a consequence of the Fall, and forced to struggle with instincts and emotions in its efforts to make sense of its surroundings through its distinctive but often inadequate powers of reasoning. So when Jupiter and Juno are seated on their thrones, Martianus notes that the face of Jupiter shows "immutable happiness" while Juno looks "troubled" (*DeNupt*, p. 20). Eriugena comments:

> The difference between Jupiter and Juno, that is, between fire and air, he says, is that the ether[6] is pure and serene and filled with the light of day while the air can sometimes be sad, so to speak, with disturbed clouds and driving rain, while at other times, in fine bright weather, it appears to be smiling, which is the reason the face of Juno is painted to give the impression of change and variation. (*AM*, p. 42)

This easy movement between the domains of mind, matter, cosmos, and divinity is a feature of Eriugena's Neoplatonism, often supported, as it is here, by attending to the remarkable way in which all four are drawn together in the experience of beauty, whether in nature or in art.

Sophia and Psyche

The story begins. Mercury has grown up and it is time for him to get married. So, accompanied by the Muse Virtue he sets out on a journey around the universe to find a suitable bride. His first love is Sophia, for reasons Eriugena explains:

> Anybody who pays close attention to the laws of allegory will discover that in this passage Mercury stands for fluent speech or abundance of eloquence. This is why Mercury himself is called "Hermes" or "speech" by the Greeks. For it is eloquent and fluent speech that provide the best proof and the crowning glory of the rational nature that is known to be unique to the human. And since speech itself, to the extent that it is fluent and enhanced by the rules of eloquence, appears to run from person to person, it is reasonable to

---

6   Ether: the invisible fire that was believed to fill the area between the sun and the earth's atmosphere.

accept that this is the meaning of the name *Mercury*. So *Mercurius* is said to be *medius currens* (running in the middle)[7] since speech runs back and forth between people, and not just in a way that is devoid of effect or results, for it is believed that it can actually be destructive unless, like an inviolate virgin, it is strengthened and modulated by modest and temperate love through the beautiful and restraining power of wisdom. So it is not in a fanciful sense but elegantly and truthfully that Mercury is said to be in love with the inviolate beauty of wisdom. As Tully[8] said in the first book of *De Rhetorica*:

> Eloquence without wisdom is never of use and sometimes does harm;
> wisdom without eloquence is sometimes of use and never does harm.

Since the tempered chastity of wisdom flees from the contagion of redundant speech and uncontrolled verbosity, it is not without reason that it is described as having sought out the company of eternal virgins—as conveyed by the image of Pallas—and never wants to be without it. (*AM*, pp. 9–10)

Unfortunately for Mercury, Sophia was actually a daughter of Pallas Athena, and there was no certainty she would be willing to abandon the family tradition of virginity. And even if she did, Mercury would then find himself married to his own niece, since Pallas is his sister. Sophia, therefore, has to be ruled out.

---

7   The "etymologies" or word meanings that abound in Eriugena and other writers of his time have little to do with historical linguistics. They are imaginative reconstructions of the words in question, and at best they provide some images that the writer wishes the reader to associate with them. This is not to say that Eriugena invented his etymologies, however. Like the one he offers here for "Mercurius," most of them can be found in earlier writers.

8   Cicero.

Mercury now sets his eye on Psyche, daughter of Apollo, the sun, and the Muse Entelecheia. She stands for the soul (*anima*), not merely in its spiritual sense but in the more basic sense of "being alive"— the sense it has in the English words "animate" and "animated." Martianus lists some of the gifts that were given her by the Gods and Goddesses when they assembled to celebrate her birth:

> Jupiter placed on her head a crown he had taken from his favourite daughter, Eternity; Juno added a hair band made from a shining vein of the purest gold; and Tritonia Pallas Athena] even opened her brooch and with her petticoat and flame-red breast-band she—herself a holy and wise virgin— covered the other virgin in the clothes from her breast. (*DeNupt*, p. 6)

Eriugena explains the gifts. "The crown," he says, "stands for the immortality and eternity of the rational soul," repeating the same phrase used above in his explanation of Mercury's name. Then he turns to the hair band:

> This passage has more to do with mythology than it has with the study of nature. Why does it say that Juno, who stands for the air around us, gives a hair band (namely density of virtues) to the rational soul? As a myth, it says that the human soul receives eternity from Jupiter and the connective powers of reason from Juno. Yet there are those who argue, not unreasonably, that there is a natural bond linking the intellect with fire, and reason with air. (*AM*, p. 11)

The hair of the head is a symbol of moral character for Eriugena. A few lines later he says "The capacity to identify virtues, which are not unreasonably taken to be somewhat like the hair of the soul, comes from the soul itself, which not merely distinguishes between virtue and vice, but also between one virtue and another by clear definitions" (*AM*, p. 11). It is not out of the question, he suggests, that the hair band and the crown are related to each other in the same way that Jupiter is to Juno, i.e. as intellect is to reason, and fire to air. The hair band (it seems to have been toothed) divides the hair up and gathers it together at the same time, just as the complementary operations of analysis and synthesis simultaneously divide and gather the thoughts of the human in rational inference. It is a symbol of human reasoning, therefore, while the crown is a symbol of divine intellect that has no need of reasoning. By the same logic, human reason is associated with the air of the earth's atmosphere rather than the fire of the sun, and so with Juno rather than Jupiter.

Yet in spite of its lower status, it is only here on earth, in Juno's domain and the disturbed air of the atmosphere, that the beauty of Creation becomes visible to the human:

> Brilliance of all kinds and the variety of diverse colours belong to the air. Although the cause of colours resides in the rays of the sun, the latter produce no visible colour until they are mixed with the air. Colour is created in the freshness of the air, or in water, or in earth through the medium of water, wherever light falls on it. (*AM*, p. 11)

This is the core of Eriugena's aesthetic: the beauty of the natural world is the light of the divinity made visible in it.

Pallas Athena

Before he explains Athena's unusual gift to Psyche, namely some of the clothes she is wearing, Eriugena draws attention to the name by which Martianus refers to her here, *Tritonia* or "three names":

> *Tritonia* is *Pallas* and *Minerva* and *Athena*. She is called *Athena* as in Ἀθάνατος [*Athánatos*], i.e. immortal; similarly *Minerva* as in Μενέρυα [*Menérya*], i.e. incorruptible, *Pallas* as in Ἀπαλός [*Apalós*], i.e. always new, and *Tritonia* as in Τρίτη ἔννοια [*Trítē énnoia*] i.e. the third knowing.[9] For philosophers ascribe the power of immortality to the aspect of the soul that takes up a third of human nature; while there are three rational components of nature, αἴσθησις [*aisthēsis*], λόγος [*lógos*], νοῦς [*noũs*], i.e. perception, reason, mind. It is not inappropriate

---

9   See footnote 7 above on Eriugena's etymologies.

therefore that Tritonia gives her petticoat, i.e. the virtuous-
ness that is most intimate and close to her nature, as a gift to
the rational soul. (*AM*, p. 11)

Clothes, like hair, are also symbols of what lies within. "Not
inappropriately",[10] he says, "the covering of the sacred breast of
Minerva stands for the elegant shield of wise counsel that surrounds
the human soul wherever it goes" (*AM*, p. 12). The triad *Perception–
Reason–Mind/Understanding*, the three levels of mental activity, will be
prominent in all of Eriugena's work. It does not come from
Martianus, however, but from the Greek theologian Maximus the
Confessor.[11]

Turning to the "flame-red breast-band" of Athena, Eriugena
switches his attention once more to matters of anatomy and
physiology, just as he did when explaining Hymen's name earlier.
This time his topic is the thorax, the heart, the lungs, and the
oxygenation of the blood:

> Just as the heart and the lungs have a safe haven within the
> walls of the chest, so does the vital centre, inflamed by winds
> of the spirit, govern from the citadel of a city, not only
> through bodily senses but also through rational convictions.
> And he aptly adds that the breast is dressed in red, since the
> humours by which bodies are nourished and grow naturally
> are initially gathered around the precordium through a
> natural process occurring within the hidden pores of the
> breast. And there, under the intense fire of the heart, which
> while living without mixing with the breezes of the lungs,
> bursting into glowing flames, as it were, from the blood-like
> colour of the scarlet-tinted flames, they take on an
> extraordinary shade of red. (*AM*, p. 12)

---

10 *Non incongrue*, a typical Eriugenian phrase. Double-negative adverbials
    at the beginning of sentences, most notably *non irrationaliter* (not unrea-
    sonably), are a feature of his Latin, and similar constructions such as
    quid mirum si (why should one be surprised if). See Jeauneau, 1978,
    p. 125, note 53.

11 Below, pp. 92–94.

Although Eriugena is referring primarily to matters of anatomy here, he still makes no rigid distinction between matter and mind. The thorax is the seat of vitality in *all* its forms, bodily and mental, exerting its control over the human through the anatomical functioning of the heart and lungs but also through perception and reasoning.

Urania and Vulcan

Martianus now tells us that Psyche was also given a mirror by Urania, the Muse of astronomy, that she in turn had received from Sophia:

> With great kindness and generosity, Urania gave her the shining mirror she had received from Sophia, who hung it among her gifts in the privacy of her rooms so that she could come to know herself and inquire into her origins. (*DeNupt*, p. 8)

Eriugena, whose copy of Martianus gave "Anie" instead of "Uranie," writes:

> "Anie" as in ἀνά ἔννοια [*aná énnoia*], i.e. recognition. "Anie" can also be understood as ἀνεῖσα [*anieîsa*], i.e. freedom. For virtue, through the recognition of its origins—created in the image and likeness of its Creator, or the awareness of free will, the greatest gift that has been given to it, and the mark of nobility that places it above other animals—has been conceded to and bestowed on rational nature from the treasury of the divinity. What I mean is that in virtue, as in a mirror shining brightly, the human soul sees the dignity of its nature and its primordial origin that was previously engulfed in clouds of ignorance due to original sin; and since it is through the studies and gifts of wisdom that virtue, through recognition of its origins and awareness of free will, is shared with human nature, it is apt that Sophia is described as having given the mirror of spiritual awareness

to Anie and fixed it immovably in the privacy of her rooms. (*AM*, p. 12)

The idea that virtuous behaviour is a kind of mirror in which the human recognizes its likeness to the Creator—which is not contained in Martianus's text—comes from Gregory of Nyssa.[12] The reference to original sin is unexpected, since it was not usual to mix Christian doctrine with the teaching of the liberal arts and Eriugena generally observes the practice. As always, he assumes that the sharing out of virtue to the human race is done through "the studies and the gifts of wisdom," i.e. education and the world of learning.

Psyche also received a gift from Vulcan, blacksmith of the Gods, a set of miniature lamps that never go out. "The blacksmith of Lemnos," as Martianus calls him, "lit some little flames for her, inextinguishable and everlasting so that she would never be bothered by dreary darkness or the blindness of the night" (*DeNupt*, p. 6). Eriugena writes:

Lemnius is actually Vulcan, named figuratively from the island of Lemnos on which he is said to have lived, and in the same way that his brother Jupiter is a symbol of ethereal fire, so does Vulcan stand for its earthly equivalent. Poets portray him in their stories as the husband of Venus, wishing him to be understood as a symbol of sexual passion, so that he is also called Lemnius as in *limnium*, i.e. a swamp. This is called λίμνη [*límnē*] or "standing water" by the Greeks, namely water that has gathered on marshy ground, so that you may understand that sexual passion is to be found only in the swampy ground of carnal desire where it is mixed with love. (*AM*, p. 13)

The theory that human passion is the result of an unnatural "mixture" of emotion and thought, symbolized here by the mixing of earth and water in marshy ground, is also taken from Gregory.[13]

12 Below, pp. 31–32.

13 Below, pp. 36–37.

Just as he did with Urania's mirror, Eriugena now provides a "higher reading" for Vulcan's lamps:

> In a higher and more naturalistic reading than Martianus seems to have uncovered here, Lemnius, namely earthly fire, stands for ability in general, from which little flames are lit by the rational part of nature in order to drive back the darkness of ignorance. Just as fire invisibly penetrates every corporeal creature, similarly, the natural gift that is common to rational nature in its entirety is distributed individually to all mortals born into this world, so that they should not be wholly ignorant of their maker and their natural dignity, but should rather search unceasingly for themselves and their God with the interior light showing the way as they track down the truth. (*AM*, p. 13)

The distribution of rational consciousness, in its entirety, to every individual member of the human race is also a prominent theme in Gregory,[14] while the invisible fire that penetrates all things most likely comes from Dionysius the Areopagite.[15]

On occasion, Martianus himself gives "higher readings" in *De Nuptiis*, or at least hints at them. Concerning the chariot that Mercury gave to Psyche as a gift he says: "The Cyllenian [Mercury] himself gave her a chariot with winged wheels in which she could travel at incredible speeds, except that Memory had made it heavier by tying chains of gold around it" (*DeNupt*, p. 8). Eriugena takes up the theme:

> This is in praise of the humbler aspect of rational nature that we refer to as "memory." Everything that the human is permitted to understand through the use of reasoning within the divine laws concerning knowledge of the truth, is fixed and guarded in memory as if by golden chains, namely the study of wisdom. For the thoughts of the human soul would soon disappear if they were not held fast by the chains of

---

14 Below, p. 34.

15 Below, pp. 75–77.

memory. And for the same reason it is in memory, and in no other part of the human, that knowledge of the things we perceive is retained, lest it should slip away like a shadow. (*AM*, p. 14)

The fleeting contents of the mind are secured by memory *and* "the study of wisdom", i.e. the liberal arts. Cosmic and physical interpretations of Mercury's chariot are to be found here also, since Martianus's readers would have associated Mercury's speed with the rapid orbit of the planet, and his evanescence with the instability of the substance, i.e. quicksilver.

Aphrodite

Aphrodite, Goddess of love, now arrives at the scene and Martianus turns from gifts for the mind to gifts for the body:

> Aphrodite brought on allurements for all of the senses, teaching her [Psyche] how to enjoy and be nourished by the spreading of ointments, the aroma of flowers on every side, and the delights of honey. She also showed her the need for gold and jewellery and how to bind her limbs to show graceful femininity. And then, when she was resting, she brought her the rattles and bells that are used to put babies to sleep. And so that time would never pass without bringing her pleasure and delight, she instructed Passion to stimulate and caress the lower parts of her body. (*DeNupt*, pp. 4–5)

Eriugena comments:

> "Aphrodite," i.e. made from foam.[16] In the stories, Venus is said to have been born from the foams coming from Saturn when he was castrated. From a strictly physical point of view they refer to the foams of bubbling seeds—whether of animals or other things—from which is born everything that appears to have its origins in this world, where it is to be understood that the gifts of the higher Gods mentioned

---

16   From the Greek ἀφρός [*aphrós*] (foam).

earlier stand for the endowments and natural virtues of the human soul which come exclusively from the First Cause and Principle of good people. On the other hand, what he means by the seductive treasure-chest of Venus is everything that comes from the corruptible and mortal creature which, as a result of original sin, is mixed with and placed among the natural virtues of the soul. From here comes passion in its general and specific senses, avarice, insatiable lust, and other allurements too numerous to list that are signified, not inappropriately, by the loveliness of flowers, the perfumes of precious ointments, meaningless tinkling, and also by a certain kind of useless drowsiness that comes over bodies when they are resting. (*AM*, p. 13)

A good deal of Eriugena's thinking on the subject of good and evil is contained in these lines. In connection with Vulcan above, he spoke of lust being "mixed" with love, and here again he talks of the rational virtues, the natural endowment of a rational creature, having emotions "inserted" among them and "mixed" with them as a result of the fall, with unfortunate consequences. What exactly is involved in this kind of "mixture," and why it occurs so frequently in the human species, will be dealt with in more detail in the next chapter, on Gregory of Nyssa.

Hell

Unfortunately for Mercury, there was a more fundamental problem with Psyche: she had just gone off with "the winged archer," i.e. Cupid. Mercury and Virtue now decide they cannot continue like this, so they set out on the long journey to the sun (Apollo) to take his advice on what to do next.

They see many marvels on the way, among them a cave that contains the Destinies (*Fortunae*) of each member of the human race, past, present and future. Around the Destinies flow seven multi-coloured rivers, symbols of the seven planets in the form of celestial rivers of water, milk, fire, and various molten metals. The scene painted by Martianus is peaceful for a while, but suddenly changes:

Then the different speeds and violence of the waves over-powered each of them [the Destinies] singly with unexpected force, throwing them headlong downwards and swallowing them in gushing whirlpools, with the result that Destinies were often poured from one river into another, or the one that had long been pounded by the first was thrown back onto the bank by the second, or else drowned in the river. But these blood-red and purple whirlpools did not make off with all of the Destinies. For those who were suddenly snatched were often lifted up on the crest of the shining wave of the milk-white stream, or else carried aloft on a high wave that threw them back into the raging blood-red stream or spat them out to be swallowed in a torrent of molten pitch. This is how the crowd of Destinies was thrown back and forth where the rivers met. For none of them flowed directly forward without interference from the others, nor was any of them entirely free from the whirlpool. (*DeNupt*, p. 8)

Eriugena has no patience with this:

From here to GURGITE FERIATA[17] consists of poetic hallucina-tions, full of mistaken ideas, even if they are considered by those who concoct them to be supported by a reasonable argument that leads them to believe, most mendaciously, that somewhere within the ambit of this universe (in the rings of the planets, or in certain rivers) unfortunate souls are harassed by these things after the death of the body, and are punished, or cleansed, and are either kept there forever because they lived badly, or set free from such things because they lived well. (*AM*, pp. 21–22)

He has no explanation for this passage except to say that it must refer to the constant interchange of earthly happiness and unhappiness that is caused by the "mixtures" in human conscious-ness that he has been talking about:

---

17 The passage above.

These mixtures of all things refer to nothing more than the happiness or misery of souls. For it is not exclusively between destinies that such things are found but also within each person. The mind of any individual person is not always in the same state but at one time like this, and at another like that: sometimes it thinks of good things and if it perseveres with this it will be happy; sometimes it thinks of evil things and if it perseveres with that it will drown and not reach the bank. For this reason Plato said all souls turn back into stars, or into people, or into horses, or into some other likeness. Gregory of Nyssa, brother of Basil, says that a certain youth claimed he was like a man at one time, like a woman at another, or even like a bird, or a fish, or a frog. Gregory said this on account of the excessive unhappiness of souls. (*AM2*, p. 122)

Somewhat implausibly, Eriugena says that Martianus is not really suggesting that people are punished after they die but is referring only to the unhappiness they experience while they are alive.

Philologia

When Virtue and Mercury meet Apollo he suggests that Philologia, the Muse of scholarship, would be the ideal wife for Mercury. Martianus says that Virtue was pleased to hear this for two reasons:

She recalls that Philologia is a close relative of hers, an esteemed patroness of Prophecy and a generous donor of so many resources and enhancements to Wisdom. In any case, said Virtue, until recently Psyche was basically an uncivilised and wild creature, and whatever beauty and grace she now had was due to the refining effect of Philologia on her, and the great affection she had shown her by constantly seeking to make her immortal. (*DeNupt*, p. 11)

Eriugena comments:

Not unexpectedly, Philologia recalls that Virtue is a relative of hers, for it is not possible to separate the study of reason from virtue, or virtue from the study of reason, since they are always joined to each other of necessity … It is not without justification that Philologia is said to be the patron of Prophecy, for the art of divination comes from no source other than diligent application of reason … All of the disciplines by which Sophia, i.e. wisdom, is sought out and achieved were discovered and set in order by the study of reason. (*AM*, p. 27)

As for Martianus's unkind reference to Psyche as a "wild animal," he says:

How well and how accurately he puts it when he says that a human soul lacking the laws of reasoning is like a wild and shaggy animal under the fur of ignorance, untamed and unrestrained by any of the teachings of wisdom, thus making it clear that whatever nobility shines forth in a rational animal comes exclusively from the practice of reason. (*AM*, p. 27)

Eriugena is aware that Martianus could now be accused of academic elitism, but he considers the charge unfounded:

Here he teaches clearly that it is the study of wisdom that makes the soul immortal, and if anybody should say against this that dull souls do not study wisdom and are therefore mortal, it must be said in reply that all of the arts which the rational soul uses are naturally present in all souls, whether they use them well or misuse them badly or never practice them at all, and in this manner every human soul is made immortal by the studies of wisdom that are innate in it. (*AM*, p. 27)

This is the same point that he made above in connection with Vulcan's lamps, one for every member of the species, regardless of the use they choose to make of it.

Book 1 of *De Nuptiis* Concluded

The Gods are called together to give their blessing to the marriage of Mercury and Philologia. There is one obvious objection: Mercury is a God and Philologia a mere mortal. But Jupiter says that in the world of learning such things are of no importance:

> For the virgin he loves is learned indeed
> and his equal in study, and though born
> of earth, is destined to ascend to the stars;
> often she flies before him in rapid circles
> travelling repeatedly beyond the terrestrial globe.
> Can youth be an obstacle to this noble lady?
> Think again, ye Gods, and recall the rattles
> of your childhood that still remain on the earth
> enshrined in the hidden depths of temples.
> Let them be married as equals, as is ordained,
> to add children of mine to the host of the stars! (*DeNupt*, p. 27)

Jupiter tells the assembled Gods that the earth should not seem like a foreign place to them in the first instance—evidently there was a tradition that they had spent their earliest years on earth. Anyway, it was the world of learning that raised them to the stars, and in this regard Philologia may be considered the equal of Mercury, even his master at times.

Eriugena comments:

> Although Mercury is fast, he says, the virgin is faster still. For the study of reason outstrips all corporeal motion and comprehends the globe of this entire world from the pinnacle of reasoning; and this is why he says "travelling repeatedly beyond the terrestrial globe." (*AM*, p. 53)

Here he touches on the unique capacity of the mind, as a part of nature, to reflect on the world in which it is embedded and thus to escape from it, as it were, and look at it from outside, flying around it in "rapid circles" as Martianus puts it here. In this way, mind appears to achieve a certain domination over matter, even when the matter in question is the entire universe. This capacity of the mind to "stand back" from things, the topic of "intentionality" as it is called in contemporary philosophy, will come up again in Eriugena.[18]

With regard to the Gods having been reared on earth, Eriugena paraphrases Martianus's text (shown here in small capitals), as he often does, and then explains it:

> O GODS, WHOSE RATTLES your origins and your upbringing YOU RECALL ARE STILL RETAINED ON THE EARTH although you are of the earth, by reason of your virtue you have been transformed into Gods. It is not surprising therefore if the studies of the virgin Philologia bring about her transformation from a human into a goddess. (*AM*, p. 54)

Deification, envisaged as an ascent to the stars, was often associated with the study of the liberal arts and the pursuit of learning generally in pre-Christian philosophy. Sentiments similar to those expressed by Martianus here can be found also in Boethius's *The Consolation of Philosophy*,[19] another humanities textbook, in prose and verse, that Eriugena knew well. There Philosophia says to the author:

> For I have swift-flying wings
> that rise to the highest heavens
> and with them your quick mind
> can view the wretched earth below,
> pass by the great globe of air
> glance back at the clouds
> go up beyond the peak of fire
> that burns rapidly in the ether
> until it ascends to the houses of the stars
> and merges its orbit with that of Phoebus. (*CCSL* 94, p. 65)

---

18 Below, pp. 160-162.

19 Book 4, Poem 1.

Eriugena, like Martianus and Boethius, takes it for granted that salvation can be achieved through learning alone. This was a tradition that had long been rejected by the Latin Church, although there is evidence that it still lingered in some of its more remote corners. "The quarrel between letters and religion," as Flower politely refers to it (1966, p. 45), was reaching its climax in Ireland in the ninth century, when Eriugena was educated there. It seems that many distinguished scholars were still to be found there like the one described by Bede as "passionately addicted to letters, but little given to the study of eternal salvation" (*ibid.* p. 44). It is in this context, no doubt, that we should understand the famous comment that Eriugena makes on the word *philosophia* in Book 2 of Martianus where he states his own position quite bluntly: "Nobody enters heaven except through philosophy" (*AM*, p. 64). But while the doctrine of deification through learning alone was defunct in the Latin Church in Eriugena's time, it was still alive in the East.[20]

The assembled Gods and Goddesses are persuaded by Jupiter's words, and they agree to reassemble at dawn to celebrate the marriage of Mercury to Philologia. So ends Book 1 of *De Nuptiis*. Book 2 deals with the wedding, and Books 3 to 9 with the seven liberal arts, one book for each.

Epilogue

Although I have looked at only handful of passages from Martianus, all of them taken from the beginning and end of Book 1 of *De Nuptiis*, they are sufficient to make three points that will be important in understanding the rest of Eriugena's work. First, he is a great admirer of *De Nuptiis* and its author, well able to enjoy the text, as its original readers would have done, and eager to learn from it. Admittedly this is no more than would be expected from any open-minded Christian scholar reading a pre-Christian humanities text. Eriugena, however, is not just explaining *De Nuptiis*, he is also teaching from it. Not only that, he frequently appears to give the same credence to Martianus as he would to Scripture or the Church Fathers. This struck some as very odd, and it was not long before it was pointed out to him.

20 See the commentary of Maximus on the Transfiguration, below pp. 95–97 ff.

Secondly, Eriugena generally keeps his Christian beliefs to himself in his commentary on Martianus, in keeping with accepted practice in the teaching of the Liberal Arts. Over the nine books of *De Nuptiis*, his notes contain hardly any references to the Bible (Lutz, 1939, p. xxv) or to Christian teaching, with the occasional exception, such as his references above to original sin.[21] This makes his outburst against Martianus's fiery whirlpool for the damned all the more remarkable, particularly since the picture of Hell it depicts would not have been greatly different from that of the Latin Church in Eriugena's time. Evidently Eriugena does not agree with either of them and has strong views of his own on the subject. What exactly he did believe about the "Destinies" of humans, and why the matter was so important to him, will become clear in the next two chapters.

Thirdly, Eriugena's presentation of *De Nuptiis* is never restricted to the seven liberal arts as taught by Martianus, but includes the disciplines of physics, anatomy and biology as well. This more comprehensive and naturalistic perspective in his work comes principally from Gregory of Nyssa.

---

21 Above, pp. 13, 17.

Chapter 2

Gregory of Nyssa

Gregory of Nyssa (c. 330–400), saint, theologian and philosopher of the Orthodox Church, was a younger brother of Basil of Caesarea. Together with their friend Gregory Nazianzen they are often referred to as "the Cappadocians" because of where they came from, the Roman province of Cappadocia now in east-central Turkey. Basil was educated in Athens and Alexandria, and his main interests were in philosophy, physics and biology. Less is known about the education of Gregory, except that he was greatly influenced by Basil, while the influence of Aristotle and Galen (the anatomist) are also clear in his work and, in matters of theology, Origen of Alexandria.

Eriugena translated Gregory's book *Περι Κατασκευής του Ἀνθρώπου* [*Peri Kataskeués tou Anthrópou*] (Concerning the Construction of the Human) into Latin and used it extensively in his own work, as he did with all of his translations from Greek.[22] The work was referred to in Eriugena's time as *De Imagine* (Concerning the Image), a reference to its main theme, namely that the human is created "in the image" of God. Gregory wrote *De Imagine* to complete Basil's *Hexameron*, a work on the six days of Creation he was unable to finish and comes to an end before the creation of the human on the sixth day.

The Structure of Creation

Although *De Imagine* is exclusively about the human, Gregory begins with a summary of the creation of the physical universe. This allows him to maintain the link with Basil's work, and also gives him a chance to set out some general principles of physics that he will apply both to the physical universe and to the life of the human. This

---

22 About a quarter of Gregory's text is quoted by Eriugena in *Periphyseon* (O'Meara, 1988, p. 56).

continuity of physical and mental life is a first principle of his method of enquiry into human nature, which accordingly he refers to as *physiologia*. This psycho-physical perspective was adopted by Eriugena in all of his work and he will later refer to *Periphyseon* as a work of *physiologia*.[23]

Gregory begins his account of the creation of the universe as follows:

> Scripture says, "This is the book of the Creation of heaven and earth," when all the things we see around us were completed and set apart from each other, and each had withdrawn to its own place, when the heavenly body enclosed and encircled everything within itself, and the central position was taken up by the heavy and downward-moving bodies, namely earth and water, each setting limits to the other. So the art and power of the divinity was embedded in the nature of things, like a binding and an identity for everything that is created, reining them all in through twin forces. For it was through rest and motion that it arranged for the creation of things not yet created and the survival of those that were, driving the sphere of the sky with great speed in a circle—as if it were on a fixed path, like the rim of a wheel—all around the massive, unchanging and immovable part of nature, preserving what is distinctive to each through their effects on each other. So the great speed of the encircling body tightens the mass of the earth within, while the latter, fixed and unyielding, continually intensifies the whirling motion of the things that are flying around it, with the result that the same degree of concentration is produced in the characteristic functioning of the immobile entity and the mobile rotation around it. For the earth never moves from its fixed base, and neither does the sky lessen its momentum or reduce its speed. (*DeIm* 1, 128CD)

Like Martianus, writing two centuries later, Gregory presents Creation as a tension of opposites. But whereas Martianus's

23 Below p. 117.

opposites (male *vs* female, mind *vs* matter, fire *vs* air, water *vs* earth, and so on) are unlimited in number and lack an overall structure, Gregory's are more abstract and closer to physics, and they form a hierarchy since they all derive from one particular opposition, that between motion and rest. From this *alone* come all of the others, and through them, the vast diversity of the natural world:

> Moreover, these things were set in order first of all by the wisdom of the Creator in order to be, as it were, the starting point for the mechanism that lies behind all of Creation. This, I imagine, is what the great Moses[24] means by "In the beginning God created heaven and earth," namely that everything we see in the world around us is generated from movement and rest and brought into existence by the divine will. (*DeIm* 1, 128D–129A)

For Gregory, "heaven" and "earth" in the first line of Genesis stand, respectively, for movement and rest, the opposing poles of the original tension from which all of Creation comes in due course.

This holds true not only for the inanimate world, he says, and also for living things. In the case of the human, four different forms of life are to be found, material, nutritive, perceptual and intellectual, and the basic tension between rest and movement is to be found in all four, most obviously so in the material and nutritive life of the body:

> The material and fluid life of bodies, constantly on its way forward through movement, derives its capacity to exist precisely from the fact that it never stops moving. Just as a river flowing under its own current appears to fill up the channel it happens to be running through, yet one never sees the same water in the same place because some of it is flowing away and more flowing in, so too does the material part of our life here on earth undergo change through the continual alternation of opposites through a certain kind of movement and flux, for it cannot resist change and, being

---

24 Moses was often taken to be the author of *Genesis* until recent times.

unable to stay still, is compelled to alternate unceasingly
between things that are similar.[25] And if it ever did stop
moving, then it would certainly cease also to exist. (DeIm 13,
165A)

He uses Heraclitus's famous paradox ("You can never step into the
same river twice"[26]) to make the point that constant change is an
essential feature of life. Moreover, it is a form of change that lacks
any direction from within, but rather takes its shape from "the
channel it happens to be running through."

In addition to its incessant movement, life is also characterized by
a balance of opposites—an idea similar to that of *homeostasis* of
modern biology:

So emptying follows fullness, and filling in turn replaces
emptiness. Sleep relaxes the tension of wakefulness, and
accordingly waking tightens up what had become loose. And
neither of these lasts forever, but rather each recedes
according as the other arrives, while nature renews itself
through their exchange, sharing each part in turn so as to
pass smoothly from one to the other. For if the organism is
engaged constantly with its activities, a tear or a rupture will
occur in the parts that are overstrained, whereas continual
relaxation of the body brings about a collapse and dissolution
of the entire system. Being in touch with each to a moderate
degree at the right time, therefore, is what gives nature its
capacity to survive, moving continually to the opposite state
to get a break from the other. So, when it finds the body
under the strain from being awake it takes steps to reduce
the tension by sleep, giving the sensory organs a break from
their activities—as if it were releasing horses from their
chariots after the races. (DeIm 13, 165A–C)

---

25 He is talking about random movements originating inside the body
that occur even when the external environment remains the same or
"similar."

26 See Kirt, 2010, p. 367.

Through its nutritive or material life the human participates in the physical life of the universe, and is therefore subject to its fundamental laws, namely continuous change and a balance of opposites. In other works of his, Gregory relates this constant movement to a passage in the letter to the Philippians where Paul describes himself as a runner trying to win a race: "I can assure you, my brothers, I am far from thinking that I have already won. All I can say is that I forget the past and strain ahead for what is still to come" (*Phil.* 3, 13). Later in this chapter we will see the role that "straining ahead" plays in Gregory's understanding of morality and deification.

The Merging of the Senses

Unlike the divine and angelic mind, the human mind is embedded in the physical world, interacting directly with it through vision, hearing, taste, touch and smell. The sensory systems of the human were often thought of by the Neoplatonists as the mind's contact with the physical environment, and were sometimes compared to *quadrupedes* or beasts of burden, i.e. horses or cattle, their four feet firmly planted on the ground that consists of four elements, fire, air, earth and water, drawing the body along behind them, under the direction of immaterial intellect.[27] But Gregory also knew from his anatomical studies that the pathways linking the sensory organs to the brain are carefully designed to *avoid* interfering with each other, as if to ensure that only sensations of pure vision, pure sound, and so on, are delivered to the brain, each uncontaminated by the other. So he wondered how the different modalities of sensation are fully integrated in the image of the world that is presented to us in consciousness:

> When you see honey, and hear it mentioned, and when you taste it, or recognise its fragrance through smelling, or touch it with your finger as proof, it is the same thing that is recognised through each of the senses. (*DeIm* 10, 153B)

He concluded (correctly) that the integration of the senses is done in the brain, and provides a sophisticated model that suggests how

27   See also below, p. 169.

it might be accomplished, based on the neuroanatomy of that time. In particular, he believed that the membrane (*hymén*) that surrounds the brain, the meninges, is "a kind of plinth or root for all of the sensory organs" (*DeIm* 12, 157A), thus attributing to it a role that actually belongs to the cerebral cortex that lies directly beneath it. This is the same description of the meninges that is contained in Eriugena's first note on Martianus' *De Nuptiis* in connection with the name of the Goddess Hymen.[28]

Gregory is captivated by the integration of the different senses in consciousness because he believes that this is the origin of beauty. This is not an unusual reaction for anatomists interested in the sensory systems. In a recent study of the "the merging of the senses" two contemporary anatomists comment on the appeal that the topic has for them:

> But aside from the egocentricity that induces us to engage in the study of the senses, there is also a very real issue of aesthetics involved in this endeavour. For it would be difficult not to be intrigued by the elaborate architecture, remarkable diversity, and exquisite sensitivity of the nervous system's sensory processes and the external organs that serve them... On reflection it seems curiously appropriate that beauty should be a characteristic of the very systems from which aesthetic appreciation is derived. For this attribute is not intrinsic to the objects, but, as most eloquently stated by David Hume, it is an attribute of "the mind which contemplates them." This contemplation, which involves sensory integration, is directed toward the creation of a harmonious synthesis, and as such perhaps, represents the most satisfying product of a merging of the senses. (Meredith & Stein, 1993, pp. ix, 174)

As we will see, the "exquisite sensitivity" of the nervous system and its organs of sensation, and their role in creating the beauty we see in nature, was also a life-long preoccupation of Eriugena's.

---

28 Above, p. 5,

As for the mystery of consciousness, Gregory has nothing to say about it except that it is a form of participation in the life of God that has been granted to the species. Moreover, the participation is active since each mind must create the beauty it experiences. Given that human consciousness is the primary manifestation of the divinity in Creation, Gregory was therefore a little sceptical of those who passed it by in order to pursue higher things:

> The Apostle asks "Who could ever know the mind of the Lord?" (*Rm* 11, 34). But to this I add "Who could ever know their own mind?" Those who consider the nature of God to be within their grasp, let them tell us whether they understand themselves, whether they know the nature of their own mind. (*DeIm* 11, 153D)

And so he sets out in *De Imagine* to show exactly how the human mind is structured and how it functions, as a part of Creation and a sharing in the life the Creator.

God, Mind, and Nature

In a striking passage that became central to Eriugena's work, Gregory says that the human mind is a kind of mirror in which the image of God can be seen, while Creation may also be seen as a mirror, "the mirror's mirror" as he puts it, in which its creator, the human mind, can see itself:

> And in this regard I think there is a more physical interpretation from which we can learn something about these somewhat subtle teachings. For since the Divinity itself is the most noble and supreme good of all, towards which all things are moving insofar as their impulse is towards whatever is good, we say that the mind, insofar as it has become an image of what is the greatest good, also remains itself in beauty so long as it participates as far as possible in its resemblance to the archetype; and conversely—to the extent that it fails in this regard—is stripped of its former beauty. In the same way that we said the mind was adorned by its

31

resemblance to the beauty of the archetype, having been constructed as a kind of mirror to accept the form of that which is seen in it, we think that the part of nature it regulates enjoys a similar relationship with the mind and is itself adorned by the beauty that is adjacent to it—as if it had become the mirror's mirror—and by this means the material aspect of existence, in which it is observed, is controlled and sustained. (*DeIm* 12, 161CD)

Gregory suggests that the forces attracting the human towards God—in other words, the forces of deification—may be compared to the light of the sun passing through the mind of the human into Creation in a single operation that constitutes and sustains the mind, and through it, the human body also and its contact with the rest of Creation. Consciousness, therefore, is a form of participation in the divinity, while the beauty of Creation is a form of participation in the life of the mind, from which it follows that the only requirement for deification to take place is a certain harmony or alignment of the mind with the divinity, on one side, and with Creation on the other. "So if each is in touch with the other the sharing of true beauty proceeds proportionately through them all, transmitting goodness from the higher to what is adjacent to it" (*DeIm* 12, 161D).

Although he relies a lot on visual images, Gregory stresses that the beauty he is talking about is not primarily for the eye: "Divine beauty does not show itself by looking resplendent in any particular shape or striking appearance, but is contemplated as goodness, in a state of happiness that cannot be put into words" (*DeIm* 5, 137A). Yet the goodness observed in human behaviour is not entirely unlike the beauty that an artist can create when painting a portrait:

Just as painters transfer the likenesses of persons to their tablets using certain colours, retaining correct and recognisable tints in their portraits so that the beauty of the original will be accurately transferred to the copy, in like manner it seems that our own Creator, laying on virtues as if they were colours and filling out the portrait to capture his own goodness, makes his nobility visible in us" (*DeIm* 5, *PG* 44 137A).

So the innate appeal of good deeds is similar to the beauty of the visual world, since in both cases it is an image of the divinity that is seen:

> The colours, so to speak, of the picture in which the true likeness is painted are many and varied, not just red or white or a mixture of both, or a black line to indicate the eyebrow and the eyes, or degrees of shading to show the hollows of the face, and whatever other techniques the painters have developed, but rather, instead of these, honesty, tranquillity, serenity, aversion from all evil, and other attributes of the sort by which similarity with the Divine grows in humans. With colours like these the maker of his own image has left his mark on our species. (*DeIm* 5, 137AB)

This is the same interpretation that Eriugena gives to the mirror Urania received from Sophia, in which she can see her real self in her good deeds "as in a mirror shining brightly."[29]

Gregory also broadens his notion of "image" in another way, by drawing attention to the undeniable fact that images of all kinds, however life-like they may be, must nonetheless remain forever different in some respects from the things they represent:

> For if the image were to bear a total likeness to the prototype of goodness, not differing from it in any way, then it would no longer be an image of any kind but would turn out to be absolutely the same as the thing itself, indistinguishable from it in every respect. (*DeIm* 16, 184C)

Referring to the image of Caesar on the coin mentioned in the Gospel (*Mark* 12: 6), he says that the coin can be an image of Caesar precisely because it is *merely* a piece of copper that has been altered, through the work of the sculptors and metalworkers, to make it into

---

29 Above, pp. 13–14.

an image of a person, Caesar. The same applies to the image of the divinity in the human. Here the image of the Creator has to be recreated in a medium that is utterly different from it, since "the former is uncreated, while the latter exists through its being created"(*DeIm* 16, 184C). Strictly speaking, therefore, the likeness of the human mind to its Creator will reside in the actions that are required to *transform* something that is created, finite, and constantly changing, into an image of something uncreated, infinite and immutable.

In effect, the likeness to the divine image has to be constantly recreated in the responses of individuals to the changing circumstances in which they find themselves. And although Gregory believed that the human race, as a species, was constantly changing for the better, he says that the divine image is nonetheless present in its entirety in the life of every single individual who ever lived or will live. This is because the essence of the image lies in its beauty, and beauty cannot be allocated to any particular part of the thing that is beautiful. Either it is present in the species as a whole or it is not present at all:

> The image is not in any particular part of our nature any more than beauty is to be found in a particular feature of things; rather, the same phenomenon extends also to the species as a whole. The proof of this is that mind is implanted in the same way in everybody: all have the power of thinking and deciding and everything else in which the divine nature is represented in all that is brought into being in accord with it. The human as it appears in the first creation of the world and the one that will be at the completion of everything are the same: they both carry the divine image in their own right. (*DeIm* 16, 185C)

This passage seems to be the source for Eriugena's "higher and more physical reading" of the miniature lamps given by Vulcan to Psyche in *De Nuptiis*, where he says that they stand for the gift of reason to each individual, all lit from a single flame.[30] It is in these terms also

---

30 Above, p. 15.

that he answered those who said that Martianus appeared to be saying that salvation was strictly for scholars and intellectuals.[31].

But if differences from the original are an essential feature of images, there must still be real similarities, and in the case of the image of God in the human, the greatest of these, according to Gregory, is the mind's inability to understand itself, for this is also an essential feature of the divinity. "Since the nature of our own mind, which is our image of the Creator, is beyond understanding, it bears a close resemblance to that which lies above it, conveying that which is beyond understanding through its own unknowability to itself" (*DeIm* 11, 156AB). The heart of Gregory's account of deification, therefore, lies not in the acquisition of knowledge, even in the broadest sense of the word, but in the mystery of consciousness and the unfulfillable longing that accompanies it:

> To really see God is never to be able to satisfy the longing for him. For it is necessary to look through everything that can be seen, and to be burned up with the desire to see more. No boundary will every be reached that could cut off the growth of the ascent towards God, for no limit will be found to beauty, nor will the longing for beauty ever be brought to an end by something that satisfies it. (*PG* 44, 404D–405A)

Although this text comes from Gregory's *Life of Moses*, which was not known to Eriugena, it is a particularly clear statement of two principles that are fundamental to Gregory and Eriugena alike. The first is that the divinity is unbounded and therefore indefinable *even to itself*,[32] and following from that, the form that deification takes in human consciousness cannot be exclusively a matter of knowledge or understanding, since these require closure of content, and a resulting distancing or detachment of the one who knows from what is known. Instead, deification cannot take any more definite form than open-ended longing of the sort that accompanies the awareness of goodness and beauty, while in the domain of behaviour it cannot

31 Above, p. 20.
32 Below, pp. 178–179.

be more definite than the undirected "straining ahead" that Gregory spoke of above, and the race that cannot be won.

Good and Evil

While Gregory believed that deification was inevitable, he acknowledged that there are times when the natural sharing of divine energy with the human mind, and through it with the rest of Creation, is disrupted.

> But when this good and natural fusion is ruptured, or if things are actually reversed and the higher imitates the lower, then the shapelessness of matter itself (when it is isolated from nature) is revealed, and by this shapelessness the goodness of nature that is bestowed on it by the mind is also destroyed. (*DeIm* 12, 161D–164A)

This is seen most clearly when human reason and animal emotion are brought together in certain "mixtures" that are mutually destructive. Gregory takes the example of anger, an emotion that can be very powerful in animals but always passes quickly. Human anger, on the other hand, through an unnatural collaboration with the human mind, can be "cultivated" until it grows into an enduring resentment:

> The way that anger wells up in us is indeed similar to an animal impulse, except that the power of thought joins forces with it and makes it into something more. From this comes vengefulness, envy, deceitfulness, treachery and hypocrisy. All of these are the products of a perverse tillage of the mind. For if emotion is stripped once more of the support it receives from thought, then the anger that is left behind quickly fades and weakens, like a bubble that bursts as soon as it is formed. So the greed of pigs is transformed into arrogance, and the nobility of the horse becomes the beginnings of pride, and all the things in animal nature that come from mere absence of rationality are turned into vices through a perverse use of the mind. (*DeIm* 18, 193AB)

Yet the human cannot live without emotions, and in any case it is within the powers of the mind to interact constructively with them:

> On the other hand, if thought takes control of such impulses they are transformed into virtues. Anger turns to courage, cowardliness to caution, fear to free compliance, hatred to distaste for wrongdoing, and the power of love to a longing for what is truly good. (*DeIm* 18, 193BC)

Rational thinking is described by Gregory here as "taking control" of emotion, but strictly speaking what is being controlled is the interaction between the two, since the result is a state of mind that owes as much to emotion as it does to thought. So he talks, for example, about the transformation of the emotion of pride into a kind self-conscious high-mindedness that is admirable. "For pride lifts our minds above misfortune and protects them from enslavement to evil. Even the great Apostle applauds elation of this sort, constantly urging us to "think about those things which are above" (*Col* 3, 1) (*DeIm* 18, 193BC).

Goodness in the moral sense is therefore merely another aspect of the goodness of Creation that draws all things towards it through the "embedded mind." It prevails as long as the deity is reflected in the mind, and the mind in nature, while evil arises only when the transmission of goodness through this "series," as Gregory calls it, is temporarily interrupted so that either mind or nature becomes degenerate "through the removal of the goodness that lies adjacent to it"(*DeIm* 12, 11)—in other words, when the mind loses contact with the presence of the divinity in Creation. Yet at no point in this "broken" relationship is the mind attracted to evil, since this is a physical impossibility for Gregory. The most that can be said is that the mind is drawn by an *impression* of beauty that it has created by an unnatural manipulation of its own feelings:

> If evil had nothing to colour it over in beauty it would fail to arouse desire in the person it tries to deceive. For of its nature evil is a compound, death concealed underneath, like a

hidden trap, and the impression of beauty in its treacherous exterior (*DeIm* 20, 200A)

This is the first principle of Gregory's moral theory, which will be further developed by Maximus and Eriugena. It was encountered above in Eriugena's notes on Martianus, where he refers to lust as an unnatural mixture of love and sexual desire, symbolized by water-logged earth,[33] useless as water and useless as earth, and also in the passage where he refers to the gifts from the "treasure-chest of Venus" as being "mixed with and implanted among" the natural virtues[34] as a result of the Fall.

The Return

Despite its brief victories, evil is doomed to defeat. For the universe is bathed in infinite goodness and beauty, while evil exists only in temporary pockets of darkness such as the tiny conical shadow of the earth, in which nothing can remain for long before its innate restlessness brings it back unexpectedly into the light once more:

> Just as the experts in astronomy tell us that the universe is completely flooded in light while darkness is like the conical shadow cast by the interposition of the mass of the earth, cut off from the rays of the sun behind the spherical shape of the earth, while the sun, many times its size, wraps its rays around it on all sides and brings the converging light together at the apex of the cone, so that if somebody had the power (let us imagine) to go beyond the limit of the shadow he would undoubtedly be in daylight without a trace of darkness. Similarly, I think this is how we should look at ourselves also. In other words, when we surpass the limit of evil, having reached the furthest point of the shadow of sin, we will find ourselves living in the light once more, since goodness, of its nature, is infinitely larger than the limit of evil. (*DeIm* 21, 201C–204A)

---

33 Above, p. 14,
34 Above, p. 17.

Moreover, the return of the light is not due to any intervention of rational consciousness. Only the incessant random movement of all living things is needed to ensure that the mind will quickly re-emerge into the light since "our unstable nature does not remain constant even in evil" (*DeIm* 21, 201B):

> If something in constant movement is proceeding towards what is good, then it will never stop moving forward towards the things that lie ahead since the path to be travelled is infinite. For it will not find any limit to what it is seeking which, if it were attained, would bring its movement to an end. But if its impulse takes it in the opposite direction, then, when it has finished its journey towards depravity and reached the furthest limit of evil, being in constant motion it finds no resting place for the drive that is natural to it, and since the entire domain of evil has been traversed, of necessity it directs its movement towards what is good. For since evil does not extend to infinity but is enclosed by necessary limits, it follows that good takes over when the limit of evil is reached. And so, as I said, the continuous movement in our nature finally redirects its journey towards the good, chastened by the memory of its misfortunes and less likely to find itself in similar circumstances again. (*DeIm* 21, 201BC)

The human is still free to disrupt the ascent for short periods, but the outcome is predetermined and inevitable. "The resurrection is to be looked forward to because it follows not so much from its announcement in Scripture as it does from the sheer necessity of things" (*DeIm* 21, 201A).

And when union with the divinity is achieved, then the human will have returned once more to its original condition:

> Paradise again, that tree again, the Tree of Life, the splendour of the Image once more, and the glory of the beginning. And I am not thinking of the things that God has placed at the disposal of humans in order to live for now, but

of the longing for a kingdom of a different kind, the very idea
of which can never be put into words. (*DeIm* 21, 204A)

This is Gregory's conception of the deification of the human,
described in almost identical terms by Eriugena in the closing pages
of *Periphyseon 5* under the heading "the second aspect of deification."[35] But he did not have to wait this long to put Gregory's views
on deification to work. In 850, when he was still known only as a
teacher of the humanities in the palace school, he was given an
unexpected opportunity to make use of them in a theological dispute
that was of pastoral concern to his local bishops.

---

35 Below, p. 194.

Chapter 3

The Book on Predestination

In 850, or early 851, a work of Eriugena's entitled *The Book on Predestination* was delivered to Hincmar, Archbishop of Reims, and Pardulus, Bishop of Laon. They had asked him to write a refutation of the teachings being spread in the area by the monk Gottschalk of Orbais (c. 800–870) to the effect that predestination was "double" or "split." Just as one may say that certain souls are predestined to salvation by God—a statement nobody objected to—Gottschalk argued that it was equally true that certain other souls were predestined to damnation. Hincmar had difficulty with this, presumably because it suggested an uncaring God, but when he consulted the theologians he found that some of them found nothing wrong with the things Gottschalk was saying. In the fourth century, Pelagius had said that salvation was entirely a matter for individuals and had nothing to do with God, prompting Augustine (354–430) to take up a strong position to the contrary, arguing God's grace was the primary factor in the salvation of the human, and even using the expression "predestination of the damned" to refer to those who choose to reject it. So it could be argued that Gottschalk was not saying anything new.

Pardulus describes what happened next: "A lot of people wrote to us subsequently … But because there was such strong disagreement between them we instructed the Irishman Johannes in the palace of the King to write" (*PL* 121, 1052A). The decision met with the approval of both Hincmar and the Emperor, and *The Book on Predestination*, or "the nineteen chapters on predestination" as it was sometimes called, was completed without delay. It was not what anybody expected, and filled some with horror.

Brief though it is, about 120 pages, *The Book on Predestination* is a difficult work to follow on a first reading. Eriugena writes clearly and elegantly as always and has many interesting things to say, but it is hard to see how any of the points he makes could set his readers at ease on the subject of predestination to damnation. In fact, he scarcely engages with Gottschalk's views on predestination to damnation but argues instead that the very idea of double predestination is absurd to begin with. It is incompatible with God's simplicity, he says, and therefore there is nothing more to be done with it except to dismiss it with contempt. Divine predestination can only refer to divine knowledge, namely the things God knows and must therefore happen for that reason alone, and divine knowledge cannot conceivably take two different forms, one for the elect and one for the damned. Double predestination cannot happen, and even to suggest such a thing is blasphemous. The only form of predestination that exists is predestination of the blessed.

But this is not at all convincing. Predestination to damnation is clearly a possibility, for if God knows that certain souls will be damned and does nothing to prevent it he can, in a sense, be said to have predestined their damnation. Augustine discussed the predestination of the damned and did not find anything absurd about it, and Boethius discusses it in Book 5 of *Consolatio Philosophiae* (*CCSL* 94, pp. 90–105), a book that Eriugena knew well. Moreover, in Eriugena's own time predestination to damnation was of real concern to reasonable people, such as Hincmar and Pardulus. It should not have been difficult for Eriugena, therefore, to form a sympathetic understanding of their concerns and to discuss the matter with them in the usual way, by examining their reasons for believing in predestination to damnation, providing some definitions and clarifications that would be acceptable to all, moving on to the evidence from Scripture and Church teaching, and finally presenting his own case against predestination to damnation. Instead, however, he merely dismisses the idea out of hand, saying that it is an impossibility. Not only that, as one reads on, the impression grows he may also disagree with some of the most basic assumptions about salvation and damnation that were shared by both sides in the debate on predestination.

The Preface

Eriugena begins by dedicating his work to the bishops who requested it:

> To Hincmar and Pardulus, eminent Lordships, worthy and outstanding defenders of the Christian faith, and gifted from above by the Father of Lights with Episcopal grace, from your devoted servant Iohannes, greetings in the Lord. (*DePr* Pref)

Here is a surprise, in the very first sentence. The unusual and rarely-used name for God, "Father of Lights," from the epistle of St James (*Ja* 1: 17), is also quoted in the first sentence of *The Celestial Hierarchy* of Dionysius the Areopagite, a work that Eriugena translated from Greek to Latin and commented on line by line. We know from his commentary on "Father of Lights"[36] that this particular image of the divinity was of great interest to him, and so its recurrence here, as he puts pen to paper on a work of his own, can hardly be a coincidence. Rather, it is further evidence for a view that is gaining increasing acceptance (and is adopted here) that Eriugena made extensive use of the Gregory, Dionysius and Maximus from his earliest writings but did not feel free to quote them for another decade or so, when his translation project would have had the public support of the Emperor.

Addressing Hincmar and Pardulus, he notes the difference between their roles as bishops, and his own, as a humanities scholar, and goes on to express his gratitude to Charles the Bald for the "safe haven" he has provided for the study of the liberal arts in the palace school:

> Your attention is partly directed upwards towards the contemplation of truth and partly downwards towards practical matters concerning the governance of the Church. We, on the other hand, like a small boat rocked by currents from all sides among the waves and ships on the sea of our glorious master King Charles's reign, even in the haven of

---

36 Below, pp. 71–75.

tranquillity that he provides for us have scarcely any time at all to look at the records of wisdom. (*ibid*)

The reference he makes to his limited knowledge of Scripture was soon thrown back at him. Nonetheless, he hopes that the bishops will be able to make use of his work, "just as the greatest and brightest lights of the universe do not dismiss the night-work of the stars but use their rays to dispel the gloom of total darkness in order to bring their own brilliance to perfection" (*ibid*). The image of lights in large numbers, like the stars in the night sky, recurs in Eriugena, referring sometimes to the light of rational consciousness that has been granted to each individual human, and sometimes also to the lamps of scholars working late at night.

In concluding the preface he takes the opportunity to draw the attention of the bishops to a definition that he will use in everything that is to follow:

And so we also humbly request your consideration that whenever you find we have spoken of the identity of divine foreknowledge with predestination you will understand that what we have in mind is the unity of the divine substance, in which they are one. (*ibid*)

The idea of God that Eriugena is proposing here, which would make predestination an aspect of divine knowledge, would indeed rule out the possibility of predestination to damnation. But a definition is still only a definition, and this one would not necessarily have been shared, or even understood, by those who were troubled by Gottschalk's teachings on predestination to damnation.

Then he rounds off the preface with a few lines of verse in honour of the king and the bishops:

The fame of the Franks thrives under Charles their king
like the fish and the salt from the shore far out to sea.
A sect and its satanic teaching now stand condemned,
And in the care of its shepherds, a beautiful faith shines forth. (*ibid*)

The sea as the home of ships, in the tribute to Charles above, is now replaced by the sea teeming with life, two major themes of early Irish sea poetry (Muhr, 1999, p. 193).

The Nineteen Chapters

He begins Chapter 1 of *The Book on Predestination* by saying that he is writing as a philosopher and his readers will therefore need to know something about the methods of inquiry used by philosophers. These he divides into four categories that are needed to answer any question whatever:

> Although [Philosophy] is divided in many different ways, it will nonetheless be found that two-by-two principal parts are needed to answer every question, which are referred to by the Greeks as διαιρετική [*diairetiké*], ὁριστική [*horistiké*], ἀποδικτική [*apodiktiké*], and ἀναλετική [*analitiké*], which in Latin can be called *divisoria*, *diffinitiva*, *demonstrativa*, and *resolutiva*, of which the first separates the one into many through division, the second gathers the many into one through definition, the third reveals the hidden in what is evident through demonstration, and the fourth resolves compounds into elements through separation. (*DePr* 1, 1)

His interest in classifying things using two-by-two tables is well known from the rest of his work, and this particular division of the methods of philosophy sounds reasonable and interesting. The same will be true of other features of "right reasoning" that he draws attention to in the course of the book, including Aristotelian syllogisms,[37] such as:

> For if the necessity of all things is the will of God, the will of God will be the necessity of natures. But the will of God is the necessity of natures—which it has itself created. Therefore the necessity of the natures which it has created will be the will of God. (*DePr* 2, 6)

---

37 It seems that Eriugena's work provides the earliest examples of syllogisms in the Latin West (Kneale & Kneale, 1962, p. 199).

But sophisticated interventions of this sort must have been utterly baffling for his readers. He is writing for people like the bishops for whom the possibility of predestination to damnation was a matter of real concern, and who would therefore rely principally on their personal faith, their understanding of scripture, the teachings of the Church, and common sense in their reflections on the matter. In this context, Eriugena's excursions into semantics, etymology, and Aristotle's deductive logic must have appeared frivolous and ostentatious.

He begins by arguing that the predestination of humans is part of God's essence and cannot therefore come in two forms: "There is one divine predestination, just as there is one divine operation, one divine wisdom, one divine substance, one divine will" (*DePr* 2, 6). To say otherwise, therefore, is sacrilegious:

> Therefore, just as none of the faithful would dare to say that God is twinned, or split, or double, because it is impious, it is also sacrilegious to say that predestination and charity come in two forms, or are duplicated, or split. For what is believed about God is necessarily believed also about his predestination and charity. (*DePr* 3, 5)

But it is not obvious that if both salvation and damnation can be predestined, as Gottschalk claimed, that predestination as an act of God must therefore refer to two different things. This is Eriugena's position, however, announced in the first principle he laid down at the end of the preface above, and repeated continuously throughout the book—and once more in its epilogue:

> And consequently, together with all of the orthodox faithful, I anathemize those who say that there are two predestinations, or one that is twinned, or split, or double. For if there are two, the divine substance is not one; if it is twinned it is not single; if it is split it is not simple but composed of parts; if it is double, then it is multiple. And if we are forbidden to call the divine unity triple, by what insanity does the heretic dare to call it double? (*DePr* Epil 3)

As for Augustine's references to "the predestination of the damned," he points out that when Augustine uses the word "predestination" on its own it refers invariably to the predestination of the elect (*DePr* 14, 2), and then argues that "predestination of the damned" is merely a figure of speech and does not imply that God willed the damnation of souls but only that he permitted it. The figure of speech, he says, is ὑπαλλαγή [*hypallagé*] or subalternation, well known to logicians, which he illustrates using a phrase from Virgil, "to give the south winds to the fleet" (*DePr* 15, 6). This, he says, cannot mean that somebody gave the south winds to the fleet, but rather the opposite, namely that the fleet, through the actions of its sailors, was given to the south winds. Similarly, those who say that the wicked are predestined to damnation do not imply that God predestined their damnation, since it was they themselves who took the actions that led to damnation. This too is a clever argument, but for readers wondering whether—through God's actions or their own—they may have been predestined to damnation, it must have seemed like playing on words.

Predestination as Deification

The book proceeds uneasily towards its final chapters and then, in the opening sentence of Chapters 18, everything becomes clear. Eriugena's references to "true" predestination simply mean deification in the Greek tradition, namely the process by which *all* humans are united with God in the course of their lives, as described in particular by Origen of Alexandria and Gregory of Nyssa. In their account, the deification of the human is a process that cannot fail, although it may be temporarily driven off course by the perverse free will of the human. The term "predestination," therefore, can only refer to the inevitable reunion of the human with its Creator, an outcome that is already assured by the form of existence that he has granted to it through its Primordial Causes.[38] Moreover, since the Primordial Causes are eternally present in the mind of God,

---

38 The Primordial Causes of all created things are their Platonic "essences," which determine the kind of existence that is granted to them. They are the subject of Book 2 and the beginning of Book 3 of *Periphyseon*, and are dealt with in more detail in Chs. 8 and 9 below.

predestination is therefore identical with divine foreknowledge, the fundamental axiom that Eriugena laid down at the end of the Preface to the book.[39] If this is what "predestination" is to mean, then the ideas of damnation and double predestination are indeed absurd and blasphemous. For how could any part of Creation be predestined to damnation when its reunification with the Creator is already assured by the Primordial Causes that brought it into existence?

At the same time, Eriugena knows that he cannot use *The Book on Predestination* as an introduction to the Greek theology of deification. He doesn't mention the word, or the names of his Greek sources, although as we shall see shortly, he does make some cryptic references to deification in the earlier chapters of the book. Here in its final two chapters, however, he is at least prepared to say openly that an alternative theology of salvation exists in the Greek Church in which the problem of double predestination simply cannot arise.

> In my opinion, therefore, the most serious delusion of those who give a garbled and hence poisonous reduction of the opinions of the venerable fathers (notably Saint Augustine) to their own perverse interpretation, is based on ignorance of the useful arts, which Wisdom itself wished to have as its companions and fellow researchers, and in addition, the inability to read texts in Greek, in which the interpretation of predestination generates no fog of ambiguity. (*DePr* 18, 1)

The notion of "predestination" that Eriugena has been working with all along is now clear: it is the Return of all things to their Primordial Causes in the substance of the divinity. To talk of the "predestination" of an individual human, therefore, is merely to refer to its Primordial Cause, or its "predefinition" as he now calls it:

> Thus the noun ὅρασις [*hórasis*] or πρόρασις [*proórasis*] which they [the Greeks] derive from the verb ὁρῶ [*horō̃*] or προορῶ [*proorō̃*] are translated by us as *uisio* or *diffinitio* or *destinatio*, and their compounds *praeuisio*, *praediffinitio*, and *praedestinatio*. So it is

---

39 Above, p. 44.

clear that the three verbs mean the same thing, or are so close in meaning that one may be substituted for the other. (*De Pr* 4, 2)

Although these lines are not entirely clear, and may be corrupt,[40] it is certain nonetheless that the terms "Primordial Cause" and "Predestination" were synonyms for Eriugena. In *Periphyseon 2*, which is devoted to the Primordial Causes, he says that "they are also called *proorismata*, that is, predestinations" (*PP2* 616A), while in his translation of Dionysius's *The Divine Names* he himself uses the term *praedestinationes* to translate *proorismata* (predefinitions), which is one of Dionysius's many terms for Primordial Causes. The passage in question is the one Eriugena will use to bring *Periphyseon 2* to a close.[41]

As for the "fires" of Hell, he can only suggest, as he does in the case of Martianus's fiery whirlpool, that they are metaphoric references to the personal unhappiness of those who choose to resist the forces of deification. God is like the fiery ether at the summit of the universe, drawing the lower elements (air, earth and water) towards itself. Or as Eriugena puts it here, "the higher quality of fire, through a power that is in it naturally, tries to transform the qualities of lower elements into itself by natural motion, as if they were food for it" (*DePr* 19, 2). This is an old idea, found in both the Old and the New Testament, taken up by Origen of Alexandria (184–253) in his *Peri Archón* (Concerning First Principles). There, in his commentary on the verse "Yahweh your God is a consuming fire" (*Deut* 4: 24), Origen says:

> So what does God consume, given that he is a fire? … He consumes the evil thoughts of minds, he consumes shameful actions, he consumes sinful desires, whenever they embed themselves in the minds of believers, and he comes to dwell, together with his Son, in those souls which have been made capable of receiving his word and wisdom, as has been said, "I and the Father will come to live with him," (*John* 14: 23) having consumed all of their vices and passions and created

---

40 See Mainoldi (2003a, p. 190, Note *d*, p. 230, Note 173).

41 Below, pp. 147–148.

from them a temple pure and worthy of himself. (*Peri Archón* 1, 1, 2)

The same idea is to be found in Gregory, except that all-consuming fire now becomes the infinite light of divine goodness and beauty shining throughout all of Creation and drawing it towards the Creator.[42] The free will of humans is still assured by their rationality: they can resist if they wish, and may succeed for a while, plunging themselves into misery in the process. But the darkness in which they now find themselves can only be short-lived, for it is surrounded by the infinite light of the sun and the restlessness that humans share with all living creatures is sufficient to ensure that they will soon find themselves once more in the light. Or, as Eriugena paraphrases Gregory here, "No one's wickedness is allowed to extend to infinity" (*DePr* 18, 7).

Eriugena makes some concessions to the Latin notions of damnation and punishment after death. The Return of saints, he says, will be more complete in some respects than that of sinners:

> The bodies of the saints will be changed into an ethereal quality which cannot be consumed by another quality, although it can change the qualities of inferior bodies into itself. But the bodies of the ungodly will pass over into a lower airy quality and so suffer from fire which is higher. (*DePr* 19, 2)

Yet this suffering of the wicked, namely "perverse humans and angels," is caused by the same internal fire that is experienced by the blessed, except that the wicked have chosen to resist it. Nonetheless they *are* deified, although this happens solely because they were created as humans, not through their acceptance of God's grace:

> Their essential integrity is never lost or their beauty diminished and they retain their full powers, and then all of the good things in their nature shine out in a wonderful display that adds to the splendour of the universe, except for

42 Above, pp. 38–39.

the happiness of which they have been deprived, which is not due to nature but to grace. (*DePr* 19, 3)

As an aspect of the life of God, therefore, deification remains one and the same, producing different results in the case of the human only because the structure of its rational mind ensures that it will be happy when it is attracted towards God and unhappy when it is not:

> By a marvellous and indescribable natural process, hidden but nonetheless just, the same thing that is sought through the highly co-ordinated movements of the elements of the world—clasped together inseparably as if in a bond of natural love—is changed into punishment for those who hate the truth. (*DePr* 19, 2)

Echoing the opening lines of Martianus's Hymn to Hymen,[43] Eriugena now presents the basic features of salvation or the Return as it was understood in early Christianity. All of Creation, inanimate and animate, irrational and rational, immaterial and material, is in an irreversible process of returning to the original state it enjoyed in the mind of God in eternity, prior to its being created. In the case of the sub-rational world, this takes place entirely through the bond of natural love, but is supplemented in the case of humans by the corrective mental suffering that follows the form of wrongdoing that they and the angels are capable of. No division is thereby created in divine predestination itself, however, since the different outcome in the case of sinners is the result of the same forces that assure the return of all of Creation to its Primordial Causes.

The only notion of Hell and damnation that remains for Eriugena, therefore, is the one he gives in his notes on Martianus, namely the distress of the sinner.[44] This too is an interpretation he would have found in Origen's *Peri Archón*:

> So in Isaiah the prophet we find that the fire by which each person is punished is described as being his own. For he says,

---

43 Above, p. 4.

44 Above p. 19.

"Walk in the light of your fire and in the flame you have kindled" (*Is* 50: 11). These words seem to suggest that every sinner lights the flame of his own fire, and is not thrown into a fire previously lit by somebody else, or which existed before he did. The fuel and food for this fire are our sins, which the apostle Paul referred to as wood, hay and straw (*1 Cor* 3: 12). (*Peri Archón* 2, 10)

Eriugena makes some attempts to acknowledge the Latin notion of Hell more. He refers to the unhappiness of the sinner as something that lasts into eternity, and describes it as being "heaped up from the outside" (*DePr* 19, 3). But it still remains a state of mind, and necessarily so if it is to play its restorative role in the process of deification. This is another fundamental principle that he holds throughout *The Book on Predestination*, openly stated here once more in the closing line of the book: "So it can be inferred that it is not substance or its qualities that will be tormented by the fire of Hell, but the feelings of the sufferer and his stubborn spirit wrestling with eternal misery" (*DePr* 19, 4).

Reinterpreting *The Book on Predestination*

Once it is accepted that predestination *means* deification for Eriugena, although he cannot say so openly, some of the enigmatic passages in the earlier chapters of *The Book on Predestination* are now easier to understand. Obviously he cannot begin a book on predestination for a Latin readership by introducing them to the radically different approach to the topic in the Eastern Church. He can, however, suggest some limitations of the Latin perspective, and the change mind and attitude that would be needed to escape from them. Specifically, he says that instead of thinking of predestination as something to do with the fate of individuals after their deaths his readers should think of it instead in a transpersonal and cosmic sense, as the Return of Creation to the Creator, a destiny that is already being continually fulfilled and is assured, on the one hand by the structure of the universe and the work of its Primordial Causes, and on the other by the historical fact of the incarnation.

So, at the beginning of Chapter 4 he says that he will now discuss "the one, true and only immutable and eternal predestination of the divine and all-powerful will that never fails to be realized, at any time or in any place" (*DePr* 4, 1). Since this sweeping image of God's grace will be unfamiliar to his readers he has a suggestion for them: "Those, therefore, who cannot envisage God's grace, let them envisage the salvation of the world. For it is impossible that at the same time the salvation of the world exists and the grace of God does not exist" (*DePr* 4, 3). The reader, he says, should think first of salvation as an achievement that is visible in the world around them, and formally announced to the entire universe through the Incarnation. Then they can understand the grace of God as the force that made it possible:

> So let us hold most firmly that the salvation of the world has come. And for that reason, let us hold for a certainty that the grace of God has shone out. Let them hear the words of the apostle when he says: 'For the grace of God has shone out.' (*Tt* 2: 11; *DePr* 4, 3)

As usual, Eriugena's cosmic imagery is extended downwards into the mind of the human. He describes deification as a form of organic growth that can be seen in the maturation of rationality and free will according as they are "prepared, helped, secured, perfected, and crowned by the gift of grace" (*DePr* 4, 4). And yet, paradoxically, deification is also a development in which rationality and free will have no direct role to play since, as Gregory makes clear, it is not through the use of reason or any act of free will that the human finds its way back "into the light" but only the restlessness and constant movement that it shares with all forms of life.[45] The primary role for rationality is to allow the process to proceed without hindrance, until it is crowned with the gift of grace.

Eriugena develops the point, quoting John and Paul, but drawing also on Gregory, most clearly so in the image of "willing" and "running" that he evokes:

---

45 Above, pp. 38–39.

So in the Gospel, the Lord says to his disciples: "Without me you can do nothing" (*John* 15: 5)—he does not say you can will nothing; and the apostle: "Willing is open to me, but doing is not" (*Rm* 7: 18). And similarly, what the same apostle says "What matters is not willing or running but the mercy of God" (*Rm* 9: 16) is to be understood as "*although* he is intending and running." For these two are naturally present in the human, given that he wills and is therefore willing, and seeks happiness and is therefore running. But it is not within the power of willing or running to initiate good deeds or to pursue them or bring them to completion; this is the gift of a merciful God. (*DePr* 4, 8)

In other words, the Return of the human cannot be linked to any human decisions, but only to its "willing" and "running" and its longing for happiness. For this alone is sufficient to bring it back into the light of God's grace. Only then will good deeds become possible through a process of healing and growth:

Just as people placed in the blackest darkness have vision but see nothing—because nothing *can* be seen until light comes from outside—and then, as soon as the eyes, previously closed, become aware of it, and are opened and see it and everything that it brings to light all around, similarly the will of the human, as long as it is covered by the shadow of original sin and sins of its own, is trapped in its darkness, yet when divine light begins to dawn not only does it scatter the night of sin and guilt but it also heals and restores the vision of the weakened will, making it capable of contemplating the light itself through the purifying action of good deeds. (*DePr* 4, 8)

And so the Return, temporarily disrupted by ill-advised interventions of human rationality, recommences, to be achieved eventually with such completeness that even the goodness of sinners is made to "shine out in a wonderful display that adds to the splendour of the universe" (*De Pr* 19, 3)

Eriugena and Augustine

The hidden theme of deification also helps to clarify Eriugena's ambivalent relationship with Augustine. He quotes extensively from Augustine in *The Book on Predestination* (Madec, 1978, 1986), and as he acknowledges in the extraordinary opening sentence of Chapter 18,[46] it is by showing Gottschalk to be is in conflict with Augustine that he seeks to refuted him. This is hardly surprising. Eriugena was asked to treat the topic of predestination as an issue for the Latin Church, and clearly any attempt by him to involve the Greek Church in his arguments would have been an impertinence on his part, and also a betrayal of the trust that the Emperor and the bishops had placed in him. And so his compromise is to use Augustine, the authoritative voice of the Latin Church, to refute Gottschalk, while at the same time suggesting, as much as he dares, that there is a third approach to predestination in the Greek Church, different from that of Gottshalk and Augustine alike, in which predestination to damnation is an impossibility and a contradiction in terms.

This is not to suggest that there is anything devious in Eriugena's use of Augustine. In fact his decision to use Augustine as his primary source against Gottschalk is a sensible and tactful solution to the problem that *The Book on Predestination* posed for him. He had to refute Gottshalk while remaining true to his own beliefs on predestination, namely those of the Greek Church. And in any case, there is common ground between Eriugena and Augustine on the issue of double predestination. They do belong together in the rough two-by-two table of possible positions on double predestination that Eriugena presents at the beginning of Chapter 4. There he distinguishes between the Pelagians and the anti-Pelagians, the former holding that free will alone is sufficient to achieve salvation, the latter that grace alone is sufficient. The third position, he says, is that of Gottschalk, standing "in the middle," agreeing with the Pelagians that grace is of no assistance to the human, but then adding that neither is free will, and thus "shamelessly" holding God responsible for everything that is done by humans, good and bad (*DePr* 4, 2). On this reading, Augustine and Eriugena undoubtedly

---

46 Above p. 48.

do belong in the fourth category, since they affirm both the autonomy of free will and the primacy of grace.

Yet two important differences remain between Eriugena and Augustine on the subject of salvation. The first and most obvious concerns the existence of Hell. Augustine believes that deification fails for some humans, who are accordingly damned on account of their misdeeds and consequently suffer eternal punishment in Hell— a physical impossibility for Eriugena. But dramatic though this difference is, there is nothing much to be said about it since Eriugena considered the idea of Hell absurd and malicious in its origins. In fact he is not even willing to discuss it in any part of his work, except to suggest (in his comments on Martianus's fiery whirlpool) that belief in a punitive afterlife is probably the creation of disturbed human minds in moments of "excessive unhappiness".[47]

A more fundamental and far-reaching difference between Eriugena and Augustine lies in their views on the nature deification,[48] in other words, in what they believe about the forms of participation in the life of the divinity that have been granted to the human. Eriugena's notion of deification, taken principally from Origen, Gregory, and Dionysius, always retains the cosmic and transpersonal quality referred to above. Moreover it is a process that appears in mental life primarily as an awareness of the goodness and beauty of Creation and the sense of longing that goes with it, while at the same time the object of this longing, the divinity towards which the human is drawn in this way, is thought of as an endlessly changing activity rather than an essence or "nature" of any kind. For Augustine, on the other hand, the human's participation in the divinity is primarily modelled on the relationship between a knowing intellect and the object of its knowledge—limited though that knowledge must be. This difference takes us to the core of the disagreement between the Latin and Greek Churches and will be stated more precisely and openly by Eriugena in his later work.

---

47 Above, p. 19.

48 For a short account of Augustine's conception of deification, see Russell, 2004, pp. 329–332.

Predestination and the Useful Arts

One final feature of *The Book on Predestination* that is more readily understood in the context of deification is the claim Eriugena makes at the beginning of Chapter 18, where he says that one of the main reasons for misunderstandings about predestination is "ignorance of the useful arts," namely the liberal arts and the rest of the world of learning.[49] This is hard to understand at first, particularly if the "useful arts" are taken to refer to the fragments of logic and epistemology that are found in *The Book on Predestination*, beginning with his reference to the four methods of philosophy in its opening lines. For although he says that his technical arguments are an essential part of the book, he also invites the reader to skip them if they wish:

> If there is no happiness other than eternal life, and eternal life is knowledge of the truth, then there is no happiness other than knowledge of the truth. But if this syllogism doesn't carry much conviction for you, let us listen to the truth itself crying out "Anyone who loves me will be loved by my Father, and I shall love him and show myself to him (*Jo* 14: 21). (*DePr* 17, 9)

In reality, the point that Eriugena is making about the Useful Arts is not methodological but philosophical. He is *not* suggesting to his readers that closer reflection on the way their minds work will lead them to a better understanding of predestination. Instead, he is hinting at a very different notion of salvation, namely deification, in which profane knowledge has a role equal to that of religion and scripture—as it has in his Greek sources, and in the Liberal Arts themselves as taught by Martianus and Boethius. Equally, he is referring to a different kind of theology, one that is still merged with philosophy, physics, biology, and the liberal arts—as it is in Origen, Gregory, Dionysius, and Maximus, and will be in *Periphyseon*.

As will seen in what follows, this secondary objective of *The Book on Predestination*, to promote profane knowledge to a status similar to that of religion and scripture, was quickly noted and rejected out of

---

49 Above, p. 48.

hand. Yet the chapter on Maximus will show that Eriugena was not mistaken in his belief that differences between the Latin and Greek Church on a wide range of subjects, including predestination and deification, are indeed rooted in a more fundamental disagreement concerning the relationship between profane and sacred learning.

Aftermath

Reaction to *The Book on Predestination* was not long in coming. Hincmar disowned it at once, saying that it had nothing to do with him, and subsequently referring to it as "Irish porridge" (Cappuyns, 1933, p. 126). Its existence could not be concealed, however, and so a copy was sent to Prudentius, Bishop of Troyes, for a professional opinion. He was shocked:

> I was trembling, I admit, and frightened to see so many errors that were long since sleeping—in the company their authors—coming to life once more in our own time, and smoke that was already drifting away now pouring out again from a new fire and blinding the eyes of many to their sins. (*PL* 115, 1011AB)

Prudentius, a Spaniard whose own name was Galindo, and who was formerly a colleague of Eriugena, quickly noted that the Greek notion of deification was being proposed as an alternative to Western interpretations of predestination and damnation. Accordingly, he took the book as an open attack on the Latin Church:

> Having skimmed your book of perversions, John, the blasphemies and insults you have uttered so freely and so shamelessly against the grace of God and his stern justice— supposedly directed at Gottschalk but disgorged, in fact, in the faces of all Catholics—were all the more hurtful to me because I once embraced you as a friend and had a special liking for you. (*PL* 115, 1011D–1012D)

He mocks Eriugena's use of logic and philosophy. "And you threw in, of course, a certain four-fold method for the interpretation of

Scripture for which our Fathers, namely all of the Catholic commentators, outstanding in both divine and human studies, had nothing but contempt" (*PL* 115, 1294A). He was also irritated by Eriugena's professorial style:

> You on your own, the cleverest of them all, Ireland sent over to Gallia so that she might learn under your instruction the things that nobody could know without you—may God forbid that Celtic eloquence, in its drunken outpourings, should turn loose your confused fantasies. (*PL* 115, 1194A)

And although there is, of course, no reference to Martianus Capella in *The Book on Predestination*, Prudentius shrewdly singles him out for special mention: "It was your friend Capella—principally, but not he alone—who led you into this labyrinth; for you paid more attention to his ideas than you did to the truth of the Gospel" (*PL* 115, 1294A).

Prudentius used the Greek letter *théta* (Θ), for *thanatos* (death), the symbol for prisoners condemned to death, to tag the unacceptable statements he found in Eriugena's text. Here are a few of the 77 he lists, together with his corrections, prefixed with a cross:

Θ   *You say:* Every question is answered by the *quadrivium* of four rules for all of philosophy.

✛   *We reply:* That neither the *quadrivium* nor any other kind of human learning is sufficient to answer every question without the grace of God, a prudent faith, true study and knowledge of Sacred Scripture.

Θ   *You say:* That no nature perishes.

✛   *We reply:* That rational nature does not perish, but that non-rational natures do.

Θ   *You say*: That the words of Augustine prove that predestination is for the blessed only.

✛   *We answer*: That Augustine neither believed nor said such a thing.

Θ   *You say:* That God does not punish the things he has made.

✠   *We reply*: That God punishes (i.e. passes punitive judgment on) nothing *but* the things he himself made: but this is as a result of sin, something he himself did not make: in the case of Job no punishment was meted out on any sin but rather on his body only, which was made by God. In the case of our Lord Jesus Christ, punishment was not meted out on anything other than what he made himself, namely, his body.

Θ   *You say:* That misunderstanding about predestination arises from ignorance of the liberal arts and the inability to understand Greek.

✠   *We answer:* It is not a misunderstanding, but rather the truth of double predestination has been affirmed by the Fathers in a way that leaves us in no doubt that they had a perfect knowledge of the matters you mention, while a smattering of knowledge about them, beyond your abilities, went to your head and gushed forth irreverently in a host of blasphemies.

Θ   *You say:* That the fire itself will raise all bodies to glory.

✠   *We reply:* There will be no glory, only eternal torture. (*PL* 115, 1351–1366)

As a result of Prudentius's critique, and similar responses from others, *The Book on Predestination* was suppressed and condemned publicly in 855 and again in 859. Yet the episode did no damage to Eriugena's friendship with the Emperor and the bishops (Cappuyns, 1933, pp. 126–127). Apparently they were prepared to pass the whole thing off as a misunderstanding, and to the annoyance of his critics Eriugena carried on with his work in the palace as if nothing had happened. Gottschalk did not get off so lightly: he was scourged, compelled to burn his writings, and sentenced to life imprisonment (Kenny, 1997, p. 576). But if *The Book on Predestination* wasn't burned, it was certainly placed under lock and key. It seems that only two copies were ever made, one of which has been lost. The other did not see the light of day again until 1638 (Mainoldi, 2003, p. cxli).

Chapter 4

Dionysius the Areopagite

Dionysius the Areopagite was a fifth- or early sixth-century Byzantine theologian. He is said to have been a monk who lived in Syria, but in reality very little is known about him—not even his name, since he used the pen-name "Dionysius the Areopagite," a person mentioned in the Acts of the Apostles where it is said that he was converted to Christianity by St Paul in Athens (*Acts* 17: 34). The Areopagus, or Hill of Ares (Mars), is one of the hills of Athens, close to the Acropolis.

A manuscript of the complete works of Dionysius was among the gifts sent in 827 by Michael the Stammerer (770–829), Emperor of Byzantium, to his Latin counterpart, the Emperor Louis the Pious (778–840), King of Francia and son of Charlemagne. It was known in the East that the Carolingians were attempting to revive the teaching of Greek language and culture in the Latin West—an enlightened and courageous undertaking when one considers how bitter the division of Christendom had become by then. Not merely was there little or no contact between the two sides any more, but a hostile and dismissive attitude towards the Eastern Church was already well established in the academic environment in which Eriugena worked (Meyendorff, 1994, p. 53).

Nonetheless, the Emperors persevered in their efforts. The writings of Dionysius were translated to Latin shortly after they arrived in the West, and again by Eriugena (*PL* 122, 1029–1194). They are *The Divine Names*, *The Mystical Theology*, *The Celestial Hierarchy*, *The Ecclesiastical Hierarchy*, and ten letters. The books are short, almost like chapters of a single book. In the English translation of Colm Luibhéid they come to around 240 pages in all (Luibhéid, 1987).

The influence of Dionysius is found throughout the work of Eriugena, most obviously in the large extracts he quotes from him in *Periphyseon*. In effect, Dionysius became his principal authority on the subject of God. Moreover, when he had finished writing *Periphyseon*, he returned to his translation of Dionysius and wrote a detailed commentary on one of the books, *The Celestial Hierarchy (HC)*. Eriugena's commentary is a large work, but although a good edition (Barbet, 1975) has been available for 40 years, very little was written about it until recently (Rorem, 2005). It was said there was nothing new in it, and the format led to repetition and tediousness. Eriugena's method in this work was to take a sentence from his translation of Dionysius, paraphrase it to make its meaning clear, then comment on it, sometimes at length, before moving on the next sentence, and so on, sentence-by-sentence through the entire text.

Actually, the book is of great interest. For a start, it is a unique opportunity to see Eriugena at work simultaneously as translator and interpreter, and to note how he develops the ideas of Dionysius as he makes his own of them. And it can hardly be said that there is nothing new in it, for his comments here are often fuller than those he makes in *Periphyseon*. Accordingly, the extracts from Dionysius's Celestial Hierarchy to follow now are often accompanied by Eriugena's commentary on them.

The Choirs of Angels

Dionysius described himself as a φιλάγγελος [*philággelos*], "a lover of angels" (*HC* 13, 4). In the Greek tradition, he sees angels as the part of Creation that is closest to God, the first manifestation of the divine presence in Creation, and the affirmation of its continuous return to the Creator. The angels Dionysius speaks of, however, are somewhat different from their counterparts in Western Christian art: they are more abstract and transpersonal, often represented as groups ("choirs," "hosts," "multitudes") rather than individuals, or even as aspects of the created world rather than entities in their own right, let alone individual "persons" in the human sense.

There are some similarities between Dionysius's "celestial hierarchy" and Martianus's account of the Roman pantheon, notably in the themes of descent and ascent, and the continuous transformation of humans into Gods. Dionysius's hierarchy, however, is taken from the Old Testament, consisting of nine groups of angelic or immaterial intellects, arranged in three ranks according to their closeness to the divinity:

Thrones	Cherubim	Seraphim
Authorities	Principalities	Powers
Angels	Archangels	Principalities

Dionysius believed that the meaning of this hierarchy was to be found in the Bible, through a close reading of *all* of the things it has to say about the divinity and its manifestations to the human. In these passages, he says, it becomes clear that the function of the angelic hierarchy, like that of Creation itself, is to draw the mind towards "the things that are above":

> Using sensory images he placed super-celestial ideas before us in Scripture in a combination of sacred symbols of Scripture designed to lead us from perception to understanding, and from symbols representing the sacred to the bare peaks of the celestial hierarchy. (*HC* 1, 3)

In addition, the celestial hierarchy of angels is an image of the *process* of deification. It shows the created world in the final stages of its reunion with the divinity. Angels are pure intellect, having no need of perception or reasoning, and their distinctive closeness to the divinity refers to the completeness and immediacy of their intuitive knowledge of God. Hence the joy that angels are noted for, the joy of discovery, and their need to proclaim it in music and song to the rest of Creation.

There was much for Eriugena to admire in Dionysius, his close observation of the natural world, his sophisticated "method of negation" for the study of the sacred, his robust aesthetic, and his powerful description of deification in both its personal and cosmic aspects. A lot of this is captured in the fine poem that Eriugena wrote in honour of his teacher:

Dionysius the Areopagite, philosopher supreme,
Brought to Athens the glorious light of the stars.
Disturbed at first when Selena passed under Phoebus[50]
At the time when the Lord was fixed to the cross
And soon converted, stunned by the wondrous eclipse,
Filled with joy he joined the followers of Ierotheas.
Thanks to him the learned and most famous teacher
Soon was born again at the font of the heavenly spirit
And still shining with the light of celestial wisdom
Taught the Athenians, the people from whom he came.
For they say that Paul, carrier of Christ to the world,
Had laid his blessed hands upon him.
By now a trusted comrade, as his own teacher was to him,
He ruled as watchful bishop over the Cechropides.[51]
Then following Paul, flying above the stars, high up
In the Empyrion, he sees the third kingdom of heaven.
And gazes at the Seraphim supreme and the holy Cherubim
And the celestial Thrones where God himself is seated,
After the Virtues, Dominations and Powers,
The order shimmers in a sequence of sacred ranks:
Principalities, Archangels and Choirs of distant shining angels,
The third order enclosed entirely in heavenly minds,
All of the ranks within the limit of three times three
As we learn in the mystical teachings of this Father. (*Carm*, No. 21)

As he does elsewhere, Eriugena encloses his poem in an image of
deification, depicted here as an ascent into the heavens.

The Varieties of Divine Imagery

In his early studies, Dionysius was surprised to find that the most
potent images of God in the Bible go far beyond everyday notions
of beauty and goodness. They often have a rougher quality and they
come from all levels of the created world, not just the sun, the sky,
the sea, and other images of the sublime that are to be found in the
natural world, but from the more commonplace aspects of nature

---

50 Selena and Phoebus, i.e. the moon and the sun.

51 I.e Athenians, i.e. descendants of Cechrops, mythical king of Athens.

also, such as rocks, plants, trees, and animals of all kinds, while in the domain of the mind it is not just knowledge and love that are attributed to God but also anger and rage. In reality, anything at all may be an image of the divinity since, as Dionysius puts it, "nothing that exists is entirely deprived of its share of goodness, for as the true words of Scripture say, 'Everything is exceedingly good' " (*Genesis* 1: 31, *HC* 2, 3).

So Dionysius set out in *The Celestial Hierarchy* to show that the same force of attraction towards the divinity that is symbolised so obviously by the hierarchy of angels, arranged in increasing order of closeness to God, can also be found throughout Creation. His term "hierarchy," therefore, is quite general and he defines it merely as "a sacred order, both an understanding and an activity, approximating as closely as possible to the divine" (*HC* 3, 1). And so the angelic hierarchy in the book's title is merely the apex of a larger triangle that descends all the way to the lowest levels of Creation.

Dionysius begins by noting that the terms used to describe God in the Bible fall into two broad overlapping categories. Firstly, there are words such as "good," "loving", "almighty," and "glorious" that attempt to convey aspects of the divinity by extensions of everyday ideas. Then there are terms like "infinite" and "invisible" that evoke the divinity in an indirect way only, by mentioning a quality that does *not* apply to it. In theory, such terms should be of little use in theology, professional or lay, since they refer only to things that do *not* apply to God. Paradoxically, however, negations of this sort often evoke a more powerful concept of the sacred than affirmative or "similar" terms like "good" or "almighty."

Dionysius believed that such negative or "dissimilar" images provide the only secure base for a rational theology. This is because they openly acknowledge the deficiencies of human language in describing the divinity, while at the same time making it clear that "similar" images, in spite of their initial appeal, have the capacity to conceal their own inadequacies and thus to conjure up false and restrictive notions of the sacred:

No expert will deny that incongruities are more effective than similarities in directing the mind upwards towards God.

For more lavish images of the divine are likely to mislead people into thinking that heavenly beings are like humans made of gold, brightly shining, beautiful to look at, dressed magnificently in gleaming garments, throwing out flames that do them no harm, and that the Word of God has decked out heavenly minds in similar forms of beauty. (*HC* 2, 3)

To prevent such an outcome, he says, the Bible uses unexpected images of the sacred drawn from all parts of Creation to ensure that readers do not become trapped in what Eriugena refers to later as the "nursery" of religious education.[52] According to Dionysius, the function of the "incongruent" imagery of the Bible, when, for example, God is referred to as a stone, a tree, or an animal, even a worm, or when angels are described as inflicting slaughter on humans, is to return the mind to the way it would naturally think about the supernatural, and in doing so to ground divine imagery in its most primitive and powerful forms:

In order to protect people who understand only the most obvious forms of beauty, the blessed writers of Scripture, in their wisdom and their concern to raise all minds to God, humbly directed their attention downwards towards incongruent dissimilarities—not forgetting our own materialism and our tendency to settle for crude images—while also arousing the part of the soul that tends towards higher things and stimulating it by the coarseness of the presentation, with the result that even those most attracted to material beauty are unable to consider it acceptable or plausible that heavenly and divine beings could be represented by such poor images. (*HC* 2, 3)

Lifting the Mind Upwards

Initially, it came as a shock to Dionysius to discover, as he put it, that "there is nothing odd in using similarities that are also dissimilarities and incongruities in order to represent heavenly realities" (*HC* 2, 5). This was the starting point for his unique study of divine imagery:

---

52 Below, p. 125.

In fact, I might not have been released from these difficulties and encouraged to proceed to a detailed study of the sacred had I not been jolted by the repulsive appearance of the angels, for my mind was unable to settle in such discordant imagery but was prompted to reject the appeal of the material images and become accustomed to reaching up devoutly beyond the appearances of things in order to be lifted up to heights that are beyond this world. (*HC* 2, 5)

Dionysius is not talking here about secondary meanings that can be derived through metaphor or allegory, but rather about a residual "echo" of the divinity that can be found in everything that exists through careful observation of the natural world:

It is not unbecoming to create representations of heavenly entities from the lowliest parts of the material world, for even this receives its existence from beauty itself, and retains throughout its material structures some echoes of the nobility of intelligence, and by using these it can raise itself up towards immaterial archetypes. (*HC* 2, 4)

Eriugena paraphrases the sentence in his commentary and then develops it:

Representations must be constructed that are suitable rather than unsuitable for the depiction of celestial essences, even if they come from the lowest levels of terrestrial and mortal matter. This is not unreasonable, since matter itself, over all the grades of its materiality, derives its existence from the supreme good, which alone is true, and therefore has certain resonances or reflections of intellectual beauty. I say resonances or reflections, called ἀπηχήματα [*apēchēmata*] (echoes) by the Greeks, images of things we know about. In the same way that an image of the voice is reflected by a particular kind of rock or cavity, or an image of the body is reflected in a mirror, images of the intellectual beauty of celestial powers echo back from all terrestrial matter, even the lowliest. (*ExpIC* 2, 4, p. 44)

Or as Gregory said, all of Creation is a kind mirror in which the mind can be seen and, through it, the divinity.

Eriugena continues:

So it is possible for our mind to be led back by these resonances to the immaterial first forms, which the Greeks call ἀρχετυπίας [*archetypías*] (archetypes), the things to which the reflections refer, in spite of differences between the way the similarities are captured in the material things from which they are reflected, and the immaterial things that are reflected. (*ibid*)

He notes that immaterial and eternal archetypes are reflected differently at different levels of Creation, subrational, rational, and beyond rationality. The changing contexts do not obscure the archetype itself but deepen it by revealing the full extent of its meaning. Take the powerful emotion of rage, for example, when it is used as an image of the sacred:

Rage is defined differently for a lion and an angel. And when these similarities are considered not from a single perspective, but according to differences obtaining between material things and the highest of immaterial things, the distinctiveness of each is compactly and beautifully defined for intellectual powers and for material things that can be perceived. For example, irrationality is an absence of rationality in creatures that lack rationality, but in celestial essences it is a surpassing of reason and something that is beyond rationality, and to that extent it is beyond every explanation and conception of ours. (*ExpIC* 2, 4, pp. 44–45).

The archetype is therefore more clearly seen in the full range of its manifestations, which in the case of rage runs from pre-rational rage in the case of animals to partly rational rage in humans, and finally, in the case of immaterial intellects, to rage that is beyond rationality.

The Way of Negation

By involving all of Creation in divine imagery, using forms of representation that exploit their dissimilarity with the things they refer to, Dionysius also places the notion of the divinity beyond all possible definitions and assertions, beyond all understanding and all perception. The experience is described in the striking poem that introduces another of Dionysius's works, *The Mystical Theology*, a short handbook of spirituality written for a student of his, Timotheos, which was also translated by Eriugena:

> Trinity beyond essences
> and beyond divinity
> and beyond goodness,
> Lord of the wisdom of Christians,
> take us to the brightest highest peak
> of the sacred words
> beyond light and unknowing
> where lie Scripture's mysteries
> simple, unqualified, unchangeable
> in the deepest darkness of secret silence
> clarity beyond clarity in light beyond light,
> in a world intangible and invisible
> pouring beauty beyond beauty
> into minds without eyes. (*PG* 3, 997AB)

Dionysius uses the prefix *hyper* (beyond) nine times, and five other negative prefixes. But as is well known, "in poetry there is no negation, but only contrast." (Langer , 1953, pp. 242–243). The negated words are not cancelled entirely but rather "the literal sense, being a constant rejection of the emerging ideas, keeps them pale and formal—faded, "gone"—in contrast with the one positively stated reality" (*ibid.*). Yet it is the "pale" and "faded" contents of the poem that hold the reader's attention, directing it towards those things which, as Dionysius would put it, can only be known through "unknowing."

He points out to Timotheos that it will be difficult to live in a world that is beyond the meanings of everyday language, perception, and intelligence:

> This is the prayer I make for myself, and what you have to do, my friend Timotheos, in your sincere efforts to uncover the mysteries, is to abandon the senses and the powers of inference, all that is perceptible and understandable, all that is not and all that is, and, like a person lacking all knowledge, to strain upwards towards union, as far as it may be achieved, with him who is beyond all being and knowledge. By unconditionally standing aside from yourself and everything else, released from them absolutely, leaving everything behind and set free from them all, you will be raised up to the ray of divine darkness that is beyond being. (*PG* 3, 997B–1000A)

An element of reclusiveness will also be required in the endeavour:

> Take care, however, that none of this comes to the ears of the uninitiated—I refer to those trapped in the world of things, who imagine that no essence higher than objects can exist, and who think that with their own kind of knowledge they can know him who has chosen the shadows for his hiding place. (*PG* 3, 1000A)

Moreover, the initiate will also face purely intellectual difficulties. For if the notion of God is based principally on negation, the question arises whether anything at all can be said about God in the ordinary way. Is the novice condemned to total silence on the subject of God? Not so according to Dionysius. In fact *everything* can be affirmed of the divinity, since it is the Creator of all there is, provided it is also denied at the same time:

Everything that is affirmed about anything should be affirmed of it on the grounds that it is the cause of everything, and more importantly, it should also be denied of it since it is above everything; and you should not think that the denials contradict the affirmations but that [the cause of everything] is prior to every denial and affirmation. (*PG* 3, 1000B)

Not surprisingly, Dionysius was accused of pantheism. If all of Creation contains an aspect of the divine that is based only on the fact that it was created by God, then the distinction between God and Creation is greatly weakened. And although both Dionysius and Eriugena are quick to answer the objection—exactly as Dionysius does here—by adding that whatever is affirmed of the deity must, of course, be denied at the same time, this is scarcely an adequate response. For if the concept of the divinity, *prior* to all affirmations and denials, has been broadened sufficiently to encompass all of Creation, then it can be argued that the denials come too late.

For our purposes here, it is sufficient to say that Dionysius objected to certain notions of the divinity that he considered superficial and restrictive, based only on the kind of "heavenliness" that he mocks openly in *The Celestial Hierarchy*. Accordingly, he sought to rectify things by a closer study of the more naturalistic images of the sacred that he found in the Bible. This is clear from the great range of sacred symbols he studied in his work as a whole, from the heavens and the angels to the great symbols of power and beauty that are to be found in the natural world, down to the most mundane aspects of everyday life, human, animal and material.

Father of Lights

This immanence of the divinity in all of Creation is the subject of Eriugena's first note on *The Celestial Hierarchy*. His attention is drawn to the little-used divine name "Father of Lights" (from the epistle of St James) that appears in the opening lines of Dionysius's book— and also in the opening line of Eriugena's *Book on Predestination*:[53]

---

53 Above, p. 43.

"Every inheritance of value and every gift of excellence is from above, coming down from the Father of Lights" (*Ja* 1: 17). But also, every movement outwards of light from the Father, like a unifying force that comes to us repeatedly and generously, opens us out and brings us back again—as God gathers us in—to oneness and simplicity through deification. For "Everything is from him and to him" (*Rm* 11: 36) as Sacred Scripture says. (*HC* 1, 1, p. 70)

Since James uses two words, δόσις [*dósis*] (inheritance) and δώρημα [*dốrēma*] (gift) to describe God's generosity to Creation, Eriugena takes the opportunity to distinguish once more between nature and grace. He identifies "inheritance" with everything that is passed on to the individual human by reason of its being a member of the species, while "gift" refers to the additional excellence it achieves according as it is drawn closer to the image of the divine—a personal gift for every human, and one that it may choose to reject. This is the same distinction he used in the closing lines of *The Book on Predestination* where he says that all humans, even the most wicked, will be deified, except for "the happiness that will be withheld from them, which comes not from nature but from grace" (*DePr* 19, 3).

Eriugena comments on the line from James:

This sentence of the Apostle distinguishes wonderfully between divine inheritance and divine gifts, since inheritances of value are distributed when Creation in general is brought into being, and gifts of excellence through the generosity of divine grace. For everything that exists shares in divine goodness in two ways, the first of which is seen in the constitution of nature, and the other in the distribution of grace. Both are present in all of nature. Everything that exists is a substance, and shares in the grace of God through a similarity with him that is appropriate for it. And note that it doesn't just say: "Every inheritance is good and every gift is perfect." In everything that exists, inheritance comes first and is brought into being as a part of nature, to which is subsequently given, in addition, a perfect gift. And to understand the difference between inheritances and gifts, note what he says: Every inheritance of value, that is, the bringing into being of everything created, is exceedingly good—as it has been written: "And God looked, and behold, all things were exceedingly good" (*Genesis* 1: 31). But since the bringing into being of everything is not perfect unless it returns to the Creator, the text continues with "and every gift of excellence." (*ExpIC* 1, 1, pp. 1–2)

The contrast, then, is between the things inherited as a part of nature, on the one hand, and on the other, the return of nature to its origin, which is the gift of the Creator.

Eriugena now directs his attention to the phrase "Father of Lights" and in particular at the use of the plural form "lights." His first suggestion is that the lights might be taken to refer to the Trinity:

That is a triple light, and a triple good, three in one essence, Father, Son and Holy Spirit, one God, one light diffused through everything that exists, so that they might subsist in essence, resplendent in everything they are, so that everything is returned to the love and knowledge of beauty, surpassing all the things that are, so that all of them can enjoy the fullness of his perfection. And in him all things are one, and therefore it is from the Father of lights that all lights descend. (*ExpIC* 1, 1, pp. 2–3)

The word "lights" now refers to the Creator and Creation alike, but Eriugena has no problem with this:

There is also another argument showing clearly that everything in Creation, visible and invisible, is a light constructed by the Father of lights. For if the supreme good, which is God, willed all things, he therefore made them in such a way that since he in himself is light invisible and inaccessible, surpassing all perception and understanding, through the things that he made he descends into the minds of intelligent and rational creatures in the form of night-work by lamp-light, as it were. Which is what the Apostle teaches; for he says: "Ever since God created the world, his everlasting power and deity—however invisible—have been there for the mind to see in the things he has made" (*Rm* 1, 20). If he introduces inaccessible light in a way that makes it accessible to pure intellects, is it any wonder that it is understood (provided there is no reasonable objection to it) as a light illuminating souls and calling them back to a knowledge of their Creator? (*ExpIC* 1, 1, p. 3)

Lucubrationes (work done by lamp-light) is a favourite word of Eriugena's, sometimes used to describe his own work practices, as in the preface to *The Book on Predestination*[54] and the Letter to Wulfad.[55] At other time, he visualizes the presence of the Creator in Creation as the myriad of human lights, i.e. intellects, "tracking down" the truth in the darkness of irrationality.[56]

Here in his commentary on Dionysius, however, he goes much further and says that every single thing that exists (not just the minds of humans) may itself be considered as a light in the dark. To make the point he considers the most trivial pieces of matter he can think of, sticks and stones:

For example—and in order to have a paradigm from the lowest orders of nature—this stone or this piece of wood is a light for me. And if you ask how this is possible, in reply to your question reason suggests that in considering this or some other stone many things occur to me that bring light to my mind: I notice that it is something good and beautiful, that it exists according to its own form, that through its genus and species it stands apart from other genera and species, that it is constrained by its number, which is a particular singularity, and does not exceed its rank, that it seeks its own place, in accordance with the kind of weight it has. These

54 Above, p. 43.

55 Below, p. 199–201.

56 Above, p. 15.

and other similar things become lights for me when I look at this stone, that is to say, they enlighten me. (*ExpIC* 1, 1, p. 4)

One last question remains, however: these "lights" that are to be found in the material world, and which have such a profound effect on the immaterial mind of the human, how can they be said to reside *in* pieces of matter? After all, a stone is still just a stone:

> I begin to reflect on how it came to possess things like these, and I note that it is not through participation in any other created thing, visible or invisible, that they are present in it. And reason soon leads me up beyond all things to the cause of all things, from which are distributed position, rank, number, species and genus, goodness, beauty, and essence, and other inheritances and gifts. It is the same for all of Creation, from top to bottom, i.e. from the intelligent to the corporeal. By referring it and themselves to the praise of the Creator, seeking their God eagerly and longing to find him in all things, and delighting in his praise above everything there is, it is a light that shows the way forward for their thinking when carefully considered and clarified by the clear intuition of the mind's eye. So it is that the grand workshop of this world is a great light, made up of many smaller lights working together, which—with the assistance of God's grace and the power of reason—reveals the pure splendour of the things that can be understood and gazed on by the eye of the mind in the heart of the learned faithful. (*ibid*.)[57]

Divine Fire

In the final chapter of *The Celestial Hierarchy* Dionysius looks at the full range of imagery that is used in the Bible to lift the mind up to "angel-like" contemplation of the divinity, and raises the question "why it is that the writers of Scripture are attracted to images of fire

---

57 The American poet Ezra Pound (1885–1972) read these words of Eriugena, whose work he studied closely, and wrote " 'sunt lumina,' said the Oirishman to King Carolus, 'OMNIA, all things that are are lights.' " Canto LXXIV. (Byron, 2014, p. 211)

to the virtual exclusion of all others?" (*HC* 15, 2). The fire he is talking about is not the earthly fire we are familiar with, which is only one of its many embodiments, but pure fire, the physical element of fire, the source of all life, originating in the sun but also shining through all things and becoming visible in them.

In particular, he notes that the choirs of angels are constantly described as being fire-like. The reason, he says, is that throughout the cosmic hierarchy, high and low, it is "fiery images that best reveal the way in which celestial minds are similar to the deity" (*ibid.*). He then points to the many features of fire that provide suitable images of the process by which Creation is united with the Creator:

> The fire we can see is also within all things, so to speak, and moves through them without mixing with them. It exceeds them and shines through them while yet remaining hidden, unknowable in itself, and showing its own power only through contact with matter, uncontrollable and impossible to look at, yet master of all and transformer of everything it encounters into its own unique activity, sharing itself with whatever moves even a little closer to it, renewing things with warmth that kindles, giving light through unveiled illuminations, unconquered and unmixed, separating things from each other but remaining itself unchanged, rising high and sharply piercing, sublime and incapable of being degraded, always moving, moving itself and moving others, closing in on everything and never closed in by anything else, in need of nothing, quietly growing and showing its magnificence wherever it is made welcome, energetic, powerful, invisibly present in all things, seemingly absent when overlooked, but when invited, as it were, by friction, appearing naturally, spontaneously, and without warning, rising up again unexplainably, and without itself being diminished in any way, sharing itself joyfully with everything. (*HC* 15, 2, pp. 169–171)

Eriugena paraphrases and comments:

It is likely, he says, that anybody who closely studies the powers of fire will discover many properties of fire in which images of the operation of the divinity are to be found. For God is indeed in everything since he is the essence of all things, and comes through all things since he maintains them, and is withdrawn from all things since he is super-essential and above all things, and shines forth in the created world he has made since, of himself, he would be hidden and unknown had he not constructed all of Creation as a kind of medium in which he can be seen and his actions made visible; and who does not know—except through extra-ordinary ignorance or impiety—that God is immeasurable and, in himself, invisible. In a word, whatever may be said in praise of fire can be elegantly predicated of God also by metaphor. (*ExpIC* 15, 2, pp. 194–195)

In addition, fire means intellect for Eriugena, and is identified with the invisible fire of the sun that becomes visible to humans only when it mixes with the three elements of this world, air, earth and water. There, in the turbulence of the earth's atmosphere, it generates beauty in all its forms, but also embroils intellect in the frailties of human reasoning, since it is now unable to understand things intuitively, as it was meant to, but only through its animal body, in physical contact with the four elements of the material world. Hence the greatest aspiration of humans is to return again to a state of pure intellect, symbolised by the angelic choirs of the Bible. "It is for this reason," Dionysius says, "that the learned writers of Scripture imagine the celestial essences to be made of fire to signify their similarity with God and their capacity, such as it is, to imitate him" (*HC* 15, 2).

The Lion

Moving to the world of animals, Dionysius considers the image of the lion, as found in the visions of Ezekiel (1: 1–14; 10: 1–22) and later as the animal-symbol of the evangelist Mark:

The image of the lion obviously conveys leadership, strength, and indomitability, and how hard they try to imitate the secrecy of the ineffable divinity by concealing the footprints left by their mental journey, quietly and without any ceremony covering the path of their ascent to divine illumination. (*HC* 15, 8, pp. 184–185)

Evidently it was part of the folklore of the lion that it erased its footprints as it walked along. This allows Dionysius to associate the majestic appearance of the animal with the return of all things to the Creator. The lion, he says, conceals the path of its return in case it might lead others astray, since all of Creation has to find its own way back.

Eriugena adds some folklore of his own:

It is also said that lions can see in the dark, that is, they see— to the extent and in the manner that seeing is permitted to them—the super-essential brilliance of the divinity, referred to by the word "dark" because it is inaccessible. They move in circles, as it were, around the principle of all there is, and it is on the same route by which they achieve divine contemplation that they return to the den that is hidden within their own nature, as if they were following a secret path. (*ExpIC* 15, 8, p. 208)

Eriugena merges the journeys out and back, and as he often does, supplements Origen and Gregory's cosmological understanding of deification with similar innate developmental forces that lead every organism back to its own unique origin, now thought of as something that lies within it.

Dionysius brings *The Celestial Hierarchy* to a close and acknowledges its incompleteness:

This is all I will say about sacred images, and insufficient though it is to give a detailed account of what is contained in them, I believe it will make it impossible for us to be content with pathetic, concocted imagery. And if you say that I have not produced an exhaustive list of the powers, energies, and images of the angels that are to be found in Scripture, I can only answer that this is indeed true, for in the case of some of them I lacked an understanding of their transcendence and would have needed another person to show me the way, while in the case of others—the sort I dealt with above—I have omitted them partly because of concern for the size of this volume, and partly to honour by silence the mystery that lies beyond me. (*HC* 15, 9, p. 191)

Eriugena's Translation

A copy of Eriugena's translation of Dionysius was sent to Anastasius the Librarian, a Greek in charge of the library of Pope Nicholas I in the Vatican. A letter survives under the Pope's name (*PL* 122, 1025–1026) in which he complains to Charles the Bald that the translation "by a man named Iohannes from Ireland" was circulated without his approval. "In spite of his great learning," the Pope allegedly says, "the same Iohannes has the reputation of being indiscreet from time to time on certain matters." There are, however, some doubts about the authenticity of the document (Brennan, 1986, p. 430, Note 10).

Not so for Anastasius's letter to the Emperor on the same topic. He begins by expressing surprise that Dionysius, above all other Greek authors, was selected for translation into Latin, given the difficulty of the topic and Dionysius's dense prose.[58] But he was surprised by the translation too:

It is also extraordinary that this foreigner, born on the edge of the world—equally as unfamiliar with the sound of other languages, one can assume, as he was with the company of other peoples—could have understood these materials and translated them. I am referring to Iohannes from Ireland, a man of great holiness from what I hear. But then, this is the

---

58 This suggests that Anastasius was not aware of another possible reason for the selection of Dionysius for translation, namely a tradition that was still strong in the Palace of Charles the Bald that the real Dionysius the Areopagite (a contemporary of St. Paul) *was* the author of the works written under his name, and more importantly, that he was also the same person as St Denys of Paris (3rd century).

work of the other Creator, the Holy Spirit, who gave him fire as well as eloquence. For if he had not been inflamed by grace with the fire of love itself, he could not possibly have received the gift of speaking in tongues. Love was his teacher, and what he learned was for the enlightenment and advancement of many. (*PL* 122, 1027–1028)

In spite of the kind words, however, and the fine description of the Holy Spirit working through Eriugena, Anastasius felt that Dionysius made demands on the Irishman that he was unable to meet. The problem, he says, stems from "his determination to translate each word; for although I often use the same method myself, you will know from your own wide experience that the better translators avoid this kind of translation" (*ibid.*). At the same time, he does not believe that Eriugena's decision to translate word-for-word was based on his limited knowledge of Greek. "In my own opinion," he says, "his only reason for doing this was humility of mind and his reluctance to part with any feature of a word for fear of losing its exact meaning" (*ibid.*).

But whatever about Eriugena's methods and motivation, Anastasius found his translation poor:

The result is that the great man [Dionysius], who in our own analyses was found to be inherently cryptic in any case— since he sought to investigate the deep and challenging mysteries of both philosophies—has been captured by him [Eriugena] in a net of labyrinthine complexities and taken even further out of sight into darker caves, leaving the person he set out to translate still untranslated. (*ibid.*)

This seems a little harsh, taking into account what has been said on the subject by classicists in more recent times. The translation is indeed word for word, as all of Eriugena's translations are, and would frequently be difficult or even impossible to understand without reference to the Greek original. But such translations were common, written for readers who had enough Greek to follow the original text with the help of the Latin "crib." Moreover, in

Eriugena's commentary on *The Celestial Hierarchy* his word-for-word translations are usually followed by one or more paraphrases that gradually depart from the word-order of the original in an attempt to give the meaning of the sentence—a technique that Eriugena often used in his commentary on Martianus as an aid to learners of the original language. One way or another, it is certain that Eriugena had an unrivalled understanding of Dionysius—and not just in his own time. In Rorem's view (2005, p. 80) no "medieval or modern analysis ever improved on Eriugena's identification of the heart of the Dionysian enterprise."

Eventually the works of Dionysius were widely used by spiritual writers in the West. *The Cloud of Unknowing*, for example, a well-known English text from the fourteenth century (Wolters, 1961), owes a great deal to Dionysius. In fact its title is a translation of a phrase of his, ὁ γνόφος τῆς ἀγνωσίας [*ho gnóphos tês agnōsías*] (the darkness of unknowing)[59]—the same "incongruous" image of knowledge as darkness that Eriugena will use to end the letter he wrote to Wulfad, having just finished his own great work, *Periphyseon*.[60]

---

59 From his *Mystic Theology* (*MT*, 1001A). See Luibhéid (1987, p. 137, Note 9).

60 Below, p. 201.

Chapter 5

Maximus the Confessor

Maximus the Confessor is thought to have been born in Palestine around 580. He worked in the court of the Emperor, was a monk for a time, and lived a good part of his life in North Africa. A well-known theologian and spiritual advisor, he was prominent in public life too because of his participation in theological controversies. This led to his death, in 662, following his refusal to abandon his belief that Christ had both a divine and a human will. His right hand was cut off and his tongue cut out, and he was expelled from the Empire, dying shortly afterwards in Lazica on the eastern coast of the Black Sea in modern Georgia. He was called "the confessor" because of his refusal to withdraw his views, which were vindicated shortly afterwards at the Third Council of Constantinople in 681.

One of his practices was to reply in writing to queries sent to him by colleagues, two in particular, Iohannes, archbishop of Cyzicus in the northwest of modern Turkey, and Thalassius, a monk who lived in Libya. Eriugena found copies of Maximus's replies to their questions and translated them into Latin, *Ambigua ad Iohannem* and *Quaestiones ad Thalassium* as they are now called. Large extracts from them can be found in Eriugena's works, *Periphyseon* in particular, and even when there is no mention of Maximus his presence is often felt, for Eriugena depends greatly on him in everything he wrote on the topic of spirituality, sometimes referring to him as "The Monk Maximus" or "Abbot Maximus."

The Spiritual Life

Maximus's replies to his correspondents contain many of the things one would expect in any handbook of spirituality. He stresses the need for discipline and the threats to the spiritual life that are posed by laziness, self-importance, envy and so on. Yet the presentation is very different from that found in similar works in the Latin Church. Maximus does not adopt the role of a personal counsellor and there no trace in his writings of the aura confidentiality and anti-intellectualism that is often found in western manuals of spirituality. On the contrary, the texts read more like short philosophical essays, and are explicitly based on what Maximus understands from the doctors and anatomists about the functioning of the human mind and body. Like Martianus, Gregory, and Dionysius, Maximus writes in the cosmic tradition of the Neoplatonists, taking the spiritual life to be merely another aspect of the continual movement of all things towards harmony with each other and unification with the Creator. His definition of love, for example, from his *Commentary on the Lord's Prayer*, is that it is "a law of devotedness implanted in the mind, drawing together all things that are related to each other by nature" (*CCSG* 23, p. 27).

Eriugena wrote a poem in honour of Maximus, as he did for Dionysius. While the poem to Dionysius[61] took the form of a journey into the heavens, on this occasion we are taken into the study, or perhaps the hermitage, of a monk and a scholar—although Eriugena returns to Dionysius to bring the poem to a close:

Those whose wish is to honour the beauteous face of wisdom
Should closely read what is written by you, Maximus Graiugena.
Let their first inspiration be the heavenly reasons for things,
Let them abandon and disown the world of the senses,
And also the senses themselves which are often a burden
To those ascending on the inner steps of the mind's journey.
Those free of the lure of this fragile life, of the world that passes,
Of the demands of the body—let them read on.
And those swallowed up in worldly things, dull and lazy,
Keep far away from here—there's no way in for you.
Filled up with concerns of their own, swollen up and arrogant,
Let them keep away, realizing there is no place here for them.
But those versed in the arts that are known to the sharp mind,
Let them come forward with confidence—they are in their
    native land.

61 Above, pp. 63–64.

Praktiké, renowned mistress of morality, lights up this place,
Custodian of the virtues, ever vigilant and well prepared.
Physiké pursues its studies here on the hidden causes of things,
And having found them, divides and unifies them at the same
    time.
Here is *Theo*—surpassing them all in beauty—*logia*;
Denying all, that which is and that which is not, at the same
    time. (*Carm*, No. 24)

Most likely it is from the word *Graiugena* (Scion of Greece)—a word
Eriugena could have found in Virgil—that he coined *Eriugena* (Scion
of Ireland) to refer to himself. The word *theologia*, in the second last
line, is broken in two to make the point that it refers not so much to
the academic discipline as it does to the contemplation of the
divinity.

Emotion, Maturation, and Deification
The topic that dominates Maximus's replies to his correspondents
is a very practical one, how to live simply and well. Here, for
example, is his answer to a question from Thalassius concerning the
best way to deal with emotions:

Question: Are emotions evil in themselves, or do they
become so because of the way they are used? I am thinking
of pleasure, sorrow, desire, fear, and so on.
Answer: These emotions, like the others, were not created
at the same time as human nature. If they had been, they
would be required to complete its definition. Following the
teaching of the great Gregory of Nyssa, I take the view that
emotions were added as a result of the fall from perfection,
and merged with the non-rational part of human nature; and
then, immediately following the transgression, the blessed
image of the divinity was replaced by an obvious and clear
similarity with non-rational animals. (*AdTh CCSG* 7, p. 47)

He accepts Gregory's teaching that the human was not designed to
handle emotion. It was meant to be an immaterial being, like the

angels, knowing everything intuitively, without the knowledge of the senses or the need reasoning, or any interference from animal instincts. After its expulsion from paradise, however, the human had to be given an animal body to ensure the survival of the species, and was thus plunged into the world of perception and feeling, often leading to unnatural and mutually destructive "mixtures" of thought and emotion of the kind described by Gregory, in which emotions that would have been natural and short-lived in animals are turned instead into envy, resentment, and vindictiveness and other unnatural but enduring mixtures of intelligence and emotion in the case of the humans.[62]

Maximus says that the human has no choice but to "rein in" emotions of the sort mentioned by Thalassius, namely pleasure, sorrow, desire, and fear, but points out that there is also a way to use them to good effect:

> With reason hidden from view, and finding themselves instinctively drawn towards the non-rational, it was necessary and correct for humans to rein in human nature, and with wisdom and the help of God, to come to a new awareness of the nobility of rationality. Besides, in good people emotions become good as soon as they are wisely detached from bodily matters in the pursuit of heavenly goals. For example, they transform desire into a compulsive longing of the mind for divine things, pleasure into the all-embracing joy of the mind when it is under the spell of divine generosity, fear into cautious anticipation of retribution for past wrongdoings, and sadness into a corrective regret concerning present wrongdoing. In short, just as skilled physicians use a poisonous creature, the viper, to remove existing or impending infection, these emotions can be used to avoid present and future wrongdoings, and to seize and protect goodness and understanding. These things, as I said, become good when used by those who "make every thought a prisoner, captured to be brought into obedience to Christ" (*2 Cor* 10: 5). (*AdTh CCSG* 7, pp. 47–49)

---

62 Above, pp. 36–37.

Thalassius's next question raises a more general issue concerning the involvement of God in the life of the universe, raising questions about divine grace and the salvation of the human of the sort that Eriugena had to deal with in *The Book on Predestination*:

> *Question:* If the Creator made all these forms that constitute the world in six days, what is the Father doing since then? For the Saviour says, "My Father goes on working, and so do I" (*John* 6: 17). Perhaps he is referring to the maintenance of the forms once created? (*AdTh CCSG* 7, p. 51)

This was an important issue in Maximus's time since the Manichees had argued that God's involvement with Creation ended on the sixth day. After that, Creation had to look after itself. Maximus replies:

> Although God completed the first principles of Creation and the universal essences of all things once and for all, in accordance with his knowledge, he is still at work, not only to preserve the existence of all these things but to develop and consolidate the components they potentially contain, and even now, to assimilate individuals to universals through providence, to the point where he can unite the self-chosen inclination of individuals with the more general principle of rational existence through their movement towards well-being, and make them self-moving, in harmony with each other and with the totality of all things, with no difference in principle between individuals and universals. Rather, one and same principle shall be seen throughout the totality, making no distinction between the particular ways in which things are attributed to individuals, so that the divine grace that brings about the deification of the totality will be made clear. (*ibid.*)

All of creation is in a constant state of deification, presented here by Maximus as a process designed "to assimilate individuals to universals." Yet the uniqueness of the individual is preserved since, as Maximus adds, "the Word of God adapts its gifts to the constitution of the souls who receive them" (*AdTh CCSG* 7, p. 43).

Having translated this last sentence into Latin, Eriugena adds a comment of his own:

> In the same way that water is dispersed through nature's hidden channels throughout all bodies that are born and give birth in order to increase the number of bodies, the Word of God is invisibly and mysteriously distributed among rational creatures in order to increase the number of good actions and reasons for things, although it is by nature indivisible. (*AdTh CCSG* 7, p. 43)

He imagines the Word of God making its way silently through the human body, like the waters that irrigate it to keep it in good health so as to ensure the continuation of the species, while "nature's hidden channels" ensure that the uniqueness of every individual human is preserved by the events that take place within each organism, although the Word of God that is distributed throughout Creation in this way is itself indivisible and immaterial.

Eriugena's comment is another example of his tendency to picture deification as an organic process, in contrast with the more abstract images of light and knowledge found in his Greek sources, or Maximus's image here of individuals being assimilated to universals. Another example was encountered in the previous chapter, in his commentary on Dionysius, where he says that the lion's journey back to its Creator can also be considered as an instinctual part of its own nature,[63] and elsewhere in the same work he describes the deification of the individual as a life-long process of maturation, as if "like small children we formed for ourselves the divine likeness by which we are now being deified through faith—and will be deified directly" (*DExp* 7, p. 105).

The Five-Fold Division of All Things

In a famous text, Maximus proposes a five-fold division of everything there is, beginning with God and Creation, in other words the

---

63 Above, p. 78.

Uncreated and the Created, similar to the "division of nature" that Eriugena will use in *Periphyseon*. Unlike Eriugena's two-by-two classification, however, Maximus's division is a hierarchy of five divisions, each of which (apart from the first) applies to the right-hand side of the previous one:

> The saints who received the many mysteries of the Divinity from followers and ministers of the Word who were initiated there and then into a direct knowledge of the realities, inform us in a tradition handed down by those who went before them that the substance of everything that exists can be divided in five ways. The first distinguishes between uncreated nature and created nature that receives existence by being created. By means of the second, all of nature that receives its existence from God is divided into things that are known (*noéta*) and things that are perceived (*aisthéta*). By means of the third, nature that can be perceived is divided into heaven and earth. By means of the fourth, the earth is divided into Paradise and the inhabited earth, and, by means of the fifth, the human person, the workshop which is most inclusive of all things and in itself mediates in a natural way between the furthest extremes of all the divisions and is involved in a good and proper way with things when brought into existence, is divided into male and female. (*AdIo* 1304D–1305B)

Read in this order, the divisions refer most naturally to the creation and deification of universe as it appears in *Genesis* and the life of Christ. But the division may be also be read in reverse order with obvious links to events in the life of Christ:

1	Male and Female	The Virgin birth
2	Paradise and the World	The Resurrection
3	Heaven and Earth	The Ascension
4	Intelligible and Perceptual	Christ seated on the right hand of the Father
5	Uncreated and Created	Christ one with the Father

Alternatively, the five divisions in this order may be taken to refer to stages in the deification of the human, as a series of limitations that are transcended in the process by which the human returns to its Creator. The first of these is gender, and its removal in the Return is symbolised by the non-sexual birth of the Saviour. Next, virtuous living confers immortality on the species, symbolised by the resurrection, thus erasing the distinction between earth and paradise on earth. With Christ's ascension the cosmic separation of heaven from earth is brought to an end, as it will be at the end of time; and with the beatific vision, symbolised by Christ's sitting at the right hand of the Father, when human minds are no longer dependent on things perceived (*aisthéta*) but only on things understood (*noéta*) as in the angelic mind. And finally, when the process of deification is complete, everything is united in the divinity.

When read both ways, descending and then ascending, Maximus's five divisions provide a history of the universe that is divided in two, from the creation of the world to the Nativity, and back again, through the life of Christ, to the return of all things to their origins. As Maximus puts it:

> He who brought all created things, visible and invisible, into being by a single act of will, prior to all ages and the creation of what has been created, had something in mind for them that is indescribable and beyond goodness itself, namely, that he would merge with the nature of humans, without undergoing any change himself, by means of a true union of substance, he himself becoming one with human nature without changing, and thus became a human, as he alone understood it, and that he would make the human into God through union with him, thus dividing the ages wisely, distinguishing between those required for God to become human and those required for the human to become God. (*AdThal*, CCSG 7 p. 137)

Maximus's "division of the ages" captures a good deal of the theology and spirituality of Eastern Christianity. He is not merely talking about a time-line that is divided in two by the Nativity. The division occurs prior to time, and is also a division of the mind, where the line segments refer to two aspects of deification that are jointly present in the deification of the human. "So let us too divide the ages in the mind, allocating some of them to the mystery of the divinity becoming a human, and the others to the gift of deification to the human" (*ibid*).

Much of the this imagery can actually be seen in icons of the Eastern Church.[64] There too the journeys outward and back refer to complementary aspects of deification. The very same icon of the Ascension of Christ, for example, is taken to represent his Second Coming also, and the Ascension of the human race. It is noticeable too that the passion and death of Christ do not have the same prominence in Eastern iconography as they do in the West. This is because the significance of these events in the Eastern Church lies also in the double journey that is completed, the "descent into hell" as it was referred to in older versions of the Creed, namely a journey into the realm of the dead this is required before the resurrection can occur. No particular transformation of the human is associated with its death; what matters is its deification, a process that begins at birth and continues into eternity.

The theme of the double journey is beautifully expressed in some verses of Eriugena on the Nativity:

The angelic bread that Adam lost in the beginning
Is found in a humble stable in a low-roofed cave.
He who adorns the stars in a gown of shining light
Is wrapped in tatters beneath the peak of the vault.
Whom neither the senses nor the sharpest mind can know
A herd of cattle saw, gently surrounding his body.
What mind or goodness or created wisdom of angels
Can explain the descent of the Word into flesh,
And know the soaring steps of the flesh into the Word?
As the eternal God made flesh falls down to the depths
So does the flesh made true God fly lightly to the heights. (*Carm*,
   No. 25)

The theology is eastern, and the imagery. The peaked cave is a feature of Greek icons of the nativity, where the stable is located

---

64 See *icon* + *nativity*, *ascension* etc. on the internet.

inside a small cone-shaped mountain with a slanting roof, located in a mountain wilderness.[65]

Maximus used the five divisions to argue that all of creation is somehow "brought together" in a unique way in the human species, or as he puts it above, the human is "the workshop which is most inclusive of all things." This is theory of the "human microcosm," a pre-Christian idea dating back to the Pre-Socratic philosophers (Jeauneau 1969, Appendix 7). According to the theory, and given both the five divisions above and the doctrine of the incarnation, the deified human does indeed hold a unique central position in the universe. It alone, particularly when compared with angels, participates in both sides of Maximus's divisions. It is created but contains an image of the uncreated, it has angelic intellect but it is embedded in the body of an animal, it is born on earth but destined for deification, it is mortal but has an immortal soul, it is either male or female but is really neither.

The five-fold division of Maximus is the subject of a long "contemplation" of Eriugena's at the beginning of *Periphyseon 2* (529C–542C), and his microcosm will become the foundation for his account of the human in *Periphyseon 4*.

The Three Motions of the Soul

Maximus was asked many questions about the teachings of the Greek Fathers, Gregory Nazianzen in particular, referred to here as "the teacher":

> *Question:* Why does the teacher say that the body is a cloud and a veil?
> *Answer:* Because he knows that every human mind has been led astray, and deviates from its natural motion and has its movement determined by emotion and perception and the things it perceives, not having anything else by which it could be moved, and having lost completely its natural movement towards God. And so he [Gregory] divides the body into emotion and perception, referring to these two aspects of the animated body as the cloud and the veil. The cloud is bodily-

---

65 See *icon+nativity* on the internet.

based emotion, engulfing the guide of the soul in darkness, and the veil is the illusion created by perception, fixed in the array of what is perceived and blocking the way to understanding; and forgetting about these, [the soul] turns its attention to external things and discovers anger, lust, and improper pleasures in the way we have described. (*AdIo*, 1112AB)

The body acts like something "thrown over" the soul, as Origen suggested when he interpreted the animal hides that were thrown over the naked Adam and Eve when they were expelled from Paradise (*Genesis* 3: 21) as their human bodies. It is impossible now for the human mind to see things intuitively and clearly, as angelic minds do, and correspondingly difficult for the human to be aware of the image of the divinity in its own mind.

In describing the ways the human overcomes these obstacles through deification, Maximus begins by pointing out that its mind, like animate nature in general, is a form of motion, three distinct motions in the case of the human, operating together as a single hierarchy:

The soul consists of three general kinds of motion merged into one, those of mind (*nous*), reason (*logos*) and perception (*aisthésis*). The first is a simple, unexplainable motion that brings the mind closer to God in a way that is beyond comprehension and yields an acquaintance with him transcending everything he has created. The second is directed by the defining cause of something that is unknown, moving the soul in a natural way to use its powers of understanding on all of the natural explanations of those things that can only be known through their causes or forms. The third is a compound motion, in which the soul, through contact with the external world, acquires its own impression of the causes as if from indicators of visible things. (*AdIo*, 1112D–1113A)

The human mind is identified by Maximus, as it is by Gregory, with the simple and unexplainable unity of consciousness when it is experienced as a theophany, i.e. an image of God. It is indistinguishable therefore from the process of deification itself, as Maximus's definition makes clear.[66] The second movement of the soul, reason, is the capacity to make inferences from what is perceived to their unseen causes. And the function of perception, which is the mind's only contact with the material world, is to provide a "print" of the external world that appears to make reality visible but in fact provides only pointers towards realities that in themselves are immaterial and can be comprehended, insofar as this is possible, only by reason and intellect. The triad Perception–Reason–Mind was a widely-accepted division of the human mind in the Greek tradition, and was encountered in Eriugena's commentary on Martianus where he says: "Nature has three rational components *aisthésis, logos, nous,* i.e. perception, reason, mind."[67] It is the subject of a long commentary in *Periphyseon* 2 (572C–579A) and the basis for his treatment of the human mind as a symbol of the Trinity.[68]

Ideally, perception, reason and understanding should be fully integrated, in the same way that nature, mind and divinity are in Gregory's account of deification. According to Maximus, this form of integration was achieved by the saints and Fathers of the Church:

> The Fathers made their way with dignity through the present age of troubles by means of the true and unerring functioning of these natural motions, which in the case of perception is by passing up to the mind, through the use of reason, only those perceptions that have a single conceptual

---

66 Given that *nous* (mind) directs the activities of reason and perception, the term "mind" as used here has two meanings: it can refer to the mind as a whole (including reason and perception), or exclusively to the intellectual act of *understanding* that is beyond the powers of perception and reasoning. Thus Eriugena sometimes translates *nous* as *animus* (soul or mind), as he does here, to refer to the mind as a whole, and sometimes as *intellectus* (understanding, intellect)—as he does below, p. 140—to refer to *nous* or understanding.

67 Above, p. 12.

68 Below, p. 139–142,

definition; and in the case of reason, by seamlessly uniting with understanding, through a simple and undivided prudence, all those things that have definitions; and in the case of understanding—freed entirely from the motions of created things and at ease with its own natural activity—by taking everything to God. Thus all [of the saints] were made worthy of being merged with the entire divinity through the spirit, since they bore the entire image of the divinity insofar as this is possible for humans, and by attracting the image of the divinity (if one may say such a thing) to the extent that they were drawn towards it, they became one with God. For they say that God and the human are representations of each other, and to the extent that God is humanized to a human person through love of humans, so is the human itself deified through the love of God; and to the extent that the human is drawn by God through the mind towards what can be known, so does the human manifest God through virtuous living, although he is by nature invisible. (*AdIo*, 1113A)

Maximus presents deification as a harmonious integration of the three main activities of the human mind, perception, reason and understanding. He describes *logos* (reason) using Aristotle's term φρόνησις [*phrónēsis*], generally translated into English as "prudence," "good judgment," "or "thoughtfulness," and sometimes described by Eriugena as "the mind's eye." *Logos*, therefore is not a particular act or state of mind in the way that perception and understanding are, but more of a perspective and an attitude, consisting of a constellation of beliefs and dispositions that collectively ensure that inference is based on secure perception and followed up by actions that are consistent with them, leading finally to understanding, which in both Gregory and Maximus is an awareness of the divine presence in the mind of the human.

The Transfiguration

The transfiguration of the Saviour on Mount Tabor (*Matthew* 17: 1–9, *Mark* 9: 2–8, *Luke* 9: 28–36) is one of the most studied events in the life of Christ in the Eastern Church.[69] and what Maximus has to say on the subject is of great interest because it deals not only with the topics of deification and the three motions of the soul, but also with the more general philosophical issue concerning the relation between profane and sacred learning in the salvation of the human.

Here is his own short account of the event:

> And so it was that some of Christ's disciples, on account of their dedication to virtuous living, were taken up by him and climbed the mountain where he was to be revealed, and saw him transfigured, unapproachable because of the light coming from his face, and were astounded by the brightness of his clothes, realizing his great holiness from the respect shown him by Moses and Elias standing on either side of him. (*AdIo*, 1125D)

He says that it was their "dedication to virtuous living," that made it possible for the disciples to experience the revelation that was to come:

> Through the change that the spirit brought about in their ability to perceive things, they passed over from body to spirit before they laid bodily life aside, lifting the veils that the passions placed around their intellectual powers, and with the perceptual faculties of body and soul now cleansed, they were taught the spiritual meaning of the mysteries that were shown to them. (*AdIo*, 1128A)

He then describes what the disciples saw on the mountain, drawing on Isaiah, John, and Dionysius:

> They were taught mystically that the splendour of sanctity, radiating with such brilliance from his face and completely

---

69 See *icon* + *transfiguration* on the internet.

blinding their eyes, was a manifestation of his divinity beyond comprehension, perception, being, and knowledge, and that they knew him to be the Word made flesh from the absence of any shape or beauty, and thus resplendent with a beauty beyond the sons of the human, they were led by the hand to understand that he was the one who was in the beginning, and that he was with God, and was God, and, proclaiming him through theological denial to be completely beyond restrictions, they were guided by reflection to the glory of the only-begotten of the Father, full of grace and truth. (*AdIo*, 1128AB)

This is a synopsis of Maximus's notion of deification, based on Scripture (Isaiah and John), the negative theology of Dionysius, and his own understanding of the three motions of the soul.

He now adds some further detail, turning his attention to the illuminated clothes of Christ. These, he says, have two quite different interpretations:

The whitened garments stand for the words of Sacred Scripture, now bright, clear and distinct, understood without puzzling ambiguities or obscure symbolism, making clear the meaning that was hidden in them, with the result that they were taken to a simple and correct knowledge of God and were released from the attractions of the world and the flesh. Or [the garments may stand] for Creation itself—provided the crude assumption that it reveals itself solely in the senses and their deceitful offerings is stripped away—as it shows the power of the generative Word through the wisdom that is evident in the great variety of forms it comprises, in the same way that a garment shows something of the nobility of the one who wears it. (*AdIo*, 1128BC)

In the tradition of Dionysius, he welcomes the ambiguity created by the two interpretations of the shining garments, i.e. Scripture or Creation, since this makes it impossible to believe that the divinity is adequately described by either, although both are accurate as far as they go:

> In both cases, the meaning is consistent with the words uttered, and also appropriately obscured by uncertainty in both cases, lest we should dare to project them onto something that is beyond them, namely the Word in the case of the writings of Sacred Scripture, and in the case of Creation, the Creator and constructor of Creation. (*AdIo*, 1128C)

For those looking for guidance on the matter of correct living, therefore, Maximus says that there is nothing to choose between Scripture and Creation. One is just as good as the other:

> So I think it follows of necessity that either one or the other is sufficient for a person wishing to live a simple and blameless life in the presence of God, i.e. a spiritual knowledge of Scripture or natural contemplation (in accordance with the spirit) of what there is. Thus the two laws, natural and written, are of equal value and teach the same thing, and none is greater or lesser than the other, showing as one would expect, that the one who becomes a lover of true wisdom is the one who truly longs for it. (*AdIo*, 1128CD)

The doctrine expounded here by Maximus, that the salvation of the human can be achieved either through Scripture or through Creation, was always strongly resisted in the West—except for the special case of peoples lacking access to Scripture. Maximus makes no restrictions, and his own work shows that he freely draws on both sacred and profane knowledge. The cryptic closing line makes the same point and provides the justification for it: truthfulness is a feature of the *search* for truth, and it is only in a secondary sense that it can be attributed to the sources in which any particular individual finds it, whether in Scripture or in Creation.

Eriugena's Translation

Eriugena's translation of Maximus is open to the same criticisms as his translation of Dionysius: it is word for word, and often impossible to understand without reference to the original. Nonetheless, it is still to be found side by side with modern editions of Maximus's Greek text. The reason for this, as the editors explain, is entirely pragmatic:

> If the *Quaestiones ad Thalassium* can sometimes dishearten the modern reader because of their lofty speculations and the complexity of their style, one can readily imagine the difficulties they would pose for somebody wishing to translate them in the ninth century, at a time when knowledge of Greek was very limited and the scholarly resources that help us to read the texts were not available.... One can only admire the result of the work all the more. Although it is true, as we shall see, that this translation is often unintelligible and contains many errors, as soon as one gets used to the methods of John the Scot, it can still be a great help to today's reader in understanding the Greek text we are editing side by side with it. (Laga & Steele, 1980, ci–cii)

In Eriugena's time, few scholars, East or West, studied Maximus. Indeed, somewhat like Eriugena himself, it was only in the latter half of the twentieth century that his work become widely known (Berthold, 1985, xi). He is now ranked among the greatest of Christian theologians, for although he prefers to write short pieces, commenting on an incident from the Bible, perhaps, or some sacred image, or a line from scripture or one of the Fathers, his work has the clarity and coherence of the great Greek philosophical texts, and the same firm foundations in the observation of human behaviour that is found in Aristotle. In the chapters to follow now on Eriugena's own works, and most notably in the five chapters on *Periphyseon*, the full extent of his indebtedness to Gregory, Dionysius and Maximus will soon become clear.

Chapter 6

The *Homily* and *Commentary* on John's Gospel

Eriugena wrote two works on the Gospel of St John, a homily, i.e. a short contemplative essay, on its opening Prologue, from "In the beginning was the Word" as far as Verse 14, ending with the words "full of grace and truth," and a commentary on the entire Gospel of John that he was unable to complete. These are his last works, written around 870 or in the following years. The homily (20 pages or so) is suitable for a public reading, and in it he goes through the passage from John verse by verse and comments on each. The fragments we have (some 90 pages) from his intended commentary on the entire gospel of John cover only Chapter 2 and portions of Chapters 1, 3, and 6. In giving special attention to John's gospel, Eriugena is most likely following once again in the footsteps of Origen who wrote a commentary on John and held that "just as the Gospels are the first fruits of Scripture, the first fruits of the Gospels is that of John" (*PG* 14, 32B).

1 The Homily
Eriugena's homily begins as follows:

> The voice of the mystic eagle resounds in the ears of the Church. May the external senses grasp the fleeting sound, and may the inner mind penetrate the meaning that remains. The voice of the bird that flies on high, flying not merely above the material air or the ether or around the totality of the world of the senses, but transcending all reflection, beyond all things that are and that are not, flying swiftly on the wings of spiritual theology and contemplative insights clear and sublime. By "things that are" I mean those

that do not entirely escape perception, human or angelic, since they come after God and are counted among the things created by the single cause of all things; the things that are not are those that entirely surpass the powers of every intellect. (*HomJ* 1, pp. 3–4)

The description of the eagle is reminiscent of Martianus' poem describing Philologia as she flies in circles around the earth and upwards "beyond the terrestrial globe."[70] And in a way, Eriugena too is writing poetry here, or any rate the *Kunstprosa* that can be found throughout his work. Actually, the Latin text translated above can be laid out precisely in the form of a poem in three verses (O'Meara, 1988, pp. 195–197, based on Dronke, 1984), and although this is an exceptional case, it is still true that even in his most abstract and technical writing Eriugena is always attentive to the sounds and rhythms of the language he uses. This was noted by critics as well as admirers, and was no doubt a part of what Prudentius was getting at in his jibe about Eriugena's "Celtic eloquence."[71]

As in his poem on Dionysius, Eriugena imagines John's achievement as a journey from earth into the heavens:

The blessed theologian John flies up not only beyond everything that can be understood and spoken about, but is carried upwards also to things that are beyond all understanding and expression, and in a wordless flight of the mind he is taken up beyond everything to the secrets of the one Principle of all things, and seeing clearly the incomprehensible unified super-essentiality and distinct super-substantiality of the Principle and Word themselves, namely the Father and the Son, he begins his gospel, "In the Beginning was the Word" (*John* 1: 1). (*HomJ* 1, pp. 4–5)

The eagle rises from the earth and flies upwards through the higher zones of the universe, air and ether, into the heart of the divinity. It is also as a journey through the three motions of the soul, as

70 Above, p. 21.

71 Above, p. 59.

understood by Maximus, from Perception to Reason, and from Reason to the realm of Mind that is beyond human understanding.[72]

God and Creation

Eriugena has a lot to say about the line "All that came to be had life in him" (*John* 1: 4). The text of John he was using read: *Quod factum est in ipso vita erat*, literally "What was made in him was life." This is ambiguous: it can be read "What was made, in him was life," and "What was made in him, was life," depending on where you put the comma. Eriugena notes the ambiguity, explores both meanings, and as he usually does in the case of ambiguous references to the divinity, retains both:

> This sentence can be read in two ways. It can be broken into *What was made* to which is then added *in him was life*. Or alternatively, *What was made in him* to which is then added *was life*. So we have two meanings to think about, based on two readings. For the idea expressed by "What was made as an individual thing, discrete with regard to times and places, distinct with regard to genera, forms and numbers, as part of a composite or singly—all of this was life in him" is not the same as that expressed by "What was made in him was life and nothing else." So let the meaning be: "All the things that were made by him, constitute life in him and are one." For they were (they subsist) in him causally before existing in themselves as effects. There is a difference between the way that things that were made by him exist below him, and the way that the things he himself is are in him. (*HomJ* 9, p. 17)

Creation participates in the divinity in two ways. Prior to its coming into being it exists as an eternal Primordial Cause that is a part of the life of the divinity; and when it comes into existence it becomes a part of the life of the divinity once more, but in a different way, namely through its being created. This dual participation in the divinity holds for all of Creation:

---

72 Above, pp. 92–94.

All things that have been made through the Word live in him without change and are life, while in their temporal and spatial existence, not one of them ever was or ever will be in him. Beyond all time and space, however, all things are nothing other than one thing in him, all things visible and invisible, corporeal and incorporeal, rational and non-rational, in short, heaven and earth, the abysses and everything in them, live in him and are life in him, and subsist in him in eternity. Even things that seem to us to lack all vitality are alive in the Word. (*Hom J* 10, pp. 18–19)

The Globe of Perception

Eriugena has now extended the notion of "life" to include the inanimate world. If readers are uneasy with this, he says, they need only look around them:

And if you ask how and in what way all things created through the Word subsist in him in a living form, uniformly and causally, take examples from nature, learn about the maker from the things that have been made in him and through him: "The things about him that are invisible," as the Apostle says, "can be understood from the things that have been created." (*Rm* 1: 20) (*Hom J* 10, p. 19)

By reflecting on the structure of the created world, its pre-existence as part of the life of the divinity becomes clear when one considers the generative force that must lie behind so many of its most striking features, whether in nature in general—beginning here with the sun—or more obviously still in the life of every individual mind:

Notice how the causes of everything that is within the globe of the perceived world subsists simultaneously and uniformly in this sun which is called The Great Light of the World. From here the forms of all bodies originate, the beauty of different colours and other things that can be attributed to nature as we see it. Consider the multiple and infinite power of seeds, how a multitude of grasses, bushes, and animals are contained in individual seeds at one point in time, and how a beautiful and innumerable multiplicity of forms springs from them. See with the eyes of the mind how a multiplicity of rules are a single thing in the art of the artist and live in the soul of the person using them, how an infinite number of lines subsist in a point, and examine examples of this sort from nature. Then, as if carried aloft above all things on the wings of natural contemplation, aided and enlightened by divine grace, you will be able to study the mysteries of the Word with the eye of the mind and, insofar as it is given to humans seeking their God by reasoning, to see how all things made through the Word live in him and are life. "For it is in him," as Sacred Scripture says, "that we live, and move, and exist" (*Acts* 17: 28).[73] And as the great Dionysius the Areopagite says, "the essence of all things is the Divinity beyond essences" (*HC* 4, 1). (*HomJ* 10, pp. 19–21)

In their fallen condition, however, humans can only infer the presence of God by reading Scripture, or alternatively, by reflecting on the structure of Creation and reasoning about its origins. In its original condition, the human would have known God as angels do, by immediate intuition and direct acquaintance. This came to an end with the Fall:

> The light of divine knowledge on earth went out when the human deserted God. As a result, the eternal light shows itself in two ways in the world, namely through Scripture and through Creation. For divine knowledge cannot be revived in us in any other way except through the words of Scripture and the splendour of Creation. Study the words of Scripture and think of their meaning in your mind and you will come to know the Word. Examine the appearance and beauty of the perceptual world using the senses of the body and there you will understand the Word of God. And in all of these the Truth will reveal to you nothing other than he who made all things, beyond whom there is nothing else to contemplate

---

73 See Footnote 110 on p. 153.

since he is everything. For in all the things there are, he himself is whatever there is. In the same way that no substantial good exists outside of him, so also no essence or substance exists outside of him. (*HomJ* 11, pp. 21–22)

John the Baptist

There is a dramatic change in John's Prologue at verse six. The preceding verses described the life of the divinity in eternity before the creation of the universe; now he turns to John the Baptist, a human, fixed in time and place. Eriugena comments:

> "There was a man sent by God whose name was Iohannes." Behold the eagle descending in gentle flight from the highest peak of the mountain of theology to the deepest valley of history, from heaven to the earth of the spiritual world, by relaxing the wings of highest contemplation. (*HomJ* 14, pp. 26–27)

Scripture, he explains, can be looked at as a kind of universe, composed of elements somewhat like the fire, air, water and earth of the physical universe. When the evangelist begins to talk about John the Baptist, Eriugena imagines him descending from Scripture's highest point, close to the sun, all the way down to the earthly region at its base:

> For Scripture can be understood as a kind of universe, made up of four parts that are like four elements. Its earth, so to speak, is in the middle, and lower down, like a core, is History. Flowing all around it like water are the deeps of moral understanding which the Greeks refer to as ἠθική [*ēthikē*] (ethics). All around these—I mean history and ethics, like the two lower parts of the universe mentioned—the air of natural science revolves, the natural science called φυσική [*physikē*] (physics) by the Greeks. And encircling them, outside all of them and beyond them, is the ethereal and fiery heat of the empyric heavens, that is, of the high contemplation of

the divine nature which the Greeks call *Theology*. Further than this no intellect can go. (*HomJ* 14, p. 27)

This matching up of the four elements with the four disciplines required for a full understanding of Scripture probably comes from Maximus (Jeauneau, 1969, Appendix 3). A version of it appears also in the poem Eriugena wrote in honour of Maximus.[74]

Eriugena notes that the soaring lines of the opening verses of John's Gospel, followed by the eagle's descent to the earth, mirrors the evangelist's own journey as he began to write his Gospel:

> The great theologian (I mean John), as he begins his gospel, touching the highest peaks of theology and penetrating the secrets of heaven and the heavenly mysteries, rising up beyond all history, ethics and physics, and then, as if returning to earth, redirects the flight of his mind to the historical account of the events that took place immediately prior to the incarnation of the Word and says: "There was a man sent from God." (*HomJ* 14, p. 27)

The Region of the Shadows of Death

Eriugena comes to the ninth verse of John's prologue, "He was the true light illuminating every person coming into this world" (*John* 1: 9). Without any warning, it leads to an outpouring of nihilism and despair not found elsewhere in his writings.

He begins by posing some simple questions about the meaning of the verse. "And what is 'coming into the world'? And who is 'every person coming into the world'? And from where do they come into the world? And into which world do they come?" (*HomJ* 17, p. 31). The answer seems obvious: "this world" means the one we are in right now, and "coming into the world" means being born. But Eriugena is embarking on a "higher" reading, and is thinking instead of Creation in the deified form it took before the Fall, and will take again after the Return. In comparison with that, "this world" that the human arrives into by being born takes on a shocking appearance:

---

74 Above, pp. 83–84.

If you think the reference is to those who come into this world from the hidden folds of nature by being born at a particular place and time, what kind of enlightenment does "this life" provide for people who are born in order to die, who grow in order to rot, who are put together in order to fall apart, descending from the solitude and stillness of nature into restlessness and the turmoil of unhappiness? Tell me, if you would, what "light" is spiritual and true for people created for a life that is short and false? Is not "this world" the perfect place for people who are blind to the true light? Is it not called, with good reason, the region of the shadow of death and the valley of tears, the pit of ignorance, and the earthly house that weighs down the soul, preventing the eyes of the mind from catching sight of the true light? (*HomJ* 17, pp. 31–32)

Taken in isolation from its origin and its Return, "this life" appears to him as one that is entirely without hope.

Although Eriugena has been speaking mostly of rational Creation as it appears in the human, with John's next verse, "He was in the world" (*John* 1: 10), he returns to the more fundamental presence of God in all of Creation, the one that it has by reason of the fact that Creation exists. This includes all of its levels, supra-rational, rational, subrational, and material:

Here "world" refers not just in a general way to the created world that can be perceived but more especially to rational nature as found in humans. In all of these, and more simply put, in the created universe, the Word was the true light, i.e. it subsists and always existed since it never ceased to subsist in all things. In the same way that the voice of a person who speaks comes to an end and disappears when he stops speaking, so it is with the heavenly Father: if his Word ceased to speak, the effects of the Word, namely the created universe, would not subsist. For the speech of God the Father, namely the eternal and unchangeable generation of his Word, is the subsistence and permanence of the created universe. (*HomJ* 18, p. 33)

This is the Byzantine conception of the Word of God, *Iésous Christos o Pantokratór* (Jesus Christ the Ruler of All), the cosmic Word that reverberates through all of Creation, assuring its continued existence and drawing it back towards re-unification with the Creator. Long before Eriugena's time, this notion of the Word of God and the second person of the Trinity was rejected by the Latin Church because of its pantheistic overtones.

Deification and Incarnation

Eriugena considers three levels in the deification of Creation, three worlds (*mundi*) as he puts it, the world of pure spirits (angels and saints), the human world, and the sub-rational world, in both its animate and inanimate forms. The three worlds also constitute a hierarchy: immaterial intellect is its highest form, non-rational and material Creation is its base. Between the two lies the world of the human:

We need to distinguish three kinds of worlds. The first is taken up exclusively by the invisible and spiritual substances of the virtues (pure spirits) and anybody entering there will possess full participation in the true light. The second is its direct opposite, made up entirely of visible and corporeal natures. And although it belongs to the lowest part of the universe, the Word was in it, and it was through the Word that it was made, and it is the first step for those wishing to ascend through the senses to knowledge of the truth, for it is the spectacle of visible things that draws the rational soul towards knowledge of the invisible. The third world is that which, through the mediation of reason, brings together within itself the higher spiritual world with the lower world of corporeal things and makes the two one, something that is found only in the human in whom all of Creation is united. (*HomJ* 19, pp. 34–35)

This is a simplified form of Maximus's human microcosm, based on his "five-fold division of all things."[75] Even though angels are higher than humans in the three-level hierarchy he has presented, and also closer to God, humans are closer to the centre of Creation because they bring together aspects of Creation that are found only in isolation from each other when they exist elsewhere in the universe. According to Eriugena, this makes the human more representative of the totality, since it contains them all, and at the same time it makes the human strikingly beautiful because of the unrivalled variety of created forms that it brings together:

> For it consists of a body and a soul. It brings together a body from this world and a soul from the other world to create a single object of beauty. And the body encompasses all of corporeal nature, and the soul all of incorporeal nature, and when these are brought together in a single entity, they constitute the integrated world of the human. And that is why the human is referred to [by John] as "every," for every created thing is brought together in it as if in a workshop. (*HomJ* 19, p. 35)

The workshop (*officina*) he refers to is the "microcosm" or "little universe" of Maximus[76] in which a mixture of material and immaterial forms, taken from all parts of the universe, are "forged" together in the life of the human. Maximus's microcosm also provides that foundations for Eriugena's account of the human in *Periphyseon 4*.

In the closing pages of the homily Eriugena turns to the incarnation of the Word and the Nativity, the turning point in the history of the universe in an Eastern perspective, when the time for God to become human comes to an end, and the time for the human to become God begins:

> It was not for his own sake that the Word became flesh but for ours, since we could not have been transformed into sons of God except through the flesh of the Word. He descended

75 Above, pp. 88–91.

76 Above, p. 91.

alone, he ascends with a crowd. He who made God into a human makes Gods of humans. (*HomJ* 21, pp. 39–40)

And so the events prefigured in the legal and prophetic texts of the prophets in the Old Testament are brought to fulfilment:

> As the Apostle says "In his body lives the fullness of divinity" (*Col* 2: 9), using "the fullness of divinity" to refer to the secret meanings hidden in the shadows of the Law, which Christ, by coming in the flesh, both taught and showed to be dwelling in him bodily, that is, in truth, since he is the origin and the fullness of grace, the truth behind the symbols of the law, the end-point of the visions of the prophets. To whom be glory with the Father and the Holy Spirit for ever and ever. Amen. (*HomJ* 23, p. 43)

2 The Commentary on John's Gospel

Some of the themes in Eriugena's Homily on Prologue to John's Gospel appear again in the surviving fragments of the commentary he planned for the entire Gospel. This is to be expected, since he is commenting on different parts of the same text, and his comments were written about the same time as the homily. I will not try to summarize the ideas contained in the fragments of Eriugena's commentary that we have, but instead will confine myself to a single theme that is found there, that of the wilderness or desert.[77] The hermit, and in particular the hermit-scholar was revered in early Irish monasticism, a reverence that reached its peak in the 9th century. "The desert," as Ryan says, "was the goal held out to every monk" (1931, p. 408), a fact that is attested also by the frequency of the Old Irish word "dísert" (*desertum*) in the place names of contemporary Ireland (Flanagan & Flanagan, 1994, p. 69), referring

---

77 I use the word "wilderness" rather than "desert" to translate "desertum" since the English word "desert" conveys little of the meaning of Latin "desertum" (a deserted place) and even less of the kind of hermitage Eriugena would have been familiar with from Ireland. In addition, the etymology he will now propose for the Greek ἐρημία [*erémia*] (wilderness) suggests that he is thinking of a mountain hermitage, far away from the dwelling-places of humans *and* high above them.

originally to well-known hermitages of saints, typically located in places of striking beauty. For Eriugena, the wilderness is not so much a topic for discussion as a constant perspective that he needs only to refresh from time to time—as he did in the Homily when he spoke of the fallen human "descending from the solitude and stillness of nature into anxiety and the turmoil of unhappiness."[78]

Eriugena's Wilderness

In the Commentary, however, Eriugena does need to go into the matter a little more deeply when he comes to the words of John the Baptist, "I am a voice crying out in the wilderness" (*John* 1: 23), since he disagrees with those scholars who give an allegorical interpretation to the word "wilderness" in this context:

> Many people like to interpret this wilderness as Judaea and all of Israel. Judea had indeed been turned into a wilderness, lacking all divine worship, corrupted by shameful idolatry, following only the letter of the law, devoid of all spiritual meaning, defiled by diverse superstitions. What was previously called a proclamation—for the word "Judea" means "proclamation"—is transformed completely into a denial of the truth. So it is in this wilderness that the voice of the Word and the Word itself first made itself heard. (*ComJ* 1, 27, pp. 59–60)

But while the allegory is plausible—and skilfully developed by Eriugena to make the point—his own reflections take him in an entirely different direction. The wilderness, he says, is an image of God:

> At a higher level of contemplation, the wilderness means the inexpressible nobility of the divine nature in its remoteness from all things. All of Creation has deserted it, because it is beyond all understanding, although it never deserts understanding. And this is made clearer than the light of day by its Greek name, ἔρημος [*érēmos*], since ἐρημία [*erēmía*] means

---

78 Above, p. 106.

remoteness and elevation, which is entirely correct for the divine nature. (*ComJ* 1, 27, p. 60)

His "higher reading" is based on the contemplative disclosure of the remoteness and isolation of the divinity in the wilderness, and the secure control that it exerts over all of Creation, more striking than ever now that it appears in its unapproachable solitude. Its primary content is simply its magnificence, and this is no more in need of interpretation or elaboration than any other manifestation of the divinity in creation.

In this wilderness, Eriugena says, two cries were emitted but only one was heard. Neither was the cry of John the Baptist:

> It is in this wilderness of divine transcendence that the Word cries out, through which all things were created. Listen to Moses speaking in Genesis. "God said: Let there be light. God said: Let there be a firmament." And similarly, in all of the works of the six days, "God said" comes first, where we should understand the word "God" to refer to the Father, and "said" to the Word of God. So the Word of God cries out in the remotest solitude of divine goodness. His cry is the creation of all of nature. He himself calls all the things that are and those that are not, since through him the Father cried out, that is, created all the things he wished there to be. He cried out invisibly, before the world was created, so that there would be a world. He cried out, coming visibly into the world, so that the world would be saved. He first cried out in eternity through his divinity alone before the incarnation; then he cried out through his flesh. (*ComJ* 1, 27, pp. 60–61)

The Brazen Serpent

The theme of the wilderness occurs again in Eriugena's commentary. He notes the comparison the Evangelist makes between the crucifixion of Christ and the raising aloft of a bronze serpent in the wilderness in the famous incident recounted in the *Book of Numbers* (*Nb* 21: 6–9). On the instructions of Yahweh, Moses places a bronze serpent on a pole in order to save the Israelites from a plague of poisonous snakes. The Evangelist adds: "And the Son of Man must be lifted up as Moses lifted up the serpent in the wilderness, so that everyone who believes may have eternal life in him. (*John* 3: 13–15). Eriugena comments:

> The truth itself explains its image, the object itself identifies its shadow. Scripture records that when the people of God were in the wilderness they were attacked by serpents who constantly bit them, causing great loss of life. But Moses, on the instruction of the Lord, made a serpent of bronze and hung it on a tall tree and ordered the people who had been bitten by the dragons to look at the bronze serpent in order to be healed and delivered from the plague of serpents. All of this is the shadow of what was to come, namely an image of Christ who was to die for the salvation of all those plagued by venomous bites from the serpents of their sins. So Moses himself is Christ, the bronze serpent is the death of Christ, the tree on which the serpent was hung is the cross of Christ, on which he suffered death for the salvation of all who believe in him. (*ComJ* 3, 5, p. 87)

Eriugena notes how the images of the crucifixion of Christ and the serpent are merged:

> And the representation of the death of Christ by the serpent is done well, using the transposition of cause and effect. For the serpent was the cause of the death of Christ, and so the serpent was also standing figuratively for its effect, namely death. (*ibid.*)

Yet the "incongruity," as Dionysius would have called it, actually adds to the power of the composite image—as is shown by the fact that so many writers, painters and sculptors through the centuries, down to the present day, have been drawn to the image of the brazen serpent raised aloft in the wilderness.[79]

---

79 See *brazen* + *serpent* on the internet.

Actually, Eriugena himself may be counted among them. The Brazen Serpent appears also in verses he wrote about the escape of the Jews from Egypt through the miraculous opening that was created for them through the Red Sea:

> Pharaoh, why do you pursue the people? Begone to the depths
> Of eternal incarceration, and may the black swamp cover you
>   over!
> In the meantime we are staying on the middle road of virtue,
> With the towering waterfalls of illusion and evil on either side.
> Getting past these, the joyful soul arrives on the sandy shore
> And sees from afar its sins, overpowered and submerged.
> Then it sings a hymn of thanksgiving, triumphant and
>   overjoyed
> And joins in the chorus of praise to the glory of God.
> Then, travelling by the shores of virtue it reaches the
>   wilderness
> Where all love of this contemptible world lapses into silence,
> Where the unclean spirit will always fail to find peace
> But is forced to return to the place from whence it came.
> That is where the bronze serpent hisses as it hangs aloft.
> Its poison is harmless now, the people shall be free. (*Car*, No. 2)

He imagines the waterfalls of the Red Sea through which the Israelites escaped as a pair of "veils" of the sort discussed by Maximus, i.e. illusory products of perception, attractive to look at but barely holding back the forces of anarchy and destruction.[80] The soul must make its way past these, and along the seashore to the safety of the wilderness.

Eriugena's distinctive image of the wilderness is never far away in his writing. It will be encountered again at the beginning of *Periphyseon 2* where he will use it to explain the "bare and empty earth" mentioned in the opening lines of *Genesis*.[81]

---

80 Above, p. 94.
81 Below, pp. 135–139.

Epilogue

Strange to say, Eriugena's homily and commentary on John's gospel, the first a very brief work and the second mere fragments of a work he never completed, were the most widely read of all his writings until recent times. In neither case, however, was it known that it was he who wrote them.[82] The homily was attributed to various authors, including Origen and John Chrysostom, and was often praised—by Aquinas among others. The commentary had few if any readers until the 12th century, when large extracts were taken from it for inclusion in the *Glossa Ordinaria*, a collection of commentaries on the Bible. Since the *Glossa* was widely used, Eriugena now gained a considerable readership although he still remained anonymous. Of those parts of John's Gospel that Eriugena commented on, about 40% of the material in the Glossa is his (Jeauneau, 1999, p. 60).

One wonders what Aquinas would have felt had he known that a large extract he borrowed from the *Glossa* for his *Summa Theologica* was by Eriugena (*ibid.*, p. 62). The only time he referred to Eriugena was to point out that his claim that angels do not see God directly is heretical (*Commentarium super Epistolam ad Hebraeos* 1, 6, §86; O'Meara, 1987). This, presumably, is the reason he does not refer to him by name but only as "one of the first to study the books of Dionysius."

---

82 See Jeauneau, 1969, Ch.4; 1999, Ch. 4, 2008, lxxvi–lxxxi, 139–150).

Chapter 7

Periphyseon 1

The greatest of Eriugena's works is the five-volume *Periphyseon* (Concerning Natures).[83] In calling it *Periphyseon* Eriugena was most likely thinking of Origen's *Peri Archón* (Concerning First Principles) (Jeauneau,1996, p. *xi*). He had a high regard for Origen, and in writing *Periphyseon* he was indeed attempting a grand philosophical survey of everything, similar in scope to Origen's work, while the shift from ἀρχαί [*archaí*] to φύσεις [*phýseis*], from "principles" to "natures" (i.e. entities), also captures the naturalistic perspective of *Periphyseon* when compared with Origen's more thematic *Peri Archón*.

The name *Periphyseon* also situates Eriugena's work within the discipline of *physica* as it was then understood. This included "physics" in the modern sense, or at any rate its medieval precursor, but was also a "philosophy of nature" that sought to relate everything known about Creation, including its mental and spiritual features, to the physical elements of fire, air, earth, and water. Examples of *physica* in this sense were encountered in Eriugena's notes on Martianus, often introduced by phrases such as "from a physical point of view" or "there is a physical aspect to this."[84] The purpose of such comments is to link aspects of mental and cultural life with physical features of the universe, suggesting, for example, that the relationship of intellect to reason is similar to that between the fire

---

83 Until recent times, the work was often incorrectly referred to as *De Divisione Naturae* (The Division of Nature) following the publication of the first printed edition under this name by Gale in 1681. It was only in 1968 that the error was finally corrected, with the publication of the first volume of Sheldon-Williams's edition, published in Dublin in that year under its correct title *Periphyseon*. The title Gale used was intended only for the first section of *Periphyseon 1*.

84 Above, pp. 7, 15.

of the sun and the air of the earth's atmosphere.[85] Eriugena himself describes *Periphyseon* as a work of *physiologia* (*PP4* 741C), from the Greek verb *physiologein*, i.e. to speculate about the relationship between mind and matter, the area of research often referred to nowadays as "the material basis of mind." By comparison with its modern counterpart, medieval *physiologia* consists mostly of analogy. Yet, as Gregory's work shows, the analogies can still capture a good deal of the truth about the functioning of the brain and the sensory systems. *De Imagine* was the most outstanding example of the discipline of *physiologia* available to Eriugena, but was restricted to the study of the human. In *Periphyseon*, therefore, Eriugena's objective was to extend Gregory's *physiologia* to the study of everything, the earth, all forms of life, the human, the angels, the heavens, and the Creator.

The Four-Fold Division of Everything

Periphyseon takes the form of a dialogue between two people, a teacher (Nutritor) and a student (Alumnus). It starts out as follows:

> *Teacher*: When I am thinking, as I frequently am, and trying as best I can to understand that the primary and most comprehensive division of all things—whether they can be conceived by the mind or lie beyond its scope—is into those that are and those that are not, the general term that comes to mind for all of them is the Greek *physis* or Latin *natura*. Or do you, perhaps, take a different view?
>
> *Student*: No, I agree with you. For I have only to set my foot on the path of reasoning to see that this is so.
>
> *Teacher*: So we are agreed that *natura* is the general term for everything that is and that is not?
>
> *Student*: Yes. For there is nothing whatever that we might think about that this term would not apply to.
>
> *Teacher*: Since we are agreed that this is the general term, then I would like you to give the method for dividing it into species by making distinctions; or if you prefer, I will

---

85 Above, p. 8.

attempt the division first, and then you can pass judgment on it.

Student: I think you should start. I am impatient and waiting to hear a correct analysis of this matter from you. (*PP1* 441AB)

Like other philosophical works written in the form of a dialogue, *Periphyseon* can just as easily be read as a series of essays on loosely related topics. Without looking for the *N* for *nutritor* (teacher) and the *A* for *alumnus* (student) it would sometimes be hard to know which of the two is speaking, while some of the teacher's "turns" in the dialogue transform themselves into "contemplations" that can go on for several pages without any response from the student.

The term *natura* that Eriugena proposes for things of every description is indeed quite general. As the Student says, it refers to anything "one might think about." The first task, therefore, is to divide all the things we might think about into their principal varieties. Eriugena opts for a two-by-two division (1) Not Created and Creating, (2) Created and Creating, (3) Created and Not Creating, and (4) Not Creating and Not Created. This echoes the first of Maximus's five divisions, Created and Not Created (above, p 87), except that Eriugena makes no use of the other four. Instead, he derives his entire scheme from the verb "create" and its passive "being created," combining them in all possible ways with the negative particle. The categories are interpreted by Eriugena as (1) God, (2) the Primordial Causes, (3) Creation, and (4) Salvation.

This particular two-by-two classification interested Eriugena from the time he first encountered it in Martianus Capella in a purely mathematical setting. There it appears as a partition of the numbers from 2 to 10 into the four sets {2, 3, 5}, {4}, {6, 8, 9, 10}, and {7} based on the distinction between prime numbers {2, 3, 5, 7} and the non-prime or composite numbers {4, 6, 5, 9, 10}. The partition is mentioned—but not presented—by Martianus as proof that Athena "was generated without intercourse and did not herself have any offspring" (*DeNupt*, p. 17). The full "proof" is given by Eriugena at two locations in his notes on Martianus, in Book 1 (*AM*, pp. 36–37) to explain Martianus' phrase "teste arithmetica" (as mathematics shows) to support his claim that the number seven stands for Athena, and again in Book 6 on Geometry on the association between Athena with the number seven (*AM*, p. 131–132). For by taking "prime" (i.e. divisible only by itself and 1) to mean "not created," and imagining that a number "creates" all the numbers that are multiples of it, we then have

(1) creating and not created {2, 3, 5},
(2) creating and created {4},
(3) created and not creating {6, 8, 9, 10},
(4) not creating and not created {7},

which "proves" that seven is the sacred number of Athena, since she too had no father and remained childless. (*AM* 36, 131).

Eriugena retains the four creation-categories throughout *Periphyseon* but was forced to abandon his plan to devote one book to each. Human nature proved too large a topic to be included with the rest of Creation in *Pereiphyseon 3*, and so an additional book was needed, *Periphyseon 4*, dealing exclusively with the human. The final structure of *Periphyseon* is therefore:

Book 1: God
Book 2: The Primordial Forms
Book 3: Creation—without the Human
Book 4: The Human.
Book 5: Salvation

It must be added, however, that Eriugena's creation-categories sometimes give little indication of the topics he will actually discuss in the books. As he well knew, he tends to explore minor topics too readily and at excessive length, frequently losing touch with the main theme. Only a few pages into *Periphyseon 1* we have the following exchange:

Student: Return to the point. These things seem reasonable enough.

Teacher: May I ask what point you mean? When we try to comment on secondary issues we very often forget about the main one. (*PP1* 453BC)

And quite apart from the Teacher's lengthy digressions, *Periphyseon* is also shaped by two additional divisions that have nothing to do with the four creation-categories. These are the *Hexameron*, a commentary on the six days of creation as described in *Genesis*, that Eriugena begins in *Periphyseon* 2[86] and continues into the early pages of *Periphyseon 5*, and the Neoplatonic notions of Coming Out and Return which make the last two books (on the "return" or salvation of the human) very different from the previous three. Convenient lists of the topics discussed in each book of *Periphyseon* have been provided by a number of authors.[87]

God

Periphyseon 1 is concerned with nature that is "Uncreated and Creating," namely God. On this subject, Eriugena depends greatly on Dionysius and makes constant use of his distinction between "similar" and "dissimilar" images of the divinity and his "method of negation." This is necessary to overcome a fundamental difficulty that is unique to theology, namely that it appears to be a subject on which nothing at all can be said since God is beyond words and statements of all kinds.

First, however, he discusses the origins of the word "God," *deus* in Latin, θεός [*theós*] in Greek:

> The etymology of this word is taken from the Greek. It comes either from the verb θεωρῶ [*theōrō̃*] (i.e. I see) or the verb θέω [*théō*] (i.e. I run) or even more likely—since their referent is the same—it is correctly taken to derive from both. When *theos* is derived from the verb *theóró* it means someone who sees, for he sees in himself everything there is

---

86 Below, p. 135.

87 O'Meara (1988, pp. 80–154), Sheldon-Williams (1968, pp. 28–33; 1972, pp. 1–2, 1981, pp. 3–23), Jeauneau (1995, pp. xi–xxii) and in his introductions to *PP1–5*.

and sees nothing outside himself because outside of him there is nothing. But when *theos* is derived from the verb *theó* it is correctly understood as someone who is running. For he is running in all things and is not in any sense stationary but is filling out all things by running, as is written: "his Word runs swiftly" (*Ps.* 147, 15). (*PP1* 452C)

These are striking and wholly unexpected images of God, and actually come from an anonymous Greek philosopher of the 5th century BCE or earlier.[88] It is not known how they reached Eriugena, but he is clearly at home with them since they evoke an image of God as neither a person nor an entity of any kind, but rather as an *activity* or a *force* that runs through Creation in order to keep it in existence. This view of God will be a permanent feature of *Periphyseon*, not however because of the pre-Christian fragment Eriugena uses here, but because essentially the same conception of the divinity passed down from pre-Christian Greek philosophy into its Greek Christian counterpart, where it was studied closely by Eriugena in the more explicit forms it takes in the works Origen, Gregory, Dionysius and Maximus.

Having described God as a form of movement, he quickly adds that this does not in any way contradict the idea that God is eternal and unchanging:

It is entirely correct to say of God that he is motion resting and rest in motion. For he is unchangeably immobile, never abandoning his natural stability, yet he moves himself through everything in order that the things that essentially subsist from him might be brought into existence. For by his motion all things are made. So the two meanings of the word have one and the same referent, which is God. To run through all things, in the case of God, is not different from seeing all things; rather, all things come into existence through seeing, just as they do through running. (*PP1* 452CD).

---

88 See Sheldon-Williams 1968, p. 228, note 62.

God may therefore be thought of as divine energy that runs through all things, bringing them into existence and maintaining them in that condition, or alternatively, as an act of seeing all things that has the same effect.

Theology and Metaphor

From this it follows that neither property, motion or rest, can be attributed to the divinity in the usual way, for then they *would* create a contradiction, and contradiction clearly cannot be attributed to God. To say that God is in motion or at rest must therefore be a figurative form of attribution:

> So these names, and many others like them from Creation, are used to refer to the Creator by a kind of divine metaphor, and not unreasonably so, since he is the cause of everything that is in motion or at rest. From him they begin to run so that they might be, since he is the origin of everything, and through him they are carried towards him by a natural motion so that they can rest without change for eternity, since he is the end and the repose of everything. (*PP1* 453B)

What needs to be learned above all else in the study of the divinity, Eriugena says, is that the two most common features of everyday thinking, those associated with the formation of defensible beliefs and their assertion in clear language, are no longer of much use. To make the point, he now takes the ten categories of Aristotle (substance, quantity, quality, relation, place, time, posture, condition, action and being acted on) as a comprehensive list of the most obvious and uncontroversial properties that can be attributed to things in everyday life, and then goes on to show that none of them can refer to aspects of the divinity when used in ordinary modes of attribution.

This immediately calls into question many of the things that *are* commonly said about God, by theologians and laity alike. Taking the verbs "move" and "love" as examples, and their passive forms, "being moved" and "being loved," the teacher points out that when these are used in reference to God they cannot possibly be true:

So if these verbs, whether active or passive in meaning, are no longer predicated of God in the strict sense but only by metaphor—and all things that are predicated of him by metaphor are not predicated of him in all truth but only in a certain manner—then in all truth God neither acts nor is acted upon, neither moves nor is moved, neither loves nor is loved. (*PP1* 504B)

The student is worried by this line of argument. "This last conclusion needs to be looked into in detail. In my opinion, the full authority of Sacred Scripture and the holy Fathers seems to be against it" (*PP1* 504C). If the conclusion stands, he says, then he will be obliged to say that God doesn't love or isn't loved, doesn't move and isn't moved, and so on for every verb that has an active and a passive voice. If this is the position he has to take, he fears that things will end up very badly for him:

And if I do so, can't you see how many and frequent will be the missiles from Sacred Scripture that rain down on me? I can hear the uproar from all sides, proclaiming that this is wrong. And no doubt you are aware how difficult and challenging it is to convince simple souls of things like this, given that they are so repugnant to the ears of acknowledged experts. (*PP1* 508CD)

But the teacher tells him that the only issue here is whether or not the two of them, teacher and student, are following the principles of right reasoning. The reactions of others to their conclusions are not relevant:

Do not be frightened. We have to follow reason now, which examines the truth of things and is not overruled by any authority or prevented in any way from presenting to the public and proclaiming aloud the things it has diligently sought out through complex reasoning and brought to light through its labours. (*PP1* 508D–509A)

It is true, he says, that "the authority of Scripture must be followed in all things," but unfortunately, when it comes to the subject of God, Scripture too runs into the limitations of everyday language and is forced to use "divine metaphor." The Bible is not a collection of things that can be easily understood and safely said about God. On the contrary, "the truth lives there as if in its own secret dwelling-place" (*PP1* 509A):

> It cannot be assumed, however, that when [Scripture] itself tries to convey the divine nature to us it uses verbs and nouns in their literal meanings, rather than certain kinds of simile and various figurative meanings of verbs and nouns that take into account our weakness, and simple statements that encourage our rudimentary and immature perceptions. Listen to the Apostle where he says, "What I fed you with was milk, not solid food" (*1 Cor* 3, 2). Here Sacred Scripture is at pains to provide and to impress on us something to think about that will nourish our faith on a matter that is beyond words, incomprehensible, and invisible. (*PP1* 509AB)

In the longer term, however, Scripture will encourage all of its readers, clerical and lay, to go beyond the literal meanings of words and sentences. But they have nothing to fear, for the text itself will itself will guide them towards its higher meanings:

> People who are living simple and dutiful lives and honestly seeking the truth should neither say nor think anything about God that is not found in Sacred Scripture, nor should those who have beliefs and express opinions about God use anything other than its meanings and metaphors. For who would dare offer some invention of their own concerning something that is beyond words, in preference to what it itself has set to music on its own sacred instruments, namely the writers of Scripture? (*PP1* 509B)

Scripture, he says, is like a piece of music. The composition is already complete; all that remains is to listen to it being played by expert musicians. Not one note can be changed.

Eriugena has been working towards a more formal presentation of Dionysius's views on divine imagery and his Method of Negation. He now declares his intentions openly:

> *Teacher*: But to convince you more fully and completely, I think the views of Blessed Dionysius the theologian must be introduced here, if you agree.
>
> *Student*: Of course I agree. There is nothing that pleases me more than reason strengthened by the firmest of authorities. (*ibid.*)

Reason and Theology

Eriugena now quotes an extract from *The Divine Names* in which Dionysius says: "Concerning this super-essential and hidden divinity, one must not dare to say or even think anything except those things which have been divinely expressed to us in the words of Sacred Scripture" (*DN* 588A). When scriptural references to God are being studied, Eriugena adds, the first role of reason is to insist that its own special skills, clarifying concepts and making defensible statements, are now irrelevant. Instead, it "urges in every case and proves by irrefutable arguments that nothing can be said about God in the strict sense, since he surpasses all understanding and all concepts, perceptual and intellectual" (*PP1* 510B).

This leaves the learner with very little to go on—just the bare words of Scripture and whatever can be taken from them in a special form of contemplation in which nothing is perceived, or inferred, or asserted any more:

> For if you should assert that he is this or that you will be proven wrong, since he is none of those things that can be asserted or understood. And if you should say that he is neither this, nor that, nor anything else, you will be found to have spoken the truth, for he is none of those things that are and are not, and none can approach him without first

"committing themselves to the journey of the mind, setting aside all of the senses and the operations of the intellect, and things that can be perceived and everything that is or is not, and are restored, in a state of unknowing, to unity—to the extent that it is possible—with the one who is above every essence and intelligence" (*MT* 997B), for whom there is neither a reason nor an explanation, who can neither be spoken about nor understood, nor referred to by a name or a word. (*PP1* 510CD)

The quotation is from Dionysius's advice to his pupil Timotheos[89] at the beginning of his *Mystical Theology*. Eriugena says that assertion, i.e. claiming that something is the case, based on what we know from perception, memory, inference, authority, and other sources of everyday belief must be abandoned in order to clear the way for a different kind of awareness, one that is evoked and sustained by the mere existence of things, since "everything that exists, from the highest to the lowest, may be asserted of him by a kind of similarity or dissimilarity or contrariety or opposition" (*PP1* 510D). This is a basic principle first laid down by Dionysius[90] where he says that if something has been made by God, then divine goodness can be found in it.

The suppression of assertion, however, does not make reason redundant. On the contrary, it places additional demands on it, forcing it to acknowledge the different forms of thinking that may be evoked by the concept of the divinity, and to ensure that they do not interfere with each other. Referring to ordinary people making the transition from everyday theology to the Bible, Eriugena says that the principal function of reason will be to correct, through religion and devotion, simple people previously nourished in the nursery of the Church lest they should believe or think anything unbecoming of God, or assume that all the things attributed with the authority of Sacred Scripture to the cause of all things are attributed in a literal way, whether they are the most glorious and sublime of all things, such as Life or Virtue or the names of individual

---

89 Above, pp. 70–71.

90 Above, p. 65.

virtues, or things in between, such as Sun, Light, Star, and others from the higher parts of this visible world, or from the lower movements of visible Creation, such as Breath, Cloud, Brightness, Sunrise, Thunder, Dew, Shower, Rain, also Water, River, Earth, Rock, Timber, Vine, Olive, Cedar, Hyssop, Lily, Man, Lion, Ox, Horse, Bear, Panther, Worm; also Eagle, Dove, Whale, and others without number which, through a certain transformation, and in a figurative sense, are constructed from that which is created so as to refer to that which creates. (*PP1* 511CD–512A)

He is aware that learners may prefer "higher" images of the divinity from the beginning of his list, but wants to point out, as Dionysius did, that Scripture also contains sacred images of a very different kind, namely those which are not just lacking in any element of the sublime but are actually in conflict with it:

> Even more remarkable, not only does Scripture refer to the Creator by skilful use of nature, it even uses things that are contrary to nature, such as insanity, drunkenness, stupefaction, oblivion, anger, rage, hatred, lust, and other similar things by which the minds of simple people are deceived to a lesser extent than they are by the previous metaphors based on nature. For the rational soul, although still naive, when it hears the names of natural things being predicated of God may mistakenly take them to apply to him, but it is not completely gullible, and when it hears the words for things that are contrary to nature being predicated of the Creator of all, it will either take them to be entirely false and reject them, or else accept and believe them as things that are said figuratively. (*PP1* 512AB)

Perception and Reason

The innate capacity of the human mind to look at the natural world in this way, as a θεοφάνεια [*theophania*] or a manifestation of the divinity, does not require Eriugena to add anything to his Neoplatonic theory of human knowledge in general. For in this view, it is only through rational inference from the external appearance of things to their invisible Primordial Causes that the human mind can be said to know *anything*, even the most commonplace objects and events of everyday life. Here too the senses grasp only the appearance of things, while the reality that stands behind them resides in their invisible Primordial Forms and they can only be grasped by reason and intellect.

This contrast between visible appearances and invisible realities rings out like a mantra in Eriugena's work, often linked to a line from St Paul' letter to the Romans, "Ever since God created the world his everlasting power and deity—however invisible—have been there for the mind to see in the things he has made" (*Rm* 1, 20). Running in parallel with it is his understanding of the relationship between perception and reason, *aisthésis* and *logos*, as understood by Maximus, namely that perception provides the mind only with "symbols" that are no closer to the realities they refer to than an echo is to the original sound, or a picture is to the thing that it represents. In the radical idealist position adopted by Eriugena, even the hardest realities that perception may seem to come up against, such as the "things" we see before us in nature, will turn out to be inferences to the existence of invisible realities, namely their Primordial Causes, based on perceptual images that are mere echoes of them.

To be clear about this, Eriugena takes three of the most elementary objects studied in geometry, namely points, lines, and surfaces, and shows that perception does not engage with these *at all* but only with convenient material symbols of them, for in themselves they are invisible entities that have no perceptual content whatever. They cannot be seen, only understood:

> The point from which a line begins, or at which it ends, is neither a line nor a part of it but the end of the line, and accordingly, its location is not perceived by the senses but instead it is thought of by reason alone. A perceptible point would be a part of a line but not its beginning or end. Similarly the line itself, when considered by reason, is immaterial and the beginning of a surface. Likewise, the surface is incorporeal and the end of a line and the beginning of a solid. And the solid too is immaterial and brings them to an end and completes them all. Whatever it is in these—

the visible point, line, solid, or surface—that the sense organ may have come into contact with, they are undoubtedly images of things that are immaterial and not the true substances of the things themselves, which are immaterial. (*PP1* 484BC)

Eriugena holds fast to an idealist theory of knowledge. The essence or substance of things lies in their immaterial forms, which are accessible only by an act of reasoning that takes us to the structure they *must* have in order to play the role that reason assigns to them. The geometric point, the end of the line, is mere location, a notion that becomes available to the mind only when the perceived point has entirely disappeared.

It might be argued that such a sharp distinction between sensory perception and rational inference holds only for abstract domains such as geometry or mathematics. Perhaps the objects of everyday life, including other people, animals, and inanimate objects, are "given" to the senses whole and entire, that is to say, through pure perception without the aid of inference. But however defensible this view may be,[91] it is not the view of Eriugena. As he argued above in connection with the phrase "Father of Lights," even sticks and stones must engage rational inference if we are to "know" them in *any* sense. Rational inference is not reserved for abstract topics but extends all the way down to the most concrete objects we can think of; and from there to the nature of matter itself:

And similarly for natural bodies, whether they can be perceived through the mixing of the elements of which they are composed, or whether they escape the gaze of mortals because of their subtlety: it is by the intellect alone that their limits are perceived. For the form that contains all the matter in material bodies is immaterial, while matter itself, when one examines it closely, is also constructed from immaterial qualities. (*PP1* 484C)

91 Such a view is often defended in philosophy under the heading of "common sense realism."

So there is no level of reality, such as "prime matter," that lacks its own Primordial Cause.

The purpose of Eriugena's digression into geometry is to make an important point about human knowledge and the nature of deification. Following Maximus's teaching on the three motions of the soul,[92] he takes deification to be a progression from perception (*aisthêsis*) to reason (*logos*), and from reason to mind or understanding (*nous*). The ascent of the human mind begins with perception of the material world, where echoes the divinity can be found, and proceeds, through rational analysis of the invisible entities that may be inferred from the perceptual world, to a form of mental awareness or intellect (*nous*) that "brings the mind closer to God in a way that is beyond comprehension" (*ibid.*) In this progression Maximus compares God to the invisible light of the sun that becomes visible according as it mixes with the air, in other words, only to the extent that it is perceived and understood by the rational mind, following which it absorbed by mind or intellect which is then no longer distinguishable from the presence of the divinity in it. Eriugena quoted the relevant passage a little earlier in *Periphyseon 1*:

> Just as air, when it is illuminated by light, seems to be nothing but light, not because it loses its own nature but because light becomes dominant in it, with the result that it is taken to be light, so is human nature said to be entirely God when it is joined to God, not because it ceases to be a natural entity but because it accepts participation in the divinity, with the result that it appears to be nothing but God. Similarly, when no light is present the air is dark, and the light of the sun as it exists in itself is not perceived by any sensory organ; but when solar light mixes with air, it then begins to appear, so that while it is in itself incomprehensible to the senses, mixed with air it can be perceived by the senses. (*AdIo* 1073D; *PP1* 450AB)

This is the "physiology" of *theophania* as Eriugena understands it from Maximus, namely the revelation of God in Creation and the

---

92 Above, pp. 91–94.

unique form it takes in the special case of creatures who are endowed with the powers of rational inference from perceptual images.

Eriugena comments:

> And from this you are to understand that the divine essence is incomprehensible in itself but when joined to an intelligent creature it becomes visible in a wonderful way so that it alone i.e. the divine essence, is to be seen in it, i.e. in the intelligent creature. For its excellence beyond words dominates every-thing that participates in it, with the result that it alone will be evident to those who understand it, although, as we said, it does not appear at all as it is in itself. (*PP1* 450B.)

Although he is commenting on Maximus, the language is that of Gregory, especially when he talks about the divinity becoming visible to the human in the life of its own mind. Maximus's image of deification as air transformed into pure light, i.e. perception and reason transformed into pure understanding, is the one that Eriugena will use to bring *Periphyseon* to a close.[93]

Reason and Authority

The possibility of conflict between reason and "authority," namely Church teaching, was mentioned above by the student when he talked about the missiles that would surely rain down on him if he were to say in public that God cannot perform any actions or love anything. But the teacher is unperturbed. Reminiscent of his note on Martianus, "Nobody enters heaven except through philos-ophy,"[94] he now says with equal bluntness that if authority is in conflict with reason, then authority is wrong:

> I have no fear of authority or worries about the onslaught from less capable minds that would make me reluctant to say openly those things that true reason demonstrates clearly and establishes beyond a doubt, particularly because discussion of such things takes place only between

---

93 Below, p. 198.

94 Above, p. 23.

knowledgeable people, and to their ears nothing is sweeter than true reason, and nothing more enjoyable to investigate while it is still being sought, nothing more beautiful to contemplate when it is found. (*PP1* 512B)

The primacy of reason, he says, has the strongest possible argument in its favour: it is prior to authority by nature, i.e. by reason of the kind of thing it is:

Teacher: You are not unaware, I imagine, that something that is prior of its nature is of greater value than something that is prior in time.

Student: Practically everybody knows that.

Teacher: We have learned that reason is prior of its nature, but authority in time. For although nature was created simultaneously with time, authority did not begin to exist from the beginning of time and nature, while reason arrived with time and nature from the Principle of things.

Student: And reason itself shows this to be so. Authority comes from true reason, but true reason never comes from authority. For any authority that is not approved by true reason is considered weak, while reason is rendered fixed and immutable through its own powers, and does not need to be shored up by the approval of any authority. In my opinion, true authority is simply truth that has been discovered through the power of reason and put in writing by the Fathers for the benefit of posterity. Or do things seem otherwise to you?

Teacher: Not in the least. And that is why reason must be applied first to the matters we are discussing, and authority afterwards. (*PP1* 513BC)

Authority is of importance only when it happens to contain an accurate historical record of correct reasoning in times past. So there are only two independent sources of knowledge, Scripture and reason, the latter taking two forms, past and present.

It is not clear what topics Eriugena has in mind when he talks here about his conflicts with authority, or who the "knowledgeable" people are with whom he can discuss his views openly. All of the evidence suggests that the authorities no longer had any great interest in him, having condemned *The Book on Predestination*, and that he was writing mostly for himself and a loyal circle of colleagues and students. There is no doubt, however, that he still holds firmly to the notion of deification that he was only able to hint at in *The Book on Predestination*, and is equally as inflexible on the importance of profane knowledge for the salvation of the human. The big difference is that here in *Periphyseon* he can explore profane learning at will, now that the Emperor has publicly endorsed his research on Greek theology and philosophy. As a result, large parts of *Periphyseon 1* are taken up with matters of epistemology as he explores the philosophical problems posed by theology as an academic discipline. He revisits Gregory's picture of the universe as a mixture of the elements of physics, he teaches Aristotle's categories in far greater detail than is really necessary to make the point that none of them can be attributed to God, and he gives a long summary of the liberal arts, including geometry, and the various kinds of knowledge they contain. And these are matters he *must* discuss at length here in *Periphyseon 1*, since they provide the philosophical and epistemo-logical foundations for the four books to follow.

In the closing lines of the book, Eriugena returns to the theme of the simplicity of the divinity and reminds the student again that humans cannot achieve a worthwhile understanding of God without setting aside all of Aristotle's categories, including "being," "acting" and "making," and at the same time, their passive forms also:

> *Teacher*: What else remains therefore, except that you should understand that it is absolutely necessary that just as being and acting and doing, in the strict sense, are removed from him, so must being-acted-on and being-made be removed also? For I do not see how something that is beyond doing and making could have something done to it or be made.
> *Student*: Bring the book to an end—there is enough in it. (*PP1* 524AB)

Chapter 8

Periphyseon 2

Periphyseon 2 concerns the Primordial Causes, the part of Nature classified by Eriugena as "created and creating."[95] These are ideas in the mind of God that bring into existence everything to which existence has been granted. Eriugena also calls them beginnings, reasons, ideas, forms, definitions, prototypes, exemplars, and archetypes.

The most obvious examples of Primordial Causes are in the world of living things, where they correspond to genera and species. But the notion is far more general than that, since there are also Primordial Causes of truth, goodness, matter, spirit, point, line, surface, or indeed, as the student put it in the opening lines of *Periphyseon 1*, "anything one might think about." When compared with their imperfect realizations in any particular instance, the principal characteristic of the Primordial Causes is their perfection and immutability. They are the unchanging essences of things, the "ideals" that came to prominence with the philosophy of Plato and have been a feature of Western thought ever since.

The Coming Out and the Return
Primordial Causes have a special importance in the Neoplatonic world-view since they provide both the point of departure for the Coming Out and the end-point of the Return. It is from their Primordial Causes that all things "proceed" into existence, and it is to them that they "return." Neoplatonists referred to the Coming

---

95 Eriugena's classification is somewhat arbitrary, and seems to be designed more to preserve the logic of the four creation-categories than to convey anything important about his views on Primordial Causes. The latter were generally considered to be eternal and therefore *uncreated* (see Sheldon-Williams, 1972, p. 216, Note 29), and in practice Eriugena does not depart from this tradition.

Out as the πρόοδος [*próodos*] or *processio* (the word that is found in the Nicene Creed where it is said that the Holy Spirit "proceeds" from the Father and the Son), while the Return is ἐπιστροφή [*epistrophē*] or *reditus*. The Coming Out refers to the origins of all things in the mind of God, their realization in the Trinity, and through the Word of God, in Creation, and the Return refers to the final unification of Creation with the Creator. But the Coming Out and the Return may also be thought of on a smaller scale as complementary forces that can be seen throughout Creation, most obviously in the living world in the "balance of opposites" that featured so strongly in Martianus's cosmology, and in Gregory's "twin forces" of rest and movement. Moreover, the opposing forces may also be thought of as acting simultaneously, as they are in Gregory's explanation for the constancy of the perceptual world, which he thinks of as the combined product of the efforts of the sensory systems to maximize the diversity of input from the external world, and the mind's search for its invariant source.

The Coming Out and the Return are permanent features of all of Creation, including the so-called "elements" of the material world, i.e. fire, air, earth and water. They too are the work of a single Primordial Cause that brings them into existence while at the same time drawing them back again to itself:

> Even the simplest and purest of all things, the four elements of this world that elude the senses of the body, are derived from one simple and individual cause that is understood only by the minds of the greatest scholars, i.e. from the most general essence of all substances that proceed to visible effects while always remaining within itself. It is reasonable to assume that the same is the case for their four primordial and unique properties. For while these seem to be contrary to one another—since heat is the opposite of cold, and dryness of moisture—they go back to the same cause, entirely unobservable yet subject to reason, by which I mean the most general quality of all qualities from which the elements, by a marvellous operation of nature, go forth and construct these bodies that are corruptible and prone to

disintegration, and in which they unite with each other in an indescribable harmony and tranquillity of nature in its entirety, where all opposing forces have been eliminated. (*PP2* 606C–607A)

This is the harmony of the elements once again,[96] presided over by the single Primordial Cause of all four elements. Individual elements can never be observed since any given element must mix with some of the others before it can be detected by the sensory systems of the human. Yet the elements must exist, to explain the observed mixtures, and they must have a common Primordial Cause, since otherwise there would be no explanation for the general notion of "element."

To say this, admittedly, is merely to reaffirm the idealist position taken up in the opening lines of *Periphyseon 1* when "things" or "natures" were defined as anything whatsoever that one might "think about." It is thought that creates reality for the idealist. We can indeed think about invisible elements, and give reasons to believe that such things exist—or at any rate find experts who can do so—and for Eriugena that is justification enough for talking about their Primordial Cause. The intellectual position taken up in this way is far from vacuous. In fact it is quite radical and counterintuitive in some respects, and constantly shapes Eriugena's work in ways that are surprising but still quite logical, including his final account of the deification of Creation in the closing pages of *Periphyseon 5*.

The Bare and Empty Earth

Having discussed Primordial Causes in fairly abstract and philosophical terms in the opening pages of *Periphyseon 2*, without any warning Eriugena now says, "I think our starting point should be taken from Sacred Scripture … The Most Holy Prophet, I mean Moses, on the very first page of the Book of Genesis, says "In the beginning God made heaven and earth" (*Genesis* 1: 1) (*PP2* 545BC). These are the opening lines of Eriugena's Έξαήμερον [*Hexaémeron*], a commentary on the six days of Creation as described in *Genesis*, that

---

96 Above, pp. 4–5.

runs from here to the opening pages of *Periphyseon 5*,[97] weaving its way in and out of the more abstract and philosophical account of everything that he gives in *Periphyseon* as a whole, based on the four creation-categories and the polarity of Coming Out and Return.

He directs his attention to the phrase "heaven and earth" in the opening verse of Genesis, notes a few of the varied opinions expressed by the Fathers of the Church on what exactly it refers to, and then gives his own reading:

> When I reflect on the multitude of opinions, however, what seems most likely and closest to the truth is that by the words of Scripture quoted above—those referring to heaven and earth—we are to understand the Primordial Causes of all of Creation which the Father had created in his only-begotten Son, referred to as "the Principle," before he had created everything else, and that we should take the word "heaven" to refer to the essences of intelligible and celestial entities, and the word "earth" to the Principal Causes of those things that can be perceived, from which the universe of this material world is made up. (*PP2* 546AB)

This is surprising. How can the bare earth, as it appears on the first day of Creation, stand for the Primordial Causes of the entire universe in their collective magnificence and diversity? Surely the earth, as it appears at the outset of Creation, is only one of the many manifestations of the Primordial Causes, and a rather primitive and incomplete one at that?

But Eriugena is about to give another of his "higher readings," with the help of the next line of *Genesis*: "The earth was bare and empty" (or, according to the Septuagint, "invisible and non-composite") "and there was darkness over the deep" (*Genesis* 1: 2). He notes Augustine's interpretation of the "bare and empty earth" as formless matter (*De Genesi ad Litteram* 1, 1, *PL* 34, 247) but rejects it because for him "formless matter" is a contradiction in terms. It is a first principle of his that even the most primitive form of matter that can be imagined must nonetheless emerge from its own perfect

---

97 *PP2* 545B to *PP5* 865C.

and self-sufficient form. So he turns to a passage in the *Hexameron* of Basil of Caesarea,[98] brother of Gregory of Nyssa, in which he finds an interpretation of the "bare and empty earth" that is more to his liking:

> Others think the earth that is described as being bare and empty, or invisible and without structure, is this mass of the terrestrial body, which in their opinion was bare and empty when first created for the reason that it was not yet adorned by the many genera and species of shoots, bushes and animals, and was actually invisible, either because it was flooded over by an abundance of water, or because the human who would be capable of witnessing it had not yet appeared through generation from Primordial Causes. (*PP2* 548C)

The bare earth is a cosmic wilderness for Eriugena, a holy place that captures "the inexpressible nobility of the divine nature in its remoteness from all things."[99] Now he takes the word "earth" in the phrase "heaven and earth" to stand for the Primordial Causes of the visible world as they existed in themselves, immutable and invisible, prior to their realization in the diversity of the natural world. This brings him into conflict with Augustine, but the support of Basil is sufficient for him. "Although it seems that Saint Augustine rejects this idea, we are not entirely opposed to it since it is a view held by Basil" (*PP2* 548CD).

The issue here is both ontological and aesthetic. Eriugena cannot accept that something might exist (he is thinking of prime matter) and still remain outside of the causal structure of the universe, since the latter consists of the Coming Out and the Return of all things as determined by their Primordial Causes:

> If the Primordial Causes are called "primordial" for the very reason that they are created before anything else by the creative Cause of all things, and create those things that are

---

98 Giet 1968, p. 142.

99 Above pp. 110–111.

beneath them—since Primordial Causes are created and
create as we said above—is it in any way surprising that just
as we believe and confirm by secure reasoning that formless
matter is to be counted among those things constructed after
and by means of Primordial Causes, we must concede that
it too is created by the Primordial Causes. (*PP2* 547D–548A)

Secondly, the barrenness and emptiness of the earth does not mean
incompleteness for Eriugena, as it does for Augustine when he talks
about matter awaiting its form, and the "semi-existence" it has while
in this state.[100] On the contrary, the "bare and empty earth" is the
desertum or wilderness, a holy place that manifests the glory and
tranquillity of the Primordial Causes before their Coming Out:

These words—I mean "bare" and "empty"—refer principally to the fullest and immutable perfection of the primordial entity created in the Word before anything else was
created, and less so to the variable and imperfect and as yet
formless Coming Out into this perceivable world, dispersed
in space and beginning to come into existence through
generation and longing to receive a form like the many that
are to be seen in Creation. (*PP2* 549B)

Eriugena's reading takes him deeper into the beauty and mystery
of the cosmic wilderness that he imagines stretching all the way from
the earth to the furthest stars:

The words "bare" and "empty" are often applied to material
things in a positive sense. All of the space that lies between
the earth's globe and the choirs of the stars and the outer
circumference of the earth is divided into two parts by those
who are well informed about the world and Sacred
Scripture. The lower part, is called "air" (i.e. "spirit") and
the higher part is called "ether" (i.e. "pure spirit") called
κοῦφος [*koúphos*] (empty) by the Greeks, "empty" or "bare" by
writers of Latin, since the higher part, it is agreed, is always

100 *Confessions* 12, 6; *PL* 32, 828.

purer and clearer and filled with everlasting light—except
for a small area occupied by the shadow of the earth. This is
why it is said to be empty. (*PP2* 549BC)

Eriugena is thinking also of the infinite light of Gregory's universe
except for the small cone of darkness behind the earth, combining
the perspective of the hermit with that of the cosmologist as he does
so often.

The Trinity and the Human Mind
Eriugena has just described the Primordial Forms of the created
world as he imagines them in the purely spiritual existence they enjoy
on the first day of Creation, prior to their Coming Out. By and large,
he postpones the actual Coming Out until Books 3 and 4 of
Periphyseon, where he will deal directly with everything that is "created
and not creating." He does not adhere rigidly to his plan, however.
Some 25 pages of Book 2 (almost a quarter of it) are given over to a
detailed commentary on Maximus's five-fold division of everything,
which is an account of the Coming Out *and* the Return. In addition,
he discusses two other forms of the Coming Out, those found in the
human mind and in the Trinity.

Following Gregory of Nyssa and Augustine, Eriugena takes the
human soul to be an image of God that reflects the mystery and
goodness of the divinity, and then goes on to say the three motions
of the human soul as described by Maximus, namely Soul (or Mind),
Reason, and Perception[101] are, respectively, images of Father, Son,
and Holy Spirit:

Think, then, and when every shadow of ambiguity has been
eliminated through sharpness of mind, notice how clearly
and accurately the substantial trinity of divine goodness
shines out in the motions of the human soul for those who
understand them correctly, and reveals itself unmistakably
to those who look for it honestly, as if in a mirror of their
own that has been made in his image; and although it is far
removed from every created thing and unknown to every

101 Above, p. 91.

mind, through its image and likeness it reveals itself to the eyes of the mind as if it were known and capable of being understood and actually present. (*PP2* 579AB)

This is the mirror that Sophia gave to Urania in which she can see the place among the stars where she was born, and also the mirror of Gregory, the human mind in which the image of God is seen. And the "golden chains of memory" that Martianus described, slowing down Mercury's speeding chariot[102] and holding fast the results of study, are here too, now transformed in Eriugena's physiological account into hidden anatomical structures:

Similarity to the Father is clearest in the soul, to the Son in reason, and to the Holy Spirit in perception. For just as we call the Son "The Art of the Almighty Artist"—not without good reason, since it is in him that the Father, the omnipotent artist, in his wisdom made everything that he wished to make, and preserves it in eternity and without change—so also the human intellect, by a wonderful exercise of its knowledge, perceives everything that it accepts without doubt or ambiguity from God and the principles of all things, and by using its memory stores it in its most secret folds as if in a work of art of its own making. (*PP2* 579BC)

In Maximus's triad, the highest level of Mind (*nous*), is "a simple, unexplainable motion that brings the mind closer to God in a way that is beyond comprehension."[103] In other words, *nous* refers to the deification of mental life and is therefore an image of the Father, from whom the Coming Out proceeds and to whom it returns. Similarly, Reason (*logos*) reflects the relationship of the Father to the Son or the Word of God, for just as the Father brings the created world into being through his Word, *nous* or Mind creates the world of the mind through reasoning, drawing together the materials provided by Perception to create a coherent "world" of beliefs and values.

---

102 Above, pp. 15–16.

103 Above, p. 92.

And finally, the relation that Perception has to Mind and Reason in the life of the mind is like that of the Holy Spirit to the Father and the Son :

> Just as the Father, the omnipotent constructor of all things, simultaneously and only once, built everything in his work of art—namely his wisdom and power as it exists in his Word and only-begotten Son—in a way that was primordial, causal, uniform and universal, so did he divide it up into the innumerable effects of the Primordial Causes through the Holy Spirit, who proceeds from him and the Son, some of which poured out into intelligible differences that no bodily sense can detect, while others flooded forth into the ever-changing and diverse beauty of this perceptible world, varying with differences of place and time, so also the intellect, i.e. the primary movement of the soul, which is formed through mystic contemplation of intelligible things, divides up through the inner perception of the soul everything that it creates and stores in the art of reason into discrete and unambiguous acts of cognition concerning individual things, whether intelligible or sensible. For everything that the intellect considers from a universal point of view by the use of reason, it divides up though the senses into particulars and discrete cognitions and definitions for all things. (*PP2* 579CD)

The distinctive role of the Holy Spirit is to bring the presence of God to the level of the individual, as symbolised, for example, by the tongues of fire that "separated and came to rest on the head of each of them (i.e. the apostles)" (*Acts* 2: 3). Similarly, perception may be thought of as the application of general principles of reason to particular cases.

The point of aligning Maximus's three powers of the mind, Soul, Reason and Perception, with Father, Son, and Holy Spirit is to provide Eriugena with a developmental perspective for the discussion of deification, now considered in Gregory's terms as the mind's desire to know and love itself. These two longings are intuitive and permanent in the angelic mind, but have to be continually rediscovered by humans, a life-long task that begins with the mind's first awareness of its own existence. This, he says, is an awareness that involves two components, knowledge and love, that are already found in a rudimentary form in the mind's first consciousness of itself, two quite distinct features of mental life although they exist in a state of constant interaction:

> Mind generates knowledge of self, and from it comes love both of self and of knowledge of self, by which self and knowledge-of-self are united. And although the love itself comes from the mind through its knowledge of self, it is not this knowledge that is the cause of the love but the mind itself, from which love comes into existence even before the mind arrives at a perfect knowledge of itself. (*PP2* 610BC)

And when self-knowledge arrives, it is loved like a new-born child: "This mind loves to know about itself before it gives birth to knowledge of itself, as if it were its child" (*PP2* 610C).

Unfortunately for the human, its innate knowledge and love of itself was lost through the Fall, and must now be pieced together from personal experience:

> And so, using the powers of reason it seeks, more than anything else, to know how and to what extent it knows itself, and loves both itself and its knowledge of itself; and when it converts this totality into the knowledge and love of its Creator, a most perfect image of him is produced. And this is the greatest, and virtually the only step on the way to knowledge of the truth, namely that human nature should first come to know and love itself, and then turn all of its love and all of its knowledge to the praise of the Creator and to love and knowledge of him. For if it is unaware of what is happening to itself, how can it long for knowledge of the things that are above it? (*PP2* 610D–611A)

This recalls Gregory's caustic remark concerning St. Paul's reflections on the mind of God,[104] and also gives us the essence of Eriugena's understanding of deification: the most immediate form of participation in the divinity that is granted to the human mind in its earthly existence lies in its knowledge and love of itself.

The *Filioque* Controversy

Most accounts of the separation of the Eastern and Western Christian Churches will contain a reference to the *Filioque* incident, when the word "Filioque" ("and from the Son") was inserted into the Latin version of the Nicene Creed. The phrase that previously read *Spiritus Sanctus qui ex Patre procedit* (the Holy Spirit who proceeds from the Father) was changed, initially in 589, to read *Spiritus Sanctus qui ex Patre Filioque procedit* (the Holy Spirit who proceeds from the Father and the Son). In reality, the separation of the Latin and Greek Churches was already an irreversible historical reality in Eriugena's time, and the *filioque* incident had little to do with it. Unlike the separation of the Catholic and Protestant Churches in the Reformation, the East-West separation was not a conflict between two groups who still shared a common language (Latin) but the result of slow demographic, linguistic and cultural changes, stretched over many centuries, with the result that the schism was a fact of life long before it could be linked to any specific doctrinal issue.[105] Few theologians of the Latin Church were able to read Greek in Augustine's time, in the 4th and 5th centuries, and Maximus, writing in the 7th century, doesn't have a single reference to Augustine.

Although Eriugena knew that the insertion of *filioque* was intended to hasten the day when the Latin Church could sever forever its connections with the Greek Church, the amended phrase ("the Holy Spirit who proceeds from the Father and the Son") is unobjectionable—in fact Eriugena uses it himself.[106] To incorporate it into the Creed, however, suggests that its converse, i.e. "the Son proceeds from the Father and the Holy Spirit," is *not* true, for if both

---

104 Above, p. 31.

105 See Meyendorff (1994).

106 On p. 141 above, for example. See also Sheldon-Williams (1972, p. 238, note 350.)

are true then the clarification is unnecessary and potentially misleading. In Eriugena's view, and that of the Eastern Church, both claims are equally true, and the suggestion to the contrary by the insertion of *filioque* would have been seen as a attempt to describe the Trinity in a way that would be entirely unacceptable in the East, while still being defensible in a legalistic way.

Eriugena now puts together a brief but very effective argument that the procession of the Son from the Father and the Holy Spirit is just as much a part of Christian teaching as procession of the Holy Spirit is from the Father and the Son. For this, he uses Church documents, Scripture, and the theology of the sacraments, supplemented with arguments from philosophy and physics.

His first argument is based on Scripture and the findings of the Synod of Nicea:

> With regard to the Son of God becoming a human, namely the incarnation of the Word, when we consult Sacred Scripture and the holy Creed handed down from the Holy Synod of Nicea (a city in Bithynia) and strengthened against all heresies, it is quite obvious to us and stated without the slightest ambiguity that the Word was conceived of the Holy Spirit. Also, the Angel says to Mary, "The Holy Spirit will come upon you and the power of the Most High will cover you with its shadow" (*Luke* 1: 35). And also to Joseph: "Joseph, Son of David, do not be afraid to take Mary home as your wife, because she has conceived what is in her by the Holy Spirit" (*Matthew* 1: 20). (*PP2* 611BC)

Likewise, the administration of the sacrament of baptism also confirms that the Word comes through the Holy Spirit:

> For when members of the faithful are baptized, what is it that happens on that occasion other than the conception and nativity of the Word in their hearts, from the Holy Spirit and through the Holy Spirit. Every day Christ is conceived and born and nourished in the womb of faith, as if in the bodily womb of a most chaste mother. (*PP2* 611D)

Consequently, anybody who has thought about these things will find the insertion of *filioque* confusing:

> Looking into this, and hearing the words "the Holy Spirit proceeds from the Father through the Son," those who know Sacred Scripture well will soon be prompted by their studies in theology to ask "So if the Holy Spirit proceeds from the Father and the Son, why is it not also the case that the Son is born of the Father through the Spirit?." (*PP2* 611D–612A)

Eriugena also has a higher "physiologic" reading of these matters. A little earlier in *Periphyseon 2*, in anticipation of the *filioque* issue, he compares the divinity with the element of fire, identified with the sun and its surrounding ether, and therefore invisible until it mixes with the earth's atmosphere. He then uses the physical triad Fire-Ray-Brightness to represent Father, Son, and Holy Spirit:

> *Teacher*: Tell me this: would you say that the ray comes from fire, and brightness proceeds from the ray?
>
> *Student*: I think that anybody who says this is not out of line with the best thinking on the nature of things. Fire, although invisible in itself, generates a visible ray from itself which would also be invisible if it remained in the simplicity of its own nature, and did not become mixed with things that are material and weighty. For the philosophers say that the ray of the sun cannot be grasped by animal senses because of its nature it is too subtle to be sensed. But as it descends bit by bit from the solar body towards the lower elements it gradually begins to appear, first in the purest ether where it only barely begins to shine, since the ether is by nature very similar to it, and going on further to the upper parts of our air it gradually becomes clearer, and then, the more it penetrates downwards into heavier matter the more it shines out brightly and presents itself as something that can be grasped by bodily sensation. But it is from the ray itself that the brightness of the greatest beauty is emitted, filling the entire world, rebounding from

the surfaces of all things, and laying bare colours of all kinds. And it too, because of its natural subtlety, would go undetected by bodily senses if it did not mix itself with more material elements. (*PP2* 608BC)

Attending now to the brightness of the ray, i.e. the Holy Spirit, and the relation of both the brightness and the ray to the fire, he says:

Although the ray proceeds from the fire through the ray, nonetheless the fire is its sole cause, not the ray. In the same way that the ray itself would not exist unless it were born from its cause, which is the fire, so also there would be no brightness through the ray if it did not first proceed from the cause of the ray itself. (*PP2* 608CD)

In other words: "Although we believe and understand that the Holy Spirit proceeds from the Father and the Son, we ought not to accept that the same Spirit has two causes but one and the same cause, namely the Father" (*PP2* 609BC).

As for the controversy surrounding the addition of *filioque* to the creed, Eriugena has nothing else to say. He sets the matter aside quietly:

But if one were to get in touch with Holy Fathers who added "who proceeded from the Father and the Son" in reference to the Spirit in the Latin Creed, they would respond in a reasonably way, I believe, and would have something to say about the purpose of the addition. Perhaps they already have been contacted, and have responded, except that their opinions on the matter have not yet reached us; and so we are not going to risk a rash statement on a question like this. (*PP2* 612BC)

It is unlikely that Eriugena was awaiting clarification. He was aware from his study of Greek theology of the extent of the gulf that now separated East and West, and aware also from his everyday experience in the West of the indifference with which the schism was viewed there.

Periphyseon 2 Concluded

Finally, he gives a short summary of what he has said about Primordial Causes:

> So the Primordial Causes are what the Greeks call ἰδέαι [*idéai*] (ideas), namely eternal species or forms and unchanging reasons in accordance with which, and in which, the visible and invisible world is formed and controlled, and were therefore worthy of being called πρωτότυπα [*prōtótypa*] (prototypes) by the learned Greeks, namely the principal exemplars which the Father made in the Son, and through the Holy Spirit divided into their effects and multiplied. (*PP2* 615D–616A)

He then concludes the book with four extracts from his translation of *The Divine Names* of Dionysius "lest anyone should suppose that what I have said about the primordial causes is not supported by any authority" (*PP2* 617A).

The last of these extracts is the one referred to earlier[107] in connection with *The Book on Predestination,* in which Eriugena translates Dionysius's term *pro-orismata* (predefinitions, i.e. Primordial Forms) as *predestinationes* (predestinations), thus making the idea of predestination to damnation absurd. The only thing that has been predestined for the human is restoration to unity with its Creator, an event that is already fully determined by the Primordial Cause that is responsible for its coming into existence in the first place. One might well ask how every physical and historic detail of the Coming Out of Creation can pre-exist in a God who admits of no complexity. But this, Dionysius says, is no more puzzling than the daily work of the sun:

> If the sun as it appears to us, in spite of the fact that it is a single light shining evenly, can renew, nourish, protect,

107 Above p. 48.

perfect, differentiate, assemble, incubate, fertilize, increase, transform, establish, bring forth, and awaken substances and properties of perceptible things that are so numerous and different from each other, and bring them all to life so that each of them participates in its own way in one and the same sun, while the solitary sun contains ahead of time, within itself and without differentiation, the Causes of the many participants, then surely we must concede that the Cause of the sun itself and of all created things requires exemplars for all things and a single process of unification that is beyond essences; for it also brings essences into being through the Coming Out of essence. We said that paradigms were reasons that create substances pre-existing as one thing in God, called predestinations[108] in theology and good acts of divine will, defining and creating things, in accordance with which the One Beyond Essence predestines and brings into existence everything there is. (*DN* 5, 8; *PG* 3, 824BC; *PP2* 618C–630A)

And then the teacher says, "It is already time to bring this book to an end," a sentiment with which the student readily agrees.

---

108 Eriugena's translation of *proorismata* (pre-definitions, i.e. Primordial Causes). See also his comments on the term in connection with pre-destination, above, p. 48.

Chapter 9

Periphyseon 3

Periphyseon 3 deals with everything that is "created but not creating," namely Creation in the usual sense, i.e. everything we see before us in the natural world. The book begins, however, with some concluding remarks on the Primordial Causes that were left over from *Periphyseon 2*, and a discussion on the meaning of *ex nihilo* (from nothing) as it occurs in the phrase "creation from nothing." On that matter, Eriugena provides the same "higher reading," of *nihil* (nothing) that he did with the words "desert," "bare," and "empty" earlier, saying that it refers to the Divine Essence beyond Essences in its isolation from Creation. Then he continues with his commentary on *Genesis* which takes up the rest of the book. The dialogue ends abruptly, while he is discussing fish and birds, suggesting the some pages are missing. He never gets to the creation of the human.

Naming the Primordial Causes

Since the student asked for a list of the Primordial Causes discussed in the previous book, the teacher now names ten: Goodness, Being, Life, Reason, Intellect, Wisdom, Virtue, Blessedness, Truth, and Eternity. He points out, however, that the list is infinite, and neither is there any natural order in which the Primordial Causes can be listed, since they are as one in the mind of God. Both the selection and ordering of any list of Primordial Causes are personal matters for the person making the list:

> So the order of the Primordial Causes is determined by a judgment made by the mind that is thinking about them and the extent to which an understanding of them is granted to people who discuss divine Causes. Those whose thinking is respectful and pure may choose to begin with any of them

they please, and allow the mind's eye (namely true reason) to involve the others in a particular ordering, including as many of them as possible, and bring their investigation to an end with one or another of them. (*PP3* 624C)

As for his own mind, when it produced the list above, he says:

It was to provide examples that it chose these Principal Causes to the best of its powers of concentration and put them in its preferred order; not because this is how they are by their own nature—where they are all one, contemporaneous, and undifferentiated—but because when people are searching for them and wishing to say something about them by way of illustration, they usually appear in theophanies of themselves, illuminated by divine glory, as this or that, and multiple and infinite. (*PP3* 624D)

Although the term "theophany" (revelation of God) refers in a special way to the Incarnation and the deification of Creation, in a broader sense it refers also to the everyday experience that occurs whenever Maximus's three motions of the soul, perception, reason and understanding are aligned so that "everything understood and perceived is but the apparition of what is not apparent" (*PP3* 633A). In other words, the selection and ordering of the Primordial Causes will be revealed in the form of a theophany to the person who contemplates them.

The student has no difficulty with this, but is still wondering why Goodness comes first in the teacher's list of Primordial Causes. "Although all of these things are so," he says, "I am reluctant to believe that you began your list of Principal Causes with 'Goodness-through-Itself' without having some special reason. It is not like a good thinker to say something for no reason" (*PP3* 627A). Eriugena's response is one of very few passages in his work where he appears to speak directly about himself as a scholar:

Your words might not have been so rash if you knew that I was one of those dedicated and faultless philosophers who never stray in the least from the paths of true reasoning. But since I find that I scarcely have a place even among the most distant followers of the great philosophers, I must not make any rash promises about my journeys to the higher reaches of thought. For very often those who begin such ascents without the help of a greater and clearer mind either make errors and go astray, or not being able to go any higher, they turn back to the lowlands, or choosing to honour them by their silence, or being unwilling, through cautiousness and with good reason, to assume that they could reach the heights, they have remained silent. (*PP3* 627AB)[109]

Eriugena was indeed accused of straying from the paths of true reasoning, and even of heresy and blasphemy. It was said that his education was inadequate, and in particular, that his knowledge of Scripture was deficient. He did not have a teacher, and although he continued with his writings he must have wondered whether they would be read by anybody other than his own colleagues and students.

But he must carry on:

Lest we should appear lazy in God's affairs, burying the Lord's talent in the ground, failing to collect interest on it and deserving the sentence of the wicked servant, we are going to say what we think is closest to the truth insofar as the interior light bestows itself on the ability of those who seek it, while always following the rule of humility in case we should consider ourselves to be what we are not. For it is written: "Do not be proud, but be afraid" (*Rm* 11: 20). (*PP3* 627BC)

He now explains why he began his list with Goodness:

---

109 The passage is reminiscent of. Dionysius's comments about himself as a scholar in the closing lines of *The Celestial Hierarchy*, quoted above on pp. 78–79.

This is the reason I was persuaded to begin my list of the Principles of Things specifically from Goodness-through-Itself. I saw—and not without the authority of the Fathers, Dionysius the Areopagite in particular—that Goodness-through-Itself is the most general of the divine gifts and, in a certain way, comes before the others. For the Cause of all things, the creative goodness that is God, created this Cause that is called Goodness-through-Itself before all things so that through it all things that are should be brought from non-existents into essences. So it is for Divine Goodness to call into existence the things that were not in existence. (*PP3* 627C)

Goodness-through-Itself comes first in Eriugena's list of Primordial Causes because nothing can exist without it since existence is itself a product of divine generosity.

The Word of God

Eriugena spends much of *Periphyseon 3* trying to restore the notion of the "Word of God" to the powerful cosmic form it took in early Christianity. In doing so, he draws principally on Gregory, Dionysius, and Maximus, but his account also owes a lot to Origen, particularly the latter's notion of deification as a physical process that is driven by the consuming force of divine fire at the apex of the universe, drawing all of Creation towards itself. Since Eriugena is dealing explicitly with Creation as it now stands, fixed in time and place, he is eager to point out to the student that the original and primary existence of Creation is in eternity, beyond time, as an integral part of the divinity. For it is the role of the Word of God to bring it "out" into existence in the visible universe, and to maintain it in existence there from moment to moment. He was well aware that this kind of thinking about the natural world had long been in decline in the West.

The fundamental principle he wishes to establish is that everything exists in eternity as a part of the divinity:

The evidence of both Sacred Scripture and the holy Fathers is that all things are eternally in God. "In whom we live," the Apostle says, "and move and are" (*Acts* 17: 28).[110] We are in God because of the integrity and prior existence in him of the Reason for our being; we move in God because of the prior Reason in him for living well through the powers of good action; and we live in God because of the prior Reason in him for life and existence without end. And lest anybody should think that we are one thing and our Reasons another, he did not say "in whom our Reasons live and move and are," but "in whom we live and move and are." For insofar as we do exist, we are nothing other than our Reasons themselves, existing eternally in God. (*PP3* 640AB)

In addition to the strangeness of the notion of existence from eternity for those brought up in the Latin Church, there is also a linguistic problem. The Greek word λόγος [*lógos*], the "word" in "Word of God," also means "reason" and "cause," and therefore the expression means a lot more in Greek than it does in Latin:

What is referred to in Greek as *logos* is a word or a reason or a cause. And what is written in the Greek gospel, Ἐν ἀρχῇ ἦν ὁ Λόγος [*En archēi ēn ho Lógos*] may be translated "In the Beginning was the Word" or "In the Beginning was the Reason" or "In the Beginning was the Cause." No matter which of these is said, one will not be departing from the truth. For the only-begotten son of God is Word and Reason and Cause. (*PP3* 642AB)

All three words apply to the Son's relation to the Father:

110 Unwittingly, Eriugena is relying here on pre-Christian Greek sources, as he was when he derived the word "God" from "running" and "seeing" at the beginning of *Periphyseon 1*. The description of God as the one "in whom we live and move and exist," attributed to St. Paul by Eriugena, is now thought to come from Epimenides of Crete, 6th c. BCE (Jerusalem Bible, Acts 17: 28). The primacy of movement in both fragments is notable, as is Eriugena's interest in them.

Word: because it was through him that God the Father spoke all things into existence—indeed he is the speaking and the speech and the word of the Father as it says in the gospel: "And the word I have spoken to you is not mine but that of him who sent me," as if he were to say openly: I, who am the word of the Father, who have spoken to you, do not belong to myself but to my Father who is uttering me and bringing me into existence from his secret self, and creating all things through me, namely by bringing me into existence.

Reason: because he is said to be the Principal Exemplar of all things visible and invisible and their Idea (from the Greek ἰδέα [*idéa*]), namely Species or Form, for in him the Father sees the making all things he wished to be made, before they were made.

Cause: (of whatever kind) because the origins of all things exists in him, eternal and unchanging. (*PP3* 642BC)

While the most prominent image of the Word of God in its multiple senses is that of Ἰησοῦς Χριστός ὁ Παντοκράτωρ [*Iēsoûs Christós ho Pantokrátōr*], found on the ceilings and cupolas of most Greek churches, the creative force of the Word of God is expressed in a multitude of other images also in Eriugena's work. He imagines it as a field force or a liquid flung into space that is constantly in motion and taking on new shapes. The Word of God, he says, "is poured out through all things to infinity, and its diffusion is the existence of them all. For he spreads powerfully from end to end and brings a beautiful order to everything" (*PP3* 642D). He also quotes a remarkable passage from Basil's *Hexameron* in which the Word of God is compared to a ball running downhill. Basil is commenting here on the verse "Let the earth produce the living souls of cattle, wild animals and reptiles" (*Genesis* 1: 24):

Imagine the Word of God running through Creation, beginning its work at that point, bringing it to its present state, and taking it on to the end, when the world will be completed. Like a ball that is pushed away by somebody and then encounters a downhill slope, and as a result of its own construction and the contours of the land continues on its way downwards until it is met by level ground—this is how the natural world, set into motion by a single command, made its way steadily through the part of Creation that is subject to birth and death, preserving the invariance of species through similarity of offspring until its objective is achieved. For it ensures that a horse gives birth to horse, a lion to a lion, an eagle to an eagle; and, protecting each living thing by continuity of offspring, it accompanies them to the completion of the totality. (Giet 1968, pp. 482–484; *PP3* 709BC)

While the unfolding of the Primordial Causes is in time, their creation is in eternity. It is the result of one single act of the will of God, a "push," as Basil puts it. Or in Eriugena's words, "By a single order—albeit repeated six times by the writer of Scripture—he brought all things into existence at one moment" (*PP3* 709D). The six days of Creation are fictions: everything is created at once, in the Word, and nothing further is needed for their Coming Out other than their own internal structure, determined by their Primordial Causes, in conjunction with the environment into which they arrive.

Water and Earth
Comparisons between the structure of the mind and the structure of the cosmos are fundamental to Eriugena's description of Creation. Many examples of these psycho-physical analogies are found in his commentary on Martianus, and in the Homily on the preamble to John's gospel where, following Maximus, he links the mental triad of Understanding, Reason, Perception with the physical triad of Sun, Air, and Water-Earth.

He now comes to the verse "Let the waters under heaven come together into a single mass" (*Genesis* 1: 9). This brings up the relationship between the two lower elements of the physical universe, water and earth. Essentially, it is one of mutual containment, "each setting limits to the other," as Gregory says in the opening lines of *De*

Imagine.[111] This is most obviously so in the case of seas, rivers and lakes, but Eriugena also likes to imagine water at work beneath the surface of the earth and in the bodies of all living things. There too water is bounded and structured by the earthen passages through which it now flows, except that they shape and direct it in a more sophisticated way. This reminds him of the way the flood of sensations is hemmed in and structured by the organs of perception, in order to provide the raw materials for reasoning and intellect, which he associates respectively with the higher elements of air and fire:

> And notice, in the same way that a confluence of waters cannot hold together on its own without support from a body of earth, whether it runs about internally through hidden channels, or externally in unrestrained floods, or stands still in lakes and ponds, so also the flood of appearances cannot hold together unless it is sustained in adjacent objects, whether they be hidden in the depths of the subject, as qualities and quantities are in causal relationships, or burst out into the open and are seen in material things, as with physical objects with multiple colours poured out on them, or fixed entities like forms and shapes which, combined with changeable materials, create visible objects consistent with the condition they are in, and gather them into a single entity lest they should suddenly come apart, and having lost the shape in which they are held together, dissolve and flow back into the flux of their own variability. (*PP3* 710AB)

The imagery is both anatomical and cognitive and remarkable for its accuracy. Water now stands for the physical input that is received and structured by the organs of perception, such as the stream of images sweeping over the retina, while the "hidden channels" through which the water flows stand for the nervous system and the parts of the brain that serve its sensory organs.

He distinguishes three kinds of invariants, i.e. fixed objects and qualities, that the mind is able to detect in the shifting appearances

111 Above, p. 26.

of things through the operations it performs on the stream of input. Firstly, there are the countless invisible dispositions we attribute to created things, animate and inanimate, in order to explain their visible appearances and behaviour. These dispositions lie "deep" within the mind, as he puts it, since the dispositions themselves are unobservable and are understood only through inferences that the mind makes about them. Secondly, there are the perceived qualities of things, like colours, which he correctly identifies as creations of the mind that are "poured out" onto the physical world but have no independent existence in the physical world. And intermediate between these two, there are the structural properties of things, "shapes" and "forms," such as "circular" or "animate" that may still be considered as belonging to the things in which they are manifest (in a way that colours do not) since they achieve a certain invariance over conditions and occasions of observation. It is only because the flood of stimulation is "hemmed in" in this way by the perceptual systems, as water is hemmed in by land, that the mind is able to detect such constant features in the flux of appearances.

When he thinks of water on the surface of the earth, as it is found in seas, rivers, and lakes, he is struck more by its capacity to replenish itself from an invisible source. In the case of rivers, he imagines the hidden passages through which they disappear into the earth and return again to their origins:

> Initially the entire river flows from its source, and the water that rises up first at the source is poured out continuously and unceasingly within its banks and is carried along as far as it goes. Similarly, divine Goodness, and Being, and Life, and Wisdom and everything that is in the Source of All Things pour out initially into the Primordial Causes and bring them into being, and then they flow down in a mysterious way through the Primordial Causes into their effects through the orders of the universe that lie beside them, always flowing from higher to lower, and return again to their source by a secret pathway through nature's most inaccessible pores. (*PP3* 632BC)

This is Gregory's river of life again,[112] driving forward in whatever channels it happens to find itself, but now it has also become the force of deification running through the heart of Creation from higher to lower, each of the "orders of the universe" being drawn into the one that lies above it as it returns to its Creator.

The Spirituality of Matter

As will be seen shortly, Eriugena never gets to the creation of the human in *Periphyseon 3* But he still makes good use of the book to establish some general features of inanimate and subrational Creation that will apply also to the human. In the two examples just given, he uses the physics of water and earth to provide a *physiologia* of perception and deification. Just as water has no fixed shape until it is hemmed in by earth, he says, neither can the flood of stimulation deliver up invariant objects to reason and intellect until it is blocked and shaped by its sensory organs; nor can the raw energy of the universe, which he likens to a river in full spate, become a return to the Creator until its lower orders are brought into contact with those that lie above them, and begin to be absorbed into them.

One obvious objection to the psycho-physical comparisons that constitute Eriugena's psycho-physical approach is that matter and mind, for example, water and earth on the one hand, and emotions and thoughts on the other, appear so utterly different to us that comparisons between seem to be mere metaphors. But Eriugena does not accept that matter and mind *are* radically different. He disagrees therefore with those who say that Creation was devoid of life in its first four days:

> There are those who say the elements of this world, the sky with its stars, the ether and the planets, the air with its clouds and gusting winds, and lightning and other disturbances, water also and its free-flowing movement, likewise the earth and all its plants and trees are not only entirely without a soul but are also without life of any kind, and this, they say, is the reason that there is no mention of "soul" or "life" in the work of the first four days. (*PP3* 728A)

112 Above, p. 27.

But there are others, he says, most notably Plato, who attribute both life and soul to everything that exists, and this is his own position also. Here Eriugena is thinking ahead to a problem he will face in the next book concerning the body of the human, namely whether it is to be considered as a material or a spiritual entity, or equivalently, mortal or immortal. Following Gregory, he accepts that the body is mortal and does not participate in the Resurrection, since it was required in the first instance, at the time of the Fall, only to ensure the continuation of the species. But he also believes that the human mind cannot function without its sensory systems, which are clearly a part of the body. He needs to argue, therefore, that the sensory systems, unlike all other parts of the body, are really a part of the soul, in effect a kind of "extension" of the soul into the more "subtle" parts of the body:

> If the soul is a spirit that in itself lacks all the heaviness of matter, and those elements into which the body dissolves—to the extent that they exist in themselves as indivisible entities—are close to being spiritual in nature, why should it come as a surprise if the immaterial soul controls the parts of its body that are retained in entities similar to itself? (*PP3* 730AB)

He is thinking of vision and hearing. Considered as parts of the body their receptor areas and pathways to the brain are indeed light and refined, as the soul itself is, and this is why he thinks they may be considered a part of it, and therefore immortal.

But it is not necessary to speculate about the fate of the sensory systems after death, he says, since their spiritual qualities can be inferred from an examination of the anatomy of the human body while it is still alive:

> Some of its parts are heavy, compacted, and dense, such as the bones, muscles, sinews and veins, and also the liquids that irrigate, nourish, and build up its overall bulk. All of these are brought in from water-like and earth-like substances to become part of the structure of the body. On

the other hand, some are extremely light and not hampered in the least by their weight or density, and no sooner do they receive their instructions from the soul than they arrive at once and without the slightest delay wherever they are supposed to be, such as vision and hearing; and no reputable philosopher will deny that these parts of the body derive from fire and air. "For there is a luminous quality in the eyes," as Saint Augustine says, "and an air-like, mobile, and sonorous quality in the ears." (*PP3* 730BC)

Vision and hearing, therefore, must be in close touch with the immaterial soul, which means they are constructed principally from the higher elements of fire and air that he associates, respectively, with understanding and perception.

Perception, Intentionality, and Mind
When Eriugena talks about the senses being instructed by the mind to "go" to a particular place and getting there instantly he is referring to the phenomenon of intentionality, as the term is understood in both medieval and contemporary philosophy of mind. This is the capacity some natural events, most notably acts of perception such as seeing and hearing, to "pick out" things or "refer" to them in just this way. As Eriugena puts it, the senses "go" to the things they refer to when instructed to do so: we have only to look at things, and there they are, before our eyes. So he describes vision as a kind of light that is generated deep within the body and shines through the eyes to illuminate the world outside:

Vision is a kind of light that rises up initially from the fire of the heart, ascending to the top of the head to what the Greeks call the μήνιχα [*mḗnika*] and the Latins the *membranula* that surrounds and protects the brain, having diverted through certain channels to the eyebrows and the pupils of the eye, from where it shoots outside with great speed, like rays of the sun, travelling so fast that it reaches places and things that are nearby or others at a great distance before it reaches the eyelids and eyebrows. (*PP3* 730CD)

We would say that light comes *in* through the eye, but Eriugena is talking about a different kind of light, namely intentionality or the capacity of bodily states to refer to things outside of the body, which he describes quite accurately as coming from deep within the organism and "shooting outside," freeing it from its coordinates in space and time, sweeping aside the last traces of its origins within the body—the eyelids and eyebrows that can scarcely be looked at all in spite of their physical proximity. For the retina, for example, does indeed consists of brain tissue of the sort that was initially concerned only with the regulation of the internal environment of the body but managed, as it were, in the course of evolution to look in the "other" direction and discover the world outside. He is correct also to involve the *ménika* "at the top of the head," where he believed the different senses were integrated, since he knew from Gregory's comments on the multiple sensations produced by honey,[113] that it is only through the merging of senses that object constancy, and hence intentionality and reference, are achieved.

Eriugena extends his analysis of intentionality from vision to hearing:

> Hearing is a very subtle tinkling rising upwards from the breath of the lungs and ascending to the part of the head previously mentioned, and having been diffused through its hidden passages in the *cochleae* of the ears, escapes outside and mixing itself with currents of air, in adjacent areas or further away, promptly and immediately picks up whatever reverberation occurs in it. (*PP3* 730D–731A)

In the case of smell, taste and touch, he says, it is clear that they do not manage to escape entirely from the body in the way that vision and hearing do, since their objects must be in close contact with the organs of sensation before they can be perceived. It could be argued, therefore, that it is only the effects that these objects produce on the body that are made present to the mind, not the objects themselves. Eriugena thinks this analysis is sufficient in the case of touch and taste, but he is not so sure about smell: "The other three sense are

---

113 Above, p. 29.

said to be contained within the limits of the body, although it is not absurd, in my opinion, to think that the sense of smell does extend outside" (*PP3* 731A).

Although an extensive "folklore of the five senses" was available to Eriugena from other authors, some of which he uses here, his own account stands out for two reasons. Firstly, he has a better grasp of the functioning of the anatomical structures that are involved in perception; and secondly, he has a better appreciation of the role perception plays in the achievement of intentionality. For it is initially through the activities of the different sensory systems that the mind is able to detect invariant objects in the stream of experience so as to "direct" itself towards them or to be *about* them. Although perception is still at the bottom of Maximus's hierarchy of the mind's "motions", and its objects are mere "symbols" of the realities it "passes up" to the higher powers of Reason and Mind, it is here that the ascent must begin for it is here also that intentionality is first achieved.

In fact, Eriugena cannot imagine the human mind as an intentional system *without* the work of the sensory systems, and this is why he argued so strenuously earlier that the senses do not perish with the body. For although they are clearly a part of the body, he argues that their unique interaction with the mind assures their immateriality and immortality. The mind, he says, works through the sensory systems, which are in direct contact with the material world, while the delicate control that the soul exercises over the senses would be impossible unless they too were a kind of "extension" of the soul into the body. "In a potential sense, it [the soul] is present to receive the phantasies which are everywhere formed in the instruments of its senses" (*PP3* 732B).

The Souls of Animals

Since Eriugena's conception of the mind is based on the notion of intentionality, while the latter depends on the work of the sensory systems, it follows that subhuman animals must also have immortal souls, given that their sensory systems are equally as good as those of the human, and often much better. "What human can see as clearly as an eagle or a gazelle?" he asks, and "What human can boast a sense of smell like that of the dog?" (*PP3* 738C). The only problem he faces here is that two of his Greek sources, Basil and Gregory, take a very different view. According to them, subhuman animals are made entirely of earth and consequently their "souls," such as they are, decay utterly with their bodies.

Eriugena cannot accept this. He thinks it sufficient to list the well-known sensory and mental capacities of animals, their feelings and attitudes, the loyalty they show to their own kind, their long memories—he mentions Ulysses's dog who remembered his master after an absence of twenty years—and other examples that make it clear that they have souls:

> I fail to see how all these natural abilities could be found in the irrational soul if it were made of earth, as the Fathers mentioned earlier say, born of the earth and dissolving back into it again, or anything other than a complete soul. (*PP3* 738D–739A)

Given his admiration for the Cappadocians, he would have preferred to avoid the conflict, but the matter is too important to him. He does, however, accept that there can be more than one view on the subject:

> But let nobody think we are saying these things to demolish the views of the holy Fathers, but rather because we are trying, to the best of our ability, to find out what can most reasonably be said about them ... We say these things without prejudice to anybody's view, but to encourage readers to study the matter closely and, having consulted Scripture, to hold fast to whatever seems most likely. (*PP3* 739AB)

Nonetheless, his own view is clear: if animals have perceptual systems as good as those of the human, then they have immortal souls. This is all so obvious for Eriugena that he wonders whether Basil and Gregory might have been thinking primarily of moralistic stereotypes of animals that priests sometimes use to encourage the faithful to lead better lives:

> I suspect that the saints, men of philosophy experienced in the accurate observation of nature, presented their views in public in this way because of their concern for foolish people given over completely to the flesh like brute and irrational animals, in the hope that they might not lapse into degeneracy and become slaves to its desires, and having become frightened by such vileness in an irrational creature and changed their behaviour, they might raise themselves up to the dignity of rational nature in which they were created. (*PP3* 739BC)

This is not just diplomacy on Eriugena's part. Gregory does indeed have a tendency to use animal imagery for pastoral purposes. In Chapter 15 of *De Imagine*, he uses the line from *Genesis* in which God says to the human "you shall eat all kinds of meat as they were greens of the field" (*Genesis* 1: 29) to support a strange Stoic theory that subhuman animals are really a species of mobile plants. And then he says, in a passage quoted here by Eriugena:

> Let this be a lesson to lovers of the flesh not to rely too much on what the senses perceive but to put their spiritual superiority to good use; for this is where the true soul is to be found, while the senses are shared equally with irrational animals. (*DeIm* 15; *PP3* 739C)

Other examples of Gregory's pastoral use of animal imagery can be found in other works of his. In the *Life of Moses*, where he comments on the plagues that were inflicted on the Egyptians, he describes frogs as "hateful to look at and always making noise, amphibious by nature, like jumping snakes, unpleasant not only to the eye but also with a skin that smells"—from which he concludes that they are "obviously the malignant offspring of filth in the hearts of humans, conceived, as it were, in slime" (*PG* 44, 345AB).

The End of the Book

Periphyseon 3 ends without warning, probably because some pages were lost or never written. The teacher and student are discussing the bodies of birds and fishes, and the spelling of the Greek word *kétos* (whale) when the teacher says:

> *Teacher*: … But this book, in my opinion, should be brought to an end before it becomes any longer—if you agree.
> *Student*: I agree, and in fact it would have been concluded a long time ago except for the lengthy discussions that delayed it. (*PP3* 742B)

And so *Periphyseon 3* comes to a close while there is still no mention of the topic that should have been its climax, the creation of the human.

Chapter 10

Periphyseon 4

Periphyseon 4 is the extra book that had to be added to give an adequate account of the human. A glance at its contents shows that it could hardly have been included in *Periphyseon 3* in any case, even if there were room for it. Following Gregory, Eriugena will discuss the human as an image of God, thus bringing the topic of deification to the fore and shifting the focus of *Periphyseon* dramatically from the Coming Out to the Return, even though the latter is still formally assigned to the last book. The biggest break in *Periphyseon* as a whole occurs right here, therefore, at the beginning of *Periphyseon 4*, and it is essentially the same division that Maximus makes in the "ages" of the universe into those required for God to become a human, and those required for the human to become God.[114]

The New Challenge

The teacher tells the student that the matters to be discussed in *Periphyseon 4* will be more difficult and contentious than anything they have encountered so far:

> The difficulty of the book and the confrontation and conflict between so many different opinions strike such fear into me that the three previous books, by comparison, seem like a calm sea with gentle waves, easy to sail on, offering readers an easy passage without the slightest danger of shipwreck. This book, on the other hand, is virtually impossible to navigate because of its narrow winding sea-ways, daunting because of the unstated assumptions, dangerous on account of the sand-banks of Syrte (that is, the currents of unfamiliar

---

114 Above, p. 90. See also Otten, 1991, pp. 106–117, and Jeauneau & O'Meara, 1995, p. 279, Note 8.

teachings), with a constant threat of shipwreck from the obscurity of the most subtle minds—hidden reefs that can break a ship in an instant—and the very length of the voyage, requiring the addition of a fifth book. Nonetheless, with divine clemency guiding and directing us, and filling our ship's sail with the favourable wind of the Holy Spirit, we will choose a safe and true course through these obstacles and will arrive, after a smooth journey, into the harbour we are seeking, free and unharmed. (*PP4* 743C–744A)

The student is ready:

> Set the sails and put out to sea. Reason knows these waters well, and will speed us on our way. She is not frightened by the threats of waves, she has no fear of straits and sands and reefs, and is happier testing her powers far out on the ocean of the divinity than lounging idly in calm and open waters where she has no opportunity to show what she can do. For she has been ordered to earn her bread with the sweat of her brow, and to farm the field of Sacred Scripture, thick with thorns and thistles (that is, a poor yield of insights into the divinity), and to pursue the study of wisdom that is closed to those who scorn it, in a careful course of investigation "until she finds the Place of the Lord, the Tabernacle of the God of Jacob" (*Ps* 131, 5), that is, until she returns and rediscovers the contemplation of the truth that was lost with the Fall of the human, through frequent and assiduous study of Divine Scripture and with the guidance, assistance, cooperation, and power of divine grace, and by finding it to love it, and by loving to remain with it, and by remaining with it to have peace. (*PP4* 744AB)

Eriugena's *Kunstprosa* shows the characteristic nervousness of the writer. While the editors may have something to do with it (Jeauneau & O'Meara, 1995, p. 280), he seems ill at ease, suddenly changing perspectives as if to correct earlier overstatements. Scripture is first presented as a vast and uncharted ocean, which might seem to leave too much of the work to the captain of the ship, namely Reason, and so we have the Holy Spirit filling the sails and a reference to the need for divine grace, while the image of Reason as the noble helmsman is replaced by that of the farmer on his knees pulling weeds.

More importantly, what is he afraid of? He told us in *Periphyseon 1* that scholarly conflict doesn't bother him,[115] so what then are the dire confrontations and shipwrecks he speaks of now? At a first glance, the fourth and fifth books of *Periphyseon* (he appears to be speaking of both) do not seem to be any more difficult than the first three. Perhaps, on the other hand, he has now reached the point in *Periphyseon* that he reached at the beginning of Chapter 18 in *The Book on Predestination*: the end of the work is in sight and he must now say openly what he has to say, or risk being counted among those philosophers who went no further than the foothills, as he put it, choosing instead to honour the peaks "by their silence."[116] Everything Eriugena has been dealing with in *Periphyseon* up to now can be taken, at worst, as a slightly unusual version of the standard teaching of the Latin Church. Even the *filioque* problem is dealt with peacefully. He will not be able to navigate *Periphyseon 4* and *5* so easily. The topic now shifts to the Return and Deification where the most fundamental conflict between Eastern and Western Christendom is to be found, and on these matters he knows that neither he nor the critics of *De Praedestinatione* have changed their views in the meantime.

The Human Animal

Eriugena's first task in *Periphyseon 4* is to define the human, i.e. to allocate it to its rightful place in the world of created things. The human, he says, is an animal, a member of the community of animals created all together by God on the sixth day. That is how he interprets the line from *Genesis*, "Let the earth bring forth the living soul" (*Genesis* 1: 24), taking "living soul" to mean "animal" in a sense that includes humans.

This was not the usual way to define the human in Eriugena's time. The student intervenes at once to express his surprise:

115 Above, p. 130.

116 Above, p. 148.

I find it very odd that the human is brought forth from the earth in the company of beasts of burden, reptiles and wild animals (*Genesis* 1: 24) when it alone, incomparably more than the rest of the animal world, is created in the image of God, as it says in Scripture: "Let us make the human in our own image and likeness" (*Genesis* 1: 26). (*PP4* 750D)

The teacher is sympathetic:

You have every good reason to be uneasy: these are matters that call for careful and serious investigation. But first, so that you can understand without the slightest shadow of ambiguity that the human is created within the universal genus of animal, listen to the strongest argument, namely the three-fold division of this genus into beasts of burden, reptiles, and wild animals. (*PP4* 751A)

Eriugena is embarking on one of his "higher" readings. He takes the three groups of animals mentioned, beasts of burden, reptiles, and wild animals, as symbols of the three defining features of the genus "animal." Beasts of burden (*quadrupedes*) stand for the sensory systems, their feet straining against the earth, in direct contact with the four elements of the physical world, but still under the control of reason, i.e. their human drivers. Reptiles stand for the nutrition and growth of the body, those life functions that "pervade by a silent progress the harmony of the body" (O'Meara, 1988, p. 123). Unlike the beasts of burden, reason has no power over them but neither do they interfere with it. And intermediate between these two are the wild animals, similar to the beasts of burden except that they have no drivers. They stand for the more instinctive and powerful forms of emotional life which, in their human embodiment, can resist the force of reason and sometimes overpower it completely.

The superiority of the human among animals may now be stated: in the animal kingdom it is only the human that all three elements are found, beast of burden, reptile, and wild animal. All of the others have only two: beast of burden and reptile:

With the sole exception of the human, only two of these three motions are present in animals: the one found in the senses, lacking rational self-control and therefore like a beast of burden, and the other in nutritive life, like a reptile. These the human shares with other animals, and other animals reciprocally with it. Don't you see, therefore, that the human is in all animals, and all of them in the human, and above them all is the human? (*PP4* 752BC)

In Eriugena's triad "beasts of burden, reptiles and wild animals" the term "wild animals" no longer refers to real wild animals but only to the "wild animal in the human," in other words the emotional and instinctual life of the human that is often in conflict with reason. Real wild animals have no such problem. As Gregory noted, their emotions are healthy and short-lived because reasoning is not involved. Only the human experience the "mixed" states he spoke of, partly emotional and partly rational, which are the result of the fall and constitute the most distinctive feature of the human mind.[117]

From one point of view, Eriugena is merely restating the standard definition of the human as a rational animal, adding some of Origen's allegorical interpretations of the various animals mentioned in *Genesis* and Gregory's conception of the human as an unnatural mixture of intellect and emotion. But he is also embarking on a "contemplation" of the human that has strong mythic and aesthetic features, based principally on Maximus's notion of the human as a microcosm of Creation[118] but combined also with materials from Gregory and Dionysius. Eriugena's "higher" readings always have the same twin objectives, to draw attention to mythic and aesthetic aspects of the topic under discussion and to shift the focus to the way things were before the Fall and how they will be after the Return, when the process of deification has been completed.

This last requirement, he says, will pose a problem for even the most intelligent and well-disposed readers who, like himself, are still far from being deified:

---

117 Above p. 36.

118 Above pp. 91–92.

A rational and intelligent creature is not willingly in error but can still be deceived, especially when it has not yet been brought to its most perfect form, the form it would have received as a reward for obedience by being transformed through θέωσις [*theōsis*] (i.e. deification). We should not judge human nature by the impression it makes on bodily senses—for it is in rightful punishment for the Fall that it is born sexually, in the manner of non-rational animals, into a temporary and corruptible existence that ends in death—but by the image of God in which it was created before the Fall, which puts it beyond all bodily perception and mortal understanding on account of the inexpressible dignity of its nature and its incomprehensibility. Deceived and fallen, however, and sightless in the darkness of its perverse intentions, it no longer remembers itself or its Creator. (*PP4* 760D–761A)

He is looking for an understanding of human nature that goes beyond the fleeting impressions that imperfect humans have of it from personal experience. To achieve the broader perspective, it will therefore be necessary to counter as far as possible the effects of the darkness in which the species now finds itself. This poses a moral as well as an intellectual challenge since the more complete picture of the human that he is searching for is revealed only through "the Wisdom of God, who created it, and took it into a union of substance with himself so that it would be saved in that way, and freed from all distress" (*PP4* 761B). Eriugena's understanding of the human is therefore inseparable from his understanding of deification and the lifelong transformations that it entails in the life of the human.

The Human Microcosm

Rather than saying bluntly that the human *is* an animal Eriugena generally prefers to say that the genus animal is "in the human" or that it is "created in the human." This is a cryptic statement of two basic theological truths that he held, firstly that everything, including humans and animals in the ordinary sense, was created in the Word, and secondly that the Word chose the form of a human for its own incarnation. But the statement is also a return to Maximus's microcosm, to Dionysius and his concern to retain all of Creation in his notion of the divine, and to Gregory's treatment of the human as an image of God.

Eriugena acknowledges the difficulties that some readers will have with Maximus's microcosm, i.e. the idea that the human species somehow "includes" all of Creation, or at any rate, may be taken to "represent" it in certain respects. For a start, it is not Church teaching. Nonetheless, he his going to use it as the framework for his own analysis of the human:

> Although these things seem quite difficult, since they are not simply a matter of doctrine, when speculative reasoning is applied to them they are consistent with the breadth of our analysis of the human condition, and are particularly useful in showing how it is that we are entitled to say that it is not the human who is in the genus of animals, but rather that every genus of animals was brought forth in the human from the earth (i.e. the solid part of nature); and not merely every genus of animals but in truth the created universe is made in the human. (*PP4* 774B)

The "breadth" (*amplitudo*) Eriugena wants to retain in his analysis of the human is a matter of both content and perspective. The notion of microcosm ensures that *all* of Creation must be involved in his analysis of the human, and to that extent it clearly broadens his account. But it broadens it in another way too, by adding a strong mythic dimensions to the perspective in which the human is to be considered, since the notion of "microcosm" will require us to bring together things we usually think of as different, and to find a new kind of unity in them. In other words, it requires "compositive imagining," as it has been called (Wheelwright, 1968, pp. 45–50), one of the most obvious features of imagination generally, aesthetic awareness in particular, where the notions of "harmony" and the ability of the mind to "bring things together" come to the fore.

Many composite images have been encountered in the pages of this book, from the opening lines of Martianus's *De Nuptiis* down to

Maximus's microcosm. This is because of the remarkable concern of the Neoplatonists to reaffirm the unity of Creation in spite of its many apparent contrasts and incompatibilities, and their use of allegory, etymology, arithmetic, numerology, physics, astronomy, and many other devices that allow them to make unexpected and seemingly arbitrary connections between different ideas. Eriugena realized that composite imagery would make considerable demands on his readers, particularly when they are asked to see all of Creation in the human. Nor are the demands reduced by noting that the human being to be considered now is the ideal human, the incarnate Word of God or the deified human. For all of Creation now acquires a degree of participation in the divinity that seems excessive, while the divinity itself acquires a degree of immanence in Creation that borders on pantheism.

It was not just in the Latin Church that the notion of the human as a kind of miniature universe or "microcosm" (μιχρός χόσμος [*mikrós kósmos*]) caused trouble. As it happens, Gregory of Nyssa was one of those who dismissed the idea as a relic from the pagan past. Here is how he put it in a passage from *De Imagine* that Eriugena translated:

> How pathetic and unworthy of the nobility of the human are the fantasies of some heathens who add to the glory of the human species—or so they think—by lumping it together with this world. They say that the human is a "little world" (*mikros kosmos*) composed of the same elements that everything else is made of, using an impressive name to heap praise of this sort on human nature, and forgetting that they are adorning the human with characteristics of the mosquito and the mouse. For they too are a mixture of these four elements. (*DeIm* 16, 177D–179A)

This is consistent with Gregory's view that the rational mind of the human is the only part of nature created in the image of God. Jeauneau suggests that Gregory's mockery of the word "microcosm" may be the reason Eriugena doesn't use it (1969, pp. 336–338). He had no objection to the idea, however, and not only does he use it here as the basis for his own account of the human, he even modifies

Gregory's account, based on the idea that the human mind as an image of God, to bring it into line with the notion of human nature as a microcosm.

To begin with, he quotes in full the passage in which Gregory's likens the human mind to a mirror in which the image of God can be seen;[119] and then he broadens it in a way that will permit him to say that it is not just the rational mind of the human that reflects the divinity (as Gregory intended) but the entire human, mind and body, and through it, all of Creation:

> Anybody who examines closely the words of the theologian just mentioned [Gregory], throughout the entire text of *Sermo de Imagine*, will find that the constitution of the human as a whole is constructed from three components, linked in their natural order, namely soul, vital motion (which he sometimes calls "fluid life" or "material life") and informed matter, so that the human as a whole can be understood as consisting of soul, material life and matter itself. (*PP4* 790BC)

He concedes that the version of Gregory he is now presenting is pieced together from different parts of *De Imagine*—it certainly cannot be inferred from Gregory's reference to the human mind as a mirror, since it is clear that the mirror in this case refers only to rational consciousness. But it does appear, as Eriugena suggests, that Gregory left himself open to the broader interpretation when he talked of a second mirror, "the mirror's mirror," meaning Creation and in particular, the body of the human, in which the mind could see an image of itself and thus, indirectly, an image of God.

Eriugena certainly thought so:

> Material life, which has a special involvement with matter and is therefore referred to as "material" seeing as it adheres to the mutable qualities of matter (namely the body), is still a kind of image of the soul, a mirror-image of the mirror, as he says himself. In the same way that the soul is like the divinity, vital movement (also called material life) is like the

119 Above, pp. 31–32.

soul, as if it were a second image, through which the soul shows itself even in matter. (*PP4* 790C)

He now gives his own version of the "series" or "chain" that Gregory referred to[120] when describing the alignment of God, Mind and Body that is necessary for virtuous living:

And so there is a certain chain of events in human nature by which the entire human can be said with justification to be made in the image of God, even if the image is to be found specifically and principally only in the soul. The sequence is: from God comes the soul, without the intervention of any created thing; from the soul comes vital motion; then, through the vital motion, matter receives from the soul the cause of its formation, so that matter follows vital motion, vital motion follows the soul, and the soul itself follows God, and when turned towards him protects the integrity and beauty of its own nature, and turned away from him, dissipates and deforms both itself and everything that depends on it—namely material life and matter itself. (*PP4* 790CD)

And so Eriugena retains the core of Gregory's account of the human while softening the focus on rationality, and thus arrives at an account of Creation that Gregory himself would certainly have dismissed as ἔζωθεν [*éxōthen*], "coming from outside," i.e. pagan.

Defining the Human

As for a short definition of the human, Eriugena simply says that the essence of the human is its Primordial Cause, inviting us to dwell on the idea of humanity in its original setting, as an aspect of the divinity. "We can therefore define the human as follows: It is a certain intellectual notion formed in eternity in the divine mind" (*PP4* 768B). The more usual approach, which is to describe the human in a piecemeal fashion, saying that it is "a rational animal, mortal, capable of perception and self-control" (*PP4* 768C), and so

120 Above, p. 32.

on, is of little value, since these are only the human's own fragmentary impressions of humanity in its present benighted condition:

> The notion of the human in the divine mind is none of these: there it is simple, and cannot be said to be this or that, since it goes beyond every definition and assembly of parts, while it is said of it simply that it exists, not however what it is. For the only definition that is truly οὐσιώδην [ousiŏdēn] (substantial) merely affirms that it exists, and does not say what it is. (*PP4* 768C)

In other words, the human must now be contemplated in the same way that the divinity is, through the method of negation.

To ensure that the human does not become indistinguishable from God when it is considered in this way, he considers the limits of the human mind when compared with the mind of God. Whereas the substance of the divine mind is the understanding of *everything* there is, created and uncreated, the substance of the human mind is at best an understanding of Creation. He begins with the human's understanding of other animals since *Genesis* tells us that humans were endowed with a particularly good understanding of their fellow creatures:

> So from the soil Yahweh fashioned all the wild beasts and all the birds of heaven. These he brought to the human to see what it would call them; each was to bear the name the human would give it. (*Genesis* 2: 19)

The act of naming the other animals, he says, symbolizes the human's understanding of them, and it is a form of understanding that extends also to the rest of Creation, including the elements of the physical world, the genera and species of grasses and trees, quantities and qualities, and other things multiplied by the innumerable differences between them. Knowledge of all of these is innate in the human, although it is unaware that it exists within until it is restored to its former integrity and understands clearly the magnitude and beauty of the image that was constructed in it, and knows of the things that were created in it, turned towards God and surrounded by the light of the divinity in which all things are seen clearly (*PP4* 769BC). So the essence of the human lies in the innate knowledge of Creation it had as a Primordial Cause, and will have again after its Return.

The definition is far from tidy. When the human attempts to consider humanity as an eternal idea in the mind of God that encompasses all of Creation, there is a danger that it will be overwhelmed by the flood of ideas that pours into it:

> Answering the present question requires a many-sided approach. And until it is resolved, an innumerable multitude of different questions and situations of all kinds will pour forth from all sides and without end, as if from a bottomless fountain, so that it might be compared with some justification to that fictional image of the Hydra of Hercules, whose heads grew as fast as they were cut off, one hundred appearing for every one that was cut off. This is like human nature, which is a Hydra, namely a multiple fountain of infinite depth, and who other than Hercules (namely, virtue) can see into it? "For nobody knows what things are in the human except the spirit of the human which is in it" (*1 Cor* 2: 11). (*PP4* 769D–770A)

The heads of the Hydra are the changing faces of the human, while the task of taming the Hydra falls not just to the scholar but to each individual. And it is not through learning alone that the task is achieved, but also through courageous living, represented here by Hercules, sword in hand.

An additional problem is that the human's understanding of its own mind, which is also the corner-stone of its understanding of the divinity, must remain forever incomplete. And yet this should not be regarded as a limitation but rather as its greatest achievement, a point that Eriugena makes in a passage that is unusual in that it brings Dionysius, Augustine and Gregory together—almost in the same sentence:

And stranger still and more beautiful to those who reflect on themselves and their God, the human mind is honoured more by what is not known about it than it is by what is known. For it is a greater achievement for it to be ignorant of *what* it is than to know *that* it is, in the same way that negation is greater and more appropriate praise of the divine nature than affirmation, and greater wisdom is shown in not knowing than in knowing "that of which not-knowing is true wisdom, and is known better through not-knowing."[121] So the image of the divinity in the human mind is seen at its clearest when all that is known is that it exists, while nothing is known as to what it is, when, so to speak, all knowledge of what it is denied, and the only thing affirmed is that it exists. (*PP4* 771CD)

In spite of the quotation from Augustine, Eriugena's primary source here is Gregory.[122] For in both Eriugena and Gregory it is not because of any limitations of the human mind that God is best known through not-knowing, but because it is this limitation that constitutes the closest similarity of the human mind to the deity. For it too is without limits and unknown to *itself*, and if the human mind were any more successful in its attempts to know itself, then it would become less like it and further removed from its own goal of deification:

For if it were known what it is, it would fall entirely within certain limits, and so it would not fully express the image of its Creator who is completely indefinable and cannot be thought of as being within anything since he is infinite, above essences, and above everything that can be said or understood. (*PP4* 771D)

It is here, on the subject of the human's participation in the life of the divinity, that the most important difference between Eriugena and Augustine is to be found. It was dealt with earlier in connection

121 Augustine *De Ordine* 2, 16, 44 (*CCSL* 29, p. 31)
122 Above pp. 34–5.

with Gregory's understanding of deification, and the fundamental differences between Eriugena and Augustine on the topic of predestination,[123] and also in *Periphyseon 2* in connection with divine self-knowledge, where he uses the same phrases from Augustine and Dionysius that he has just quoted now. He now gives his own understanding of what they mean:

> For I am of the opinion that what the holy fathers—I refer to Augustine and Dionysius—say most correctly about God (Augustine: "that he is known better through not-knowing;" Dionysius: "ignorance of whom is true wisdom") is not to be understood as referring only to intellects that search him out piously and diligently, but also to himself. (*PP2* 597D)

Here he parts company with Augustine, whose phrase "knowing through not-knowing" always remains a cognitive or "knowledge-like" act of mind that leads eventually to direct knowledge of God "as he is" in the beatific vision. But this is an impossibility for Eriugena. There is no God "as he is:" The divinity is indefinable even to itself. It follows, then, that the highest form of participation in the divinity that is granted to the human, if it is to be referred to as "knowing through not-knowing," cannot be a cognitive act in the usual sense which, as Eriugena points out, always requires closure of content.

The Problem of Evil

Since the forces attracting the human to God will always prevail, it is only through short-lived episodes of self-deception that evil is possible:

> In itself, evil is ugly and repulsive. If the fickle senses could see it as it is, not only would they not seek or enjoy it, they would run from it and be horrified by it. But the senses make mistakes and as a result are deceived, thinking that evil is good and beautiful, and when chosen, enjoyable. (*PP4* 826C)

123 Above pp. 55–6.

The deception is not a matter of misleading appearances, however, since appearances are also a part of nature and, to that extent, good without qualification. Evil resides at a higher level, at the level of reason, and consists of the "perverse tillage" that Gregory spoke of, a destructive interference of intellect with the natural arousal of emotion. Eriugena explains with a brief parable:

> Suppose there are two men, one wise and not in any way tempted or goaded by avarice, and another foolish, avaricious, completely transfixed and lacerated by darts of perverse greed. A vessel of pure gold is brought before them both at a particular location, decorated with the most precious of stones, beautifully designed, fit for a king. Both look at it, the sensible man and the foolish man, both acquire an image of the actual vessel through their bodily senses, fix it in their memories, think about it. (*PP4* 428BC)

Up to this point there is no difference between the two men. The difference between them emerges only when the image provided by the senses is "passed up," in Maximus's terms, from Perception, to Reason, and finally to Mind or Intellect. This "ascent" is the natural response of the human to the perception of beauty, but stops at the level of reason in the case of the avaricious man:

> But the sensible man in a simple way refers in its entirety to the Creator of all things the beauty of the vessel whose image he thinks about within himself; the lure of avarice snatches nothing from him, no addiction to money infects the purpose of his pure mind, no selfish desire contaminates it. The avaricious man, on the other hand, is in an entirely different situation. As soon as he absorbs the image of the vessel, the flame of desire is kindled, he is consumed, he is destroyed, he dies, since he does not refer the beauty of the object and its images to the praise of the one who said "Mine is the gold, and mine is the silver," but plunges himself into a foul swamp of greed and is swallowed up. (*PP4* 828C)

For the sensible man, the beauty of the vessel speaks for itself and does not permit other considerations to interfere with it. And while the avaricious man experiences this same beauty, it is cut short by the intervention of other perspectives:

> Do you not see that in both of them the image of the vessel is good and beautiful? But as seen by the sensible man it is something simple and natural and free of evil, while in the avaricious man it is a double image, compounded with the opposing evil of avarice which is mixed with it, and structured and coloured by it so that it appears to be good even though it is pure poison. (*PP4* 828CD)

So the "mixing" (Gregory's term) he speaks of lies not in perception but in the interference of reason with the normal arousal of emotion, leading in turn to the distorted perception, and then to behaviour driven by avarice.

The Tree of Good and Evil

To end the discussion on the nature of evil, Eriugena now brings together the views of Gregory and Maximus on the subject of the Tree of Good and Evil:

> Following Gregory of Nyssa, we have already said a good many things above about the forbidden tree, and now I think we must briefly say something else on the topic in order to introduce the interpretation of the great teacher, Maximus the Monk. He took the tree of knowledge of good and evil to be Creation as we see it, which the human pursued when it abandoned its Creator. It contains both the enjoyment of pleasure and the beginnings of fear and death, like fruit that is a mixture of the deceptive goodness of gratification, and the evil of the sadness that follows. For there is no gratification to be had from the world we can see that is not followed by deprivation, and deprivation is followed by fear and the sadness of death. (*PP4* 842AB)

He points out, however, gratification and deprivation need not be thought of as things that come one after another:

> Although fear and death are hidden behind the smile of enjoyment, they are present at the same time in the human soul, and they are aroused at the same time. Fear is concealed behind the kind of false beauty that pleasure has, and is like a fruit that is a mixture of apparent enjoyment and latent fear. But when the pleasure and enjoyment of the visible world recedes, fear remains, naked and by itself, born of the poverty and inadequacy of goodness as it appears to the eye. (*PP4* 842BC)

This, he says, is the reason Maximus identifies the Tree of Good and Evil with Creation, quoting in full the relevant passage from Maximus:

> And perhaps the person who says that the Tree of Knowledge of Good and Evil is nothing other than Creation as we see it before us will not be proven wrong. For pleasure and pain is what it gives, of its very nature, to those who are a part of it. Or to put it differently, since the world before us has both a spiritual content to nourish the mind, and a physical capacity to delight the senses while warping the mind, it is called The Tree of Knowledge of Good and Evil, containing knowledge of goodness when considered spiritually, and knowledge of evil when taken from the standpoint of the body. So it becomes the teacher of the passions for those who become involved with it for the body's sake, and causes them to forget the divinity. It was for this reason that God made a prohibition preventing humans from participating in Creation for a time, so that first of all (and quite correctly) they should learn of their own responsibility and immortality through the gift of grace, and, hardened into impassibility and steadfastness through this experience, and already made God-like through deification, they would be empowered through their acquaintance with

God to examine what God had created without coming to any harm, knowing about such things not as humans do but as God does, having the same knowledge of Creation through grace and wisdom that God has, through the change of mind and perception that is necessary for deification. So this is what the Tree means here, in an interpretation that is supported by all of the evidence. (*AdTh CCSG* 7, p. 37; *PP4* 842C–843A)

Maximus gives two different theories about the origins of evil, both of which go far back into the cultural heritage of Greece, and further still to the creation myths of natural religion from all parts of the globe. The first is that evil comes from haste (with its implied recklessness or *hubris*), and the second that it comes from forgetfulness. According to Maximus, if Adam and Eve had been patient and waited a little longer before eating from The Tree, then its appeal for them would no longer have been false, and partaking of it would have strengthened their will to live as they ought to. But evil is also due to forgetfulness, in particular the mind's forgetfulness of its own origins. This idea is also an old one, recurring many times in the extracts from Martianus in Ch. 1, and even more frequently in Gregory, Dionysius and Maximus in their many references to the divine origins of the created world, and the protection that this fact affords to those who are able to keep it in mind.

Eriugena is impressed by Maximus's interpretation of the Tree:

Note how beautiful and clear is his interpretation of the Tree of Good and Evil. As he himself says, it is the world as we see it, providing knowledge of what is good, and fruit for the spirit to those who understand it spiritually, in accordance with its own principles; but to those who seek it carnally, for pleasure and without temperance and who misuse it contrary to God's laws, the knowledge it brings is lethal. From which it follows that the cause of evil does not reside in the world but in the intemperance of those who abuse it. (*PP4* 843AB)

The End of the Book

Periphyseon 4 ends abruptly, as *Periphyseon 3* did, but on this occasion there is no suggestion that some text is missing. The teacher simply has too many things to say:

> *Teacher*: And so, if you agree, let us bring this book to an end before it gets any longer.
> *Student*: Of course I agree. It should have been ended long ago. (*PP4* 860C)

Chapter 11

Periphyseon 5

Periphyseon 5 deals with the Return of Creation to its Primordial Causes, an activity or a "nature" allocated by Eriugena to the category "not created and not creating." On the first page of *Periphyseon 1* (*PP1* 442A) he acknowledged that this category appears to be empty, since only God is "uncreated" and God can hardly be described as "not creating." Elsewhere in *Periphyseon*, and here again at the beginning of *Periphyseon 5*, he provides a justification of sorts for the category, saying that it refers to God as the *goal* towards which all Creation is moving. This, he says, necessitates the fourth creation category for "when I observe that all things seek the same end and impassable boundary, in which they determine the limits of their natural motion, I find it to be neither created nor creating"(*PP5* 1019B).

The Tree of Life and the Return

In the early pages of *Periphyseon 5* Eriugena continues his *Hexameron*, commenting on the account of creation in *Genesis* up to the Fall. Surprisingly, he says that the Return is announced just as Adam and Eve are being expelled from Paradise. The verse he is referring to is the one that begins:

> Now, therefore, lest he [the human] should stretch out his hand and take from the Tree of Life and eat from it and live in eternity… (*Genesis* 3: 22)

The text then goes on to describe the punishment of Adam and Eve, their expulsion from Paradise, the harsh life they were condemned to on earth, and the placing of a guard on the Tree "lest he should stretch out his hand" and attempt to eat from it again. There is nothing about the Return here, just divine retribution for the *hubris* of the human.

But this is not how Eriugena reads the verse. He reads it as a question, replacing "lest" with "is it not possible that":

> Now, therefore, is it not possible that he should stretch out his hand and take from the Tree of Life and eat from it and live in eternity? (*PP5* 859D)

Correctly understood, he says, the verse announces "the Return of humans to the same state of blessedness that they lost through sinning" (*ibid.*).

Eriugena's reading is far-fetched and indicative of a certain impatience found elsewhere in the early part of *Periphyseon 5*. In any event, the difficulty he has with the standard reading of the verse has nothing to do with grammar: he objects to it because it conjures up an image of God taking steps to deny the human access to the Tree of Life. This is an absurdity for Eriugena, the same absurdity that he first tried to point out in *The Book on Predestination*, since the Tree of Life is a symbol of deification and God wants nothing *other* than deification for the human and has ensured that this must be so. He suggests that those who interpret the verse differently should examine it more carefully:

> It seems to me that those who think that the particle *ne*, in this context, expresses negation rather than interrogation or doubt, implying that humans were expelled from Paradise so that they could not eat of the Tree of Life and live in eternity, are not looking into the matter closely enough. (*PP5* 861AB)

To partake of the Tree of Life is to be drawn towards God, he says, and the suggestion that humans might wish to eat again from the Tree of Life when they have just rejected it is self-contradictory:

> How could the humans possibly have taken and eaten from the Tree of Life and lived in Eternity after they had sinned

and were not yet freed from sin and death (which is the price of sin) when they neither took nor ate from the same tree before they sinned—as a careful reading of divine Scripture will show? If they had taken and eaten, certainly they would not have sinned or fallen, but would have lived happily in eternity. (*PP5* 861B)

In Eriugena's reading, it was not from the Tree of Life that Adam and Eve ate when they were driven by the *hubris* and forgetfulness that Maximus spoke of,[124] but from the Tree of Good and Evil, namely Creation.

For those who are still tempted to take the Tree of Life in a material sense, as a possession of some kind that God might wish to deny to the human, he adds a final rebuff:

And another thing: if this Paradise from which the human was expelled was located in space and of earthly origin, and if the Tree of Life planted at its centre was of earthly origin and perceivable by the senses and bore fruit suitable for bodily use, why did God not restrict the expulsion of the human solely to the Tree of Life and fence it off in another part of Paradise where it could not get at it? (*PP5* 861BC)

His advice to those who wish to understand what Scripture has to say on the Tree of Life is to "to refrain from thinking of Paradise and its animals in physical terms, and look for the spiritual meanings by which Scripture makes things known to us, for this is the one and the only road to the heart of the mystic writings" (*PP5* 862A).

The Return Announced

Eriugena sees a dramatic transformation in the text of *Genesis* at the point where God utters the two words "Nunc ergo" (Now therefore), the two words at the beginning of the verse quoted above, and the opening words of *Periphyseon 5* also. It is with these two words, he says, that the Return is announced for the first time in Scripture:

124 Above, pp. 180–181.

The voice of God suggests a return such as this with the words "Now therefore," or as it is put more clearly in another translation "And now God said." As if divine mercy and infinite goodness, always ready to be kind and compassionate, sighing over the fall of the divine image, mercifully accepting what has happened, enduring with patience the arrogance of humans, were to say openly, "Now therefore," that is, "Now that I see the humans expelled from Paradise, happiness turned to distress, wealth to deprivation, eternity to mortality, life to death, spirit to animal, heaven to earth, youth to old age, joy to sadness, saved to lost, the sensible son to the prodigal, straying from the heavenly flock, I feel sorry for them. For this is not what they were created for." (*PP5* 862BC)

Eriugena now imagines God turning to the choirs of angels (who have been observing all of this) to speak to them about the plight of the humans:

"They were created instead to have eternal life and happiness, and you, their neighbours and friends, now see them expelled from Paradise to the region of death and distress." God was addressing the heavenly hosts who stood by their Creator and remained in perpetual blessedness, although their number was reduced by the immorality of the humans. Note how many things are contained in the expression of divine feeling, although it is very brief, consisting of one temporal adverb, namely "now," and one causal conjunction, namely "therefore." (*PP5* 862C)

This is all in keeping with Gregory's belief that humans were angels before the Fall, and provides an additional reason for thinking of the Fall itself in mental terms only, as a loss of spiritual integrity:

I doubt that you have forgotten how in Book 4, as we followed the things said by the holy Fathers (writing in either language) on the subject of Paradise, we were able to infer conclusively—to our own satisfaction at any rate—that the Paradise from which humans were expelled was nothing other than human nature itself, created in the image of God, the dignity of which (i.e. of the image) this same human nature lost when it turned its back on divine authority. And from this it follows that the expulsion or driving out of humans is nothing other than the loss of the natural happiness they were created to enjoy. Humans did not lose their own nature, however, which was made in the image and likeness of God, and is necessarily incorruptible. They did, however, lose the happiness they would have been theirs except that they disregarded obedience to God. (*PP5* 863AB)

Eriugena holds to his distinction between nature and grace. Regardless of how they live their lives, humans are still constructed in the image of God.

The Flaming Flashing Sword

Returning to the account of the Fall in *Genesis*, he discusses the line that reads "he posted the Cherubim, and a flaming and flashing sword to guard the way to the Tree of Life"(*Genesis* 3: 24). The Cherubim and the fiery sword, he says, are not to be understood as precautions that were taken by God to prevent the human from access to the Tree of Life, but as further indicators of the spiritual nature of salvation. In fact they refer to God:

According to Dionysius the Areopagite, writing in the book *The Celestial Hierarchy*, "Cherubim" means "great knowledge" or "outpouring of wisdom." This is confirmed by Epiphanius in the book *On Hebrew Names* where he writes that "Cherubim" means "full knowledge" or "knowledge of many things." But if Scripture is trying to convey the essence of heaven to us here, then of necessity we are obliged to concede that Paradise is of a spiritual nature. For reason does not permit us to accept that a spiritual entity close to God and always in motion around him could be stationed in front of a Paradise that is a location in the earthly sense. (*PP5* 863CD)

The same holds for the fiery sword, which makes it even clearer that both the Cherubim and the sword stand for the Word of God:

> For the same reason, it is appropriate for us to take the flaming sword too to mean the Word of God itself. It burns and cuts. It burns our sins, for "God is a fire that consumes," and purges the squalor and irrationality of human existence, and divides and separates it from the things that have rightly descended on it as a result of the Fall, discolouring and deforming it and making it dissimilar to its Creator. The sword, namely the Word of God, the only-begotten Son, Virtue and Wisdom, is rightly described and thought of as something that is flashing, for although by nature it is unchanging it is nonetheless moved through its indescribable pity and mercy to intervene in the salvation of the human race. And so the Cherubim and the flaming, flashing sword, understood in this way, are permanently stationed before the eyes of our souls, namely reason and intellect. Why? "To guard the path to the Tree of Life," that is, lest we forget the path to the Tree of Life, and to ensure that we keep the memory of the Tree of Life, and the path that leads to it, unceasingly before the eyes of our hearts. (*PP5* 864D–865A)

Origen's consuming fire and Gregory's mirror, in which the human is reminded of its similarity with its Creator, are among the many images that he finds here in *Genesis*, all of them referring to one thing only, the presence of the Word of God in Creation:

> Many different symbols of the Word of God have been heaped up in these lines of Holy Scripture. It is referred to by the expressions "Cherubim," and "flaming, flashing sword," and "path," and "Tree of Life," to convey to us that the Word is never out of the sight of our hearts, that it is ever-present to enlighten us, that it never permits the memory of

blessedness that was lost through duplicity to fade completely, always wishing us to return to it, and until it does, sighing with compassion and urging us to take the road that leads there by secure steps of knowledge and behaviour. "I have come to bring fire to the earth," he says, "and how I wish it were blazing already" (*Luke* 12: 49). (*PP5* 865BC)

The Journey Back

The teacher tries to convince the student that the complementary actions of Coming Out and Return are to be seen throughout Creation. He mentions the rising and setting of the sun, the coming and going of the tides, the rotation of the skies, and the seasons of the year. In the world of living things the pattern is even more obvious and fundamental:

> Put simply, in Creation that possesses vital motion there is nothing which does not return to the origin of its motion. The end of the entire motion is its beginning; it does not finish up at any end-point other than its origin, from which it began to move and to which it always seeks to return so that it can stop there and be at rest. (*PP5* 866C)

So also for the life of the mind. The liberal arts, he says, start out from a small number of basic principles to which they endlessly return.

The student's main interest, however, is in the Return of the human. How can it come back, given that it dies and its body decays. The teacher says the Return of the human will happen in five stages:

> The first Return of humans is when the body decays and is called back to the elements of the physical world from which it was constructed. The second will be completed with the resurrection, when everybody will receive their own body from the community of the four elements. The third when the body will be changed into spirit. The fourth, when the spirit (or to be more precise, the complete human) will return to its Primordial Causes which are in God, always and

without change. The fifth, when nature itself and its Causes will be changed into God, in the way that air is changed into light. For God will be all in all when there is nothing but God. (*PP5* 876AB)

The first Return begins with death of the human, and the others with its resurrection at the end of the world. The human body is transformed into pure spirit in the Third Return, but this is not a loss for the human but rather restoration to its original form.

The teacher now combines this abstract account of the Return with Maximus's five-fold division of all there is, reading the divisions from the bottom up[125] as stages in the deification of the human:

So the ascent and the unification of the divisions just mentioned begin with the cancellation of the division of the human into two sexes. For in the resurrection sex will be removed and nature united and there will be nothing but the human, as if it had not sinned. Next, the world will be united with Paradise, and there will be nothing but Paradise. Next, heaven and earth will be united and there will be nothing but heaven. And note that the lower is always transformed into the higher. Sex is changed into the human since sex is inferior to the human; and the earth, which is inferior, into Paradise. Earthly things, since they are inferior, will be changed to celestial bodies. Then there follows the unification of all of visible Creation and its transformation into something that can be understood, so that all of Creation is made intelligible. Finally, the created universe will be united with the Creator, and will be in him and with him. And this is an end to everything visible and invisible, since all visible things will cross over into intelligible things, and intelligible things into God by a mysterious and indescribable unification—although, as we have often said, not through a mixture or dissolution of essences or substances. (*PP5* 893C–894A)

---

125 Above, p. 89.

Shadows and Echoes

So what kind of "world" will remain when Creation has been united with God? The student is bothered by Maximus's idea that the entire universe is somehow "in" the human. This suggests that all of Creation will be restored simultaneously with the resurrection of the human on the Last Day:

> *Student*: So what are we to say? That irrational animals, even the trees and the grass and every part of this world, from top to bottom, are restored in the Word of God incarnate?
>
> *Teacher*: I'm amazed that you keep on saying the same thing. Did not the Word, when it became human, accept all of Creation visible and invisible, and save everything that it accepted as a part of the human? And if it accepted all of Creation when it became human, certainly it saved all of Creation, and will continue to save it in eternity. (*PP5* 913BC)

If this is so, the student says, then the world will simply remain as it always was, namely a particular thing with a particular mass, a particular shape, and so on. The teacher corrects him, taking the special case of non-rational animals:

> I did not say that the mass and appearance of visible, bodily things would be retained in the resurrection, but rather (as we have often agreed) that they would return, with the human and in the human, to their Causes and Reasons—which were created in the human—where all of them may be more truly said to be animals than they are in their corporeal and perceptible effects. For where animals are brought into being is where they truly are animals. (*PP5* 913D)

When the human species and all of creation are returned to their Primordial Causes, he says, irrational animals will also be taken closer to their own Primordial Causes. Wherever pairs of Primordial

Causes can be classified as higher and lower; the lower will be absorbed into the higher in the resurrection.

It is only the Primordial Causes that will be raised upwards, however, and not the bodies in which they existed while they were alive, since the latter are not really "things" at all but mere shadows and echoes of their Primordial Causes:

> The same holds for all things perceivable by the senses, whether they be celestial or earthly. For all things that vary with place and time and can be detected by bodily senses are not themselves substantial entities that truly exist, but must be taken as certain kinds of transitory images and reflections of those things that really do exist. The voice and its image (ἠχώ [ēchō] in Greek) is an example of this, or physical entities and their images, formed in clear air, or reflected in water or anything else that tends to reflect them. None of these are things, but turn out to be false images of things. And so, in the same way that images of voices and reflections of bodies do not exist in their own right, since they are not substances, similarly, these bodies that we can perceive are like images of things that exist, and of themselves know nothing of existence. (*PP5* 913D–914B)

The world that is perceived by the human during its lifetime on earth, including its own body, consists only of material symbols of immaterial realities. These "symbols" are lost with the death of the body but their immaterial forms are retained for the resurrection. This is a process he described in detail in connection with the sensory systems of humans and animals in *Periphyseon 3*.[126] Now he presents it in more general terms:

> Natural reason teaches that even human bodies, which are now extended in space and move and change by increments and decrements, and also their features, be they general (shared with all human bodies) or special (circumscribing the mass of individual bodies) will not be a part of the

---

126 Above, pp. 157–162.

resurrection to come, but will pass over into a spiritual entity that cannot be circumscribed in place or time or by special features based on qualities and quantities. (*PP5* 914B)

Adam and Eve were bodiless spirits of this sort before the Fall. This is why Eriugena, like Origen before him, takes the "clothes made of skins" that were thrown over them as they were expelled from Paradise as symbols of their sexualized bodies (*Genesis* 3: 21; *PP4* 818C–819A). It is no great loss, therefore, if the animal hides have to be left behind. Eriugena notes that other theologians believe in the resurrection of the body, notably Augustine, but he is content with shadows and echoes, for nothing more is required for the unending work of the mind, which alone continues into eternity.

The End of *Periphyseon*

In the closing pages of *Periphyseon* Eriugena turns to the topic of deification and the many images of it that are to be found in Scripture before returning once more to his preferred image, the Tree of Life:

> All will return to Paradise, as we said, but not all will enjoy the Tree of Life; or at any rate, all will partake of the Tree of Life, but not equally. Only a fool does not know that things that are good by nature, which will be shared equally by all humans, are a fruit of the Tree of Life. Πᾶν ξύλον [*Pãn xýlon*], i.e. "every tree," which we spoke of earlier, refers to Christ. For he is the tree that bears as fruit everything that is good, since he is everything good, and he is also the giver of everything good. So, in general terms, all humans will enjoy its fruit through participation in natural goodness, while in a special sense his elect will enjoy the magnificence of deifications beyond everything in the natural world. (*PP5* 1015AB)

He uses the plural "deifications" here, in the same way that he used "predestinations" to refer to the salvation of individuals.[127] He realizes that the word will be unfamiliar to some of his readers:

127 Above, p. 48.

But this word (I mean "deification") is very rarely used in Latin writings, although I find that it is understood by many, Ambrose in particular. Why this is so is not clear to me. Perhaps the meaning of the term (that is, θέωσις [*theōsis*]) which the Greeks use widely to refer to the crossing over of the saints into God, not only in soul but also in body, so that they might be one in him and with him, when nothing animal, nothing corporeal, nothing human, and nothing of the natural world will be left in them, seems too exalted, and to those who are not able to rise above corporeal considerations, incomprehensible and incredible, and for this reason not to be uttered in public. (*PP5* 1015BC)

But he does not press the matter further, saying only "this is something for the experts to discuss" (*PP5* 1015C).

It is time to bring the book to an end, and the Student requests a summary of *Periphyseon* as a whole. The teacher goes back over the four-fold division of "universal nature" but pointedly leaves the topic of the Return outside of this framework: "Having considered the four-fold theory of universal nature in these four species, we decided to add some ideas about the return of effects to causes (i.e. the reasons in which they subsist"(*PP5* 1020A). For while the formal structure of *Periphyseon* is given by the four creation categories, in effect, and especially in Boooks 4 and 5, the narrative is structured also by the more general notion of the Return of all things to their Primordial Causes.

So the teacher now gives a summary of what has been said about the Return in *Periphyseon* and finishes with a short account of the final stages of deification in his own words. Essentially, all created things will return to their origins, namely their Primordial Causes, and depending on which part of Creation is being referred to, all of it, human nature, or sanctified human nature, the Return takes three different forms, more properly thought of as aspects (*modi speculationis*) of the same phenomenon:

The first of these is seen in a general way in the transformation of visible Creation as a whole (that which is contained within the boundaries of this world, namely bodies of all kinds, those that may be detected by the senses of the body and those that escape them because of their excessive subtlety) such that there is no body that is a part of corporeal nature, whether it flourishes through vital motion alone, invisibly or openly, or enjoys an irrational soul and bodily senses, that does not return to its hidden causes by means of its life. For none of those things that have been constructed as substances by the Cause of All Things will be reduced to nothing. (*PP5* 1020AB)

This is the principle that "no nature is lost" that Eriugena affirmed so strongly in the closing pages of *The Book on Predestination*, and which was rejected with equal firmness by Prudentius, speaking on behalf of the Latin Church, when he corrected it to read "rational nature does not perish, but non-rational natures do."[128]

Eriugena now considers the Return of the human:

The second aspect is to be seen in the general return of human nature in its totality, as redeemed in Christ, to its former state and condition, and (as if in a kind of paradise) to the dignity of the divine image thanks to one person, he whose blood was shed for the salvation of all of humanity as a group, so that no humans are deprived of the natural gifts with which they were constructed, regardless of whether they lived well or badly in this life. And in this way, the indescribable and incomprehensible diffusion of divine goodness and generosity will be apparent, ensuring that nothing flowing from the Greatest Good is punished in a person. (*PP5* 1020BC)

This is the cosmic "diffusion of divine goodness" that he speaks of briefly in Chapter 4 of *The Book on Predestination* and in its closing pages. It sweeps away all resistance. Even in the case of sinners, God does not punish what he himself made, and in the resurrection "all

128 Above, p. 60.

of the good things in their nature will shine out in a wonderful display
that adds to the splendour of the universe" (*DePred* 19, 3).

Finally there is the deification of the saints, whose lives are brought
to a level of fulfilment that can only be explained by the exceptional
gifts of divine grace that were given to them, in addition to their
being humans:

> The third aspect of the return is exemplified by those who
> will not only ascend to the magnificence of the nature that
> was created in them but, through the generosity of divine
> grace which through Christ and in Christ was given to his
> elect, will also pass over all the laws and boundaries of nature
> and beyond essences into God himself, and will be one with
> him and in him. (*PP5* 1020A–1020C)

The final act of deification he describes as "the submersion beyond
nature of the purest souls in God, as of incomprehensible and
inaccessible light into the shadows in which the causes of all things
are hidden" (*PP5* 1020D–1021A).

The five aspects of human life (material, vital, sensory, rational,
and intellectual) return to their Primordial Causes, each being
consumed, as if by fire, by the one that lies above it, and the return
continues from there into the three aspects of divine life, knowledge,
wisdom, and *theosis*, where all eight become the vertices of a solid
cube of pure light:

> And then "night will be as bright as day," that is, the most
> secret of divine mysteries will be revealed to blessed and
> enlightened intellects in a manner beyond words. The
> perfect solidity of the number Eight will then be achieved,
> like a supernatural cube, prefigured in Psalm 6, known as
> "The Psalm of David on the Octachord." The resurrection
> of the Lord also occurred on the eighth day, in a mystic
> reference to the blessed life that is to come after the end of
> world, following the Seven of this life, through the seven
> rotations of the days, when human nature, as we have said,
> will return to its origin by ascending through eight steps, five

within the confines of the natural world, and three within God himself, supernaturally and super-essentially. Then the Five of the Created will be united with the Three of the Creator so that nothing will appear in anything except God alone, just as the clearest air appears to be nothing but light. (*PP5* 1021AB)

Which brings the famous dialogue to its last exchange:

Student May Christ, the true light, enlighten us internally, so that we may see the light of the Father in the Holy Spirit.
Teacher So may it be. (*PP5* p. 226)

The Letter to Wulfad

When *Periphyseon* was complete Eriugena sent a copy to his friend Wulfad with a covering letter that makes a fitting epilogue to it, containing as it does the thoughts of the author on his greatest work and his hopes for it.

It begins:

Here are the complete contents of this work, five books in all. Readers who still think I have written things that are dubious or too obvious should attribute it to haste or carelessness on my part, and I would hope that with a kind heart they might make allowance for the intellect of the human, still carrying the weight of its bodily dwelling place. I believe that nothing that is entirely free of error has ever been achieved by human scholarship in this foggy life, where even good people are called good not as if they were already good while still living in the flesh, but because they wish they were good, and because they long for perfect goodness in the future, being called so only because of their attitude of mind.

But if readers are pleasantly surprised to find here something that is useful and relevant to the promotion of the catholic faith, then they should attribute this solely to God, who alone reveals the secrets hidden in the dark, and draws to himself those who seek him, no longer deceived by errors

but set free from them; and united in charity of spirit they
should join me in giving thanks to the Universal Cause of all
good things, without which we can do nothing, attracted no
longer by the urge to find fault, or inflamed by the fires of
envy which—uniquely and above all other vices—is
dedicated to sundering the bonds of charity and
brotherhood. (*PP5* 1021B–1022A)

He then dedicates the work to God, and then to Wulfad on
account of the assistance he received from him in writing it:

With full respect to all, whether they accept the results of my
labours with good will, having considered them with an open
and eager mind, or reject them with malice, passing
judgment on them without first finding out what exactly they
say, I offer this work in the first place to God, who has said
"Ask and it will be given to you; search and you will find;
knock and the door will be opened to you" (*Luke* 11: 9), and
then to Wulfad, my brother in Christ, for examination and
correction. For it was thanks to your encouragement that it
was begun, and continued with the help of your expertise to
its conclusion—such as it is. (*PP5* 1022A)

And referring to promises he made to Wulfad to deal more fully with
certain topics, he asks him to let him know if he would like further
clarifications.

Addressing readers in general, and taking into account that the
work is still unfinished, he says:

In the meantime I would ask readers to be content with the
matters already discussed, giving credit not to my powers of
intellect, which are few if any, but to the modest ability I
have to persist with my work on matters concerning the
divinity. I hope you will want to defend it—perhaps not with
those who are jealous, but at least with friends and those who
seek the truth—relying just as much on the sharpness of your

own minds as you do on the dull theories I have arrived at by lamp-light. (*PP5* 1022BC)

And finally, he has some words of encouragement for readers who might wish to promote his work:

> This will not be a difficult task, in my opinion. As soon as a work like this finds its way into the hands of true philosophers—assuming it is relevant to their investigations—not only will they accept it with an open mind, they will embrace it as if it were their own. On the other hand, when it reaches those who are quicker to find fault than to understand, I don't think there is much to be gained from discussing it with them. "Everybody must be left free to hold their own opinion" (*Rm* 14: 5) until that light appears which will turn the light of false philosophers to darkness, and transform to light the darkness of those who really knew. (*PP5*, 1022C)

Chapter 12

The End of the Story

In the words of his biographer, the only clue we have about the death of Eriugena is "the abrupt and definitive interruption of his literary activities."[129] To go by the unfinished commentary on John's Gospel, and taking into account his considerable output at that time, it must be assumed that he died around 870, or a year or two later. Jeauneau imagines him dying "pen in hand," having just finished Verse 6 of Chapter 6 of his commentary on John's Gospel, where Jeauneau himself, as editor of the text, has written *Reliqua desunt* (the rest is missing) (*ComJ*, p. 137). Certainly information about Eriugena after 870 is scant, and at present there is no reason to accept the story of his subsequent travels to England, where his students are supposed to have stabbed him to death with their pens.

We are no better off with regard to the year of Eriugena's birth. All we can do is work back from 850–851 when we know for sure that he was working on *The Book on Predestination*. Given that only a well-established academic would have been asked to undertake such a task, he can scarcely have been less than 30 years old at the time, and there is evidence that he may have been older. In their edition of Eriugena's glossaries on the Old Testament[130] Contreni and Ó Néill say "not only does it appear that John Scottus was no neophyte when he wrote *De divinae praedestinatione liber*, in the early 850s, it is highly likely that he was an accomplished scholar even before the early 840s when Prudentius of Troyes knew him at court."[131] This would place his birth no later than 800. So it can be truly said that "Eriugena's writings are his monument"(Brennan, 1986, p. 413).

---

129 Cappuyns 1933, p. 233.

130 Below, p. 198.

131 Contreni & Ó Néill, 1997, p. 78.

Life at the Palace

Some of the daily routine of Eriugena's life in the palace school can be pieced together from the rich record of "work in progress" that remains in the margins of his manuscripts. Based on Reims 875 (a draft of *Periphyseon*) and the many insertions in different hands that it contains, Dutton (2002) imagines what we might have seen had we looked into his scriptorium when he was writing his great work:

> I believe we would have seen him with wax tablets and stylus fixed to his belt for ready use, have watched as he bent over the open and unbound gatherings of R [*MS* Reims 875], here erasing text, there inscribing new materials in its margins, have seen him speak to a student who was copying a new gathering of the work as he handed him a wax tablet with a small text to be added at a point he had already marked, and we might have seen him number the new quires of the codex as they were readied.[132]

As we now know, Eriugena himself wrote some of the materials in the margins. The discovery was first made by the German palaeographer Ludwig Traube (1861–1907) who was clearly moved by the event. It was, he said, "as if I were seeing in front of me the very hand of Erasmus writing the Commentary on the Gospel of Mark as painted by Holbein."[133]

The matter, however, was more complex than he realized. The Irish handwriting he was referring to is actually in two different hands, referred to now as i^1 and i^2 (i for Irish as opposed to Carolingian). Following a lengthy debate, it is now accepted that i^1 is the hand of Eriugena (Jeauneau & Dutton, 1996). An example can be seen in the right margin of Figure 1.

---

132 Dutton 2002, p. 164.

133 Jeauneau & Dutton, 1996, p. 16; To see the picture Traube is referring to, search for *erasmus* + *louvre* on the internet.

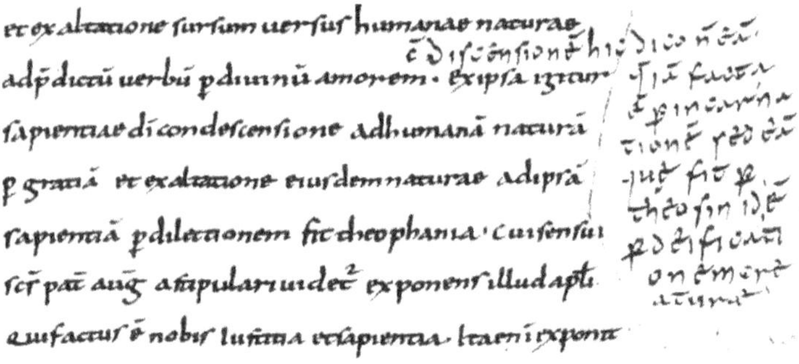

ERIUGENA

Figure 1. The handwriting of Eriugena (in the right margin) from Scot Jean Erigène *Περί Φύσεως μερισμοῦ, seu de Divisione naturae* Reims, BM, Ms 875 fol. 10r, reproduced here with the permission of Bibliothèque Municipale de Reims. From Jeauneau & Dutton (1996, p. 126) with the permission of the publisher, Brepols.

Eriugena has added some new text to be included in the next version, starting in the middle of the old text to show where the insertion is to be made, and continuing out into the margin. The words he wishes to insert are "condiscensionem hic dico non eam qua iam facta est per incarnationem sed eam quae fit per theosin, id est per deificationem creaturae."[134] The insertion translates: "The 'condiscensio'[135] I refer to here is not that which has already taken place through the incarnation but which comes about through *theosis* i.e. through the deification of Creation" (*PP1* 449A).

Since Eriugena was a minor figure in medieval philosophy until recently, it is quite likely that other writings of his will turn up. Glossaries he wrote on the Old Testament, first discovered in 1895 and published in 1997, are of special interest, not least because of

134 Written, with medieval suspensions, abbreviations, and the long s, as:
c̄difcenfionē hic dico n̄ eā q̄ iā facta p̄ incarnatonē fed eā quę fit p̄ theofin id ē p̄ deificationem creaturæ.

135 Eriugena's term "condiscensio" means "descent-ascent," referring to the joint descent of God to Creation through the incarnation and the ascent of Creation to God through *theosis*. It is a major theme of his work, found above (pp. 90–91), for example, in the closing couplet in his verses on the Nativity.

the 150 words of Old Irish they contain.[136] For example, he gives the gloss *foilenn* (seagull) for one of the birds listed in *Leviticus* (11: 16) as not suitable for eating, and glosses the Cherethites and Pelitithes mentioned in *Kings 1* (1: 38) with the military term *buiden choisc* ("a stopping gang"), evidently "special forces" of some kind. The glosses confirm that migration from Ireland to Europe in those years involved students as well as established scholars, and it is notable too, as the editors point out, that the list of Old Irish words in the glossaries includes technical legal terms that could scarcely have been acquired by Eriugena in his youth—further evidence that he may have been older than is generally supposed when he left Ireland.

From Eriugena's own point of view, the most significant feature of his working environment was the unwavering support he enjoyed from the Emperor throughout his career. Without it, it is hard to see how he could have remained in the palace after the condemnation of *The Book on Predestination*. It appears that the Emperor was prepared to ignore any difficulties that might arise between Eriugena and local Church authorities because he depended on him for the promotion of a project that was of great personal importance to him, the palace programme for the promotion of Byzantine literature and culture that was, in effect, directed by Eriugena.

The imperial protection that Eriugena acquired in this way was bitterly resented. Referring to *The Book on Predestination*, Remigius, Bishop of Lyons, wrote:

And it is more shameful still and more insulting that they should have instructed the Irishman to write for them. Even the words of Scripture are unfamiliar to him, as we have confirmed beyond doubt from his writings. And he is so full of certain fanciful theories and erroneous opinions that not alone should he not be consulted, under any circumstances, in matters concerning the true faith, but he, along with his utterly laughable and contemptible writings, unless he quickly corrects or revises them, should rather be pitied as one who has lost his mind, or else condemned as a heretic. (*PL* 121, 1055A)

136 Contreni & Ó Néill, 1997.

Similarly, Florus of Lyons writes about "certain parts of this kingdom where this enemy of truth not only goes free from punishment or imposed silence but is actually held in the highest regard and esteem" (*PL* 119, 126B). But their complaints were in vain.

The publication of Eriugena's translations of Dionysius and Maximus must have greatly strengthened his position. Once the translations were published with the approval of the Emperor, probably in the early 860s, it would have been impossible for Eriugena's critics to object to his use of Greek sources, and no longer necessary for him to refrain from naming them. No doubt Eriugena's role as Court Poet was also a big help to him in keeping his enemies at bay. The poems on Dionysius and Maximus[137] were most likely intended to draw attention to the translation projects and to announce them to the public. Other poems, such as the following (written in Greek, in Homeric hexameter) appear to have been written to celebrate some political or military achievement, to be read out no doubt by Eriugena in the presence of the Emperor.

Iohannes Greets Lord Charles

To Charles, our King of Wonders, Life and Light.
Orthodox Commander of the Franks, Glory to him and Honour.
God-like and virtuous, our trusted and peerless Monarch
hope of our fatherland, the one who has earned immortality,
wearing the golden crown and the wreath of his fathers,
the sceptre in his hand, the true staff of his kingship.
O Christ, save your servant whom I call my Lord,
Charles the greatest of Leaders, to us and to the masses,
One who is wise and strong, restrained in all and powerful,
Magnificent, splendid, the glorious leader is revealed,
Like Mercury in the heavens, the star in the diadem,
The shining sun, the evening star, the white Goddess.
Grant that Charles may live for all of the ages.
Pray for these things now, O people; let all Francia pray. (*Carm*, No. 17)

---

137 Above, pp. 63–64, 83–84.

Unlike the poems in honour of Dionysius and Maximus, this one is not structured as an ascent into the heavens, presumably because the Emperor was still a mere mortal. Instead, Eriugena uses the "heaping up" of words and images that he admired so much in scriptural references to the Word of God.[138] It is notable that while the poem is in the form of a Christian prayer, it includes pre-Christian images also. Since the king appears to be wearing a two-tiered crown, it has been surmised that the occasion may have been the annexation of Lotharingia in 869.[139]

But while Eriugena's standing in the palace cannot be doubted, it is much more difficult to reconstruct the academic environment in which he was working. Was he writing with a realistic expectation that his work would be read and discussed by scholars—as he hoped *Periphyseon* would be in his letter to Wulfad?[140] Or was he an outcast, writing only for himself and his immediate circle of colleagues and friends?

If the fate of *Periphyseon* is any indication, then the latter would appear to have been the case. Admittedly the book was not condemned on publication, as *The Book on Predestination* was; but then its publication probably went unnoticed. As soon as the work did attract some attention, in the 12th century, condemnation was not long in coming. In 1225 Pope Honorius III proclaimed it to be "alive with the worms of foul heresy" (*PL* 122, 439–440) and ordered all copies, complete or partial, to be handed over to Church authorities for burning. It was placed on the *Index of Prohibited Books* in 1684, three years after Thomas Gale's edition appeared in print in Oxford; and there it remained until the *Index* itself was withdrawn in 1966.[141]

Eriugena Today

And then, remarkably, in the second half of the 20th century there was a new interest in Eriugena that now draws readers to him from

138 Above, p. 188.

139 Herren, 1993, pp. 151–152, Poem 17. Concerning this poem, see also Jeauneau (1979, pp. 16–20).

140 Above, p. 198.

141 Eriugena's influence prior to modern times is discussed in Beierwaltes (1987), O'Meara (1988, Ch. 11), and Moran (1989, Ch. 13).

both the Latin and the Greek traditions of Christian Europe. This happened principally because of the appearance, in 1933, of Cappuyns' scholarly biography of Eriugena[142] combined with new standards of excellence in the study of medieval texts. This gave us a clearer view of the historical setting in which Eriugena worked, what his sources were, and what was new in the things he had to say.

But there was also a new eagerness to hear him. For one thing, he sounds strangely "modern," with his great interest in the invisible structures of the universe and his search for "a theory of everything".[143] In addition, he has now begun to benefit from a new variety of European Studies, one that gives greater prominence to Central and Eastern Europe and is more aware of the debt of Rome to Byzantium. From his earliest writings, the most immediate professional problem facing Eriugena was a very simple one: he was an intellectual working in the West of Christendom, but the authors he most admired were from the East, as is already evident in *The Book on Predestination*. This was probably not the result of a "conversion" or indeed a conscious decision of any kind. More likely his distinctive version of Christianity grew slowly as he tried to integrate the Christianity he brought with him from Ireland with the Carolingian Christianity he encountered in his place of work, and at the same time, with the Christianity of the Eastern Church that he found in the Greek texts in the palace library, notably those of Gregory, Dionysius, and Maximus.

Whatever the circumstances of the discovery, the outcome was decisive. As Sheldon-Williams puts it:

> He fortuitously became acquainted with three of the most characteristic and important documents of the Greek Christian Platonism; the effect of their influence upon him was to bring him as wholly into the Greek tradition as if he had been a Byzantine writing in Greek, and to make of him the agent through whom the Western world came into this valuable inheritance (Sheldon-Williams, 1967, p. 520)

142 Cappuyns (1933)
143 See Carabine (2000, p. 109).

How well Eriugena understood the Greek tradition is another matter. His reading of it would certainly have been at odds with the teachings of the Orthodox Church in the ninth century, principally on account of its "unredeemed Origenism" (Meyendorff, 1994, p. 62).[144] Yet his knowledge of the two traditions was exceptional for that time, and to the extent that he tried to find a perspective broad enough to accommodate both, it can be said that he attempted a reconciliation. But the project was doomed from the outset. He lost his readership with the condemnation of *The Book on Predestination*, and by the ninth century the Latin Church was no longer interested in closer contacts with the East.

But things have been changing on that front also, and in ways that can give us a better appreciation of what Eriugena was attempting to do:

> Thus, in Eriugena's time, his system did not succeed in bridging the intellectual and spiritual gap between the two worlds, which continued to move on their separate ways. But today, as we know more about the problems which separated them, Eriugena deserves to be rediscovered, as a lonely but prophetic and powerful voice, searching for the right solutions, but hardly succeeding in a task much too vast to be handled by his lonely, isolated genius. (Meyendorff, 1994, p. 66)

These days, however, the Latin West *is* getting to know a lot more about the division of Christendom. This is due partly to Western scholars who have maintained an interest in the Greek Church, including Eriugenian scholars,[145] but also to a new wave of writing in English from the Eastern Church and its diaspora, some of it translated from modern Greek, Romanian, and other contemporary languages of the Orthodox Church. Here we can find a history of the philosophy and theology of the Eastern Church that is more

---

144 Ontologically, God and Creation are one in Eriugena, since the substance of created things lies in their Primordial Causes, and these are eternally in God.

145 See, for example, McGinn & Otten, 1994, and Petroff, 2002.

detailed and systematic than any that was previously available in the West.[146]

The picture of the schism that is emerging is surprising. We had been told, for example, that everything important in Greek philosophy was finally transmitted to the West when Latin translations of Aristotle became available to Aquinas. But Bradshaw (2004) shows, for example, that ἐνέργεια [enérgeia], a term that was coined by Aristotle and is central to his work, was translated into Latin using three different words (operatio, actus, and actualitas) with the result that a physical notion of the participation of Creation in the life of the divinity that would, in its original form, have proved extremely challenging for the West, became diluted and lost. In its place came a purely mental and intellectual interpretation of deification first developed by Augustine and later taken up by Aquinas.

For Bradshaw, this particular failure of communication is crucial for an understanding of the schism:

> If one were to summarize the differences between the Eastern and Western traditions in a single word, that word would be συνέργεια [synérgeia]. For the East, the highest form of communion with the divine is not primarily an intellectual act, but a sharing of life and activity. This seems to have been true among both pagans and Christians during the formative period of late antiquity, stretching back to the magical papyri and Hermetica, as well as to the New Testament and early Church Fathers. It led to a tendency to think of earthly, bodily existence as capable of being taken up and subsumed with the life of God. Emphasis was placed, not on any sudden transformation at death, but on the ongoing and active appropriation of those aspects of the divine life that are open to participation. (Bradshaw, 2004, p. 265).

Although the term energeia is rarely used by Eriugena, the idea is everywhere. He envisages the Divinity as a cosmic force running through all of Creation, the voice that utters the universe and must

---

146 For a brief overview of the literature I refer to, see the prefaces and bibliographies in Bradshaw (2004) and Russell (2004).

continue to utter it to ensure its existence, the water that flows through the "hidden pores" of body, the fire that is constantly consuming all of Creation, the experience of goodness and beauty that draws everything towards itself. The participation of the human in the divinity is therefore a physical as well as a mental process, while its counterpart in consciousness can never be more than a certain openness to the mystery of Creation. Meantime, in the Latin West, human participation in the divinity was gradually becoming restricted to the domain of rational belief.

It is hardly surprising, then, that the Eastern Church can still appear different and a little alien when viewed from the West. The schism *was* based on genuine and fundamental disagreements, all the more potent because they were already entrenched—culturally, linguistically, and demographically—long before they could be put it into words. Eriugena's proposed reconciliation in the ninth century, therefore, had no chance of succeeding. But it is surely another testament to the scope and depth of his work that a new wave of contemporary writing on the separation of the Greek and Latin Churches can help us to a better understanding of what he was saying more than a thousand years ago.

Be that as it may, the first thing to be done about Eriugena is to read what he wrote. He was right when he said it would be easy. Once you get used to the language and the main ideas, his work has the freshness of poetry and the clarity of all great philosophical writing. And the theme could hardly be more attractive, since it is the goodness and beauty of Creation, for which he has no explanation except to say that it is a form of participation in the life of the divinity. Moreover, it is active participation, since beauty must be created by the mind that experiences it, and so he sets out in his great masterpiece *Periphyseon* to do a complete inventory of everything there is, so as to experience the "beauty of truth" in every form it can possibly take, in the natural world and in the derived worlds of learning and art. And all of this, he says, is no more than the work being done throughout Creation as the many "natures" it contains, animate and inanimate, live out the forms of existence that have been given to them.

Chapter Summaries

Chapter 1 *Martianus Capella* shows Eriugena at work as a teacher of the liberal arts in the palace school of the Emperor, Charles the Bald. He is using the pre-Christian "school book" *De Nuptiis Philologiae et Mercurii* (Concerning the Marriage of Philology and Mercury) by Martianus Capella, a Roman of Greek stock who lived in the 5th century) to teach grammar, logic, rhetoric, geometry, mathematics, astronomy and music. From his extensive notes for students it becomes clear that Eriugena considers the teaching of the humanities to be just as important as religion for the salvation of the human. In addition, he sets Martianus's account of the seven liberal arts in a more general theory of the physical universe, making use of his knowledge of anatomy, biology and physics from Greek sources.

Chapter 2 *Gregory of Nyssa* presents Gregory's account of the human as contained in his *The Creation of the Human*, a book that Eriugena translated in its entirety and used extensively in his own work. He took a special interest in Gregory's claim that the mystery of the human mind is the image of God in Creation, while the beauty of Creation is likewise an image of its own Creator, the human mind. The chapter presents Gregory's deterministic theory of salvation, based on the fact that the physical structure of Creation assures its Return to the Creator. This too was adopted by Eriugena in his own account of salvation, as was Gregory's understanding of human wrongdoing as an unnatural "mixture" of human thought and animal emotion resulting from the Fall.

Chapter 3 *The Book on Predestination* describes Eriugena's unfortunate intervention in 850 in a local theological controversy. Asked by the

bishops of Rheims and Laon to refute the teachings of the monk
Gottschalk of Orbais, who said that some souls were predestined to
damnation, Eriugena wrote an enigmatic rebuttal that uses
Augustine to refute Gottshalk while at the same time hinting a
radical alternative to Western notions of salvation and damnation,
based on the Greek theology of deification, that would make the
notion of predestination to damnation absurd and blasphemous in
the first place. Although Eriugena does not use the word "deification" or name his Greek sources (principally Origen and Gregory of
Nyssa) *The Book on Predestination* was taken as an attack on the Latin
Church and promptly condemned.

Chapter 4 *Dionysius the Areopagite* presents the main ideas that
Eriugena took from this anonymous 5th or 6th century Greek
theologian. Eriugena translated all of his works into Latin, and uses
him as his principal authority on the subject of God. The chapter
explains the "way of negation" by which Dionysius broadened the
conventional understanding of divine imagery, and in the case of
Dionysius's *The Celestial Hierarchy* (a work that Eriugena annotated
after he had translated it) shows him working simultaneously as
translator and interpreter. This shows the distinctive ways in which
he extends Dionysius's notion of deification, heavily based on visual
imagery, in order to provide it with a more organic and developmental structure.

Chapter 5 *Maximus the Confessor* deals with the works of Maximus
(580–662) that were translated by Eriugena. It presents Maximus's
"five-fold division of everything" that is fundamental to the
spirituality of the Eastern Church, and his theory of the human as a
"microcosm" of Creation as a whole, in the sense that all levels of
Creation are to be found in it. These are two notions that will
dominate Eriugena's account of the human in *Periphyseon 4*. Likewise
with Maximus's description of the structure of the human soul
(defined by the triad *perception–reason–mind*) and, based on it, his
account of deification.

Chapter 6 *The Writings on John's Gospel* presents two shorter works of Eriugena, his celebrated homily on the prologue to John's Gospel, and a piece from the fragments of his intended commentary on John's Gospel. The homily is a fine example of Eriugena's poetic prose and one of the best short statements of his entire philosophy. It also reveals a nihilistic outlook rarely seen in the rest of his work. The text chosen from Eriugena's commentary on John concerns the "wilderness" (*desertum, díseart*), a recurring theme in Eriugena's work that allows him to combines the perspectives of cosmologist and hermit.

Chapter 7 *Periphyseon 1* outlines the structure of *Periphyseon* as a whole (based on Eriugena's four-fold division of everything) and the contents of its first book, on "nature uncreated and creating," i.e. God. Following Dionysius, he shows that while "divine metaphor" may be used to attribute any aspect of Creation to God, strictly speaking nothing can be "attributed" to him in the ordinary sense. He accepts the difficulties this poses both in theology and the spiritual life, but claims it is the only position that can be supported by rational argument. This involves him in discussions on the relation of reason to authority, theology, and the evidence of the senses.

Chapter 8 *Periphyseon 2* deals with Eriugena's treatment of the Primordial Causes, "nature created and creating" in his terms. It also sees the beginning of his *Hexameron*, i.e. his commentary on the creation of the world as described in *Genesis*, which will continue into the early pages of *Periphyseon 5*. He does not accept the usual interpretation of "the bare and empty earth" to mean unformed matter but thinks of it as a cosmic *desertum* (wilderness) and therefore a symbol of divinity itself and of the Primordial Causes pre-existing in it. He discusses the Trinity and the "procession" of the Word, linking it to Maximus's triad Mind-Reason-Perception, and the *filioque* controversy that was already beginning to mark out the theological boundary between the Latin and Greek Churches.

Chapter 9 *Periphyseon 3* deals with "nature created and not creating", i.e. Creation in the ordinary sense. Eriugena's account, however, is principally in the Eastern tradition, most notably in its treatment of Jesus Christ, the incarnate Word of God, as the *Pantokrator* (Ruler of All), i.e. the cosmic force that assures the continued existence of the universe from moment to moment, just as the spoken word assures the continued existence of the meaning it conveys. He discusses the interaction of the material world and the sensory systems by analogy with the interaction of water and earth in nature, and finds in it further proof of the spirituality of all matter and the immortality of animal souls—a point on which he disagrees even with the Greeks.

Chapter 10 *Periphyseon 4* is about the human, a topic that proved too big to be included with the rest of Creation in *Periphyseon 3*. Eriugena's takes the human to be a "microcosm" of Creation as whole, as taught by Maximus, to which he adds materials from Gregory, Dionysius, and Augustine. To understand the human, he says, it is necessary to consider it, however inadequately, in the deified form it will take when it is re-united with its Primordial Cause in the divinity. He argues that the permanent incompleteness of the human's understanding of itself constitutes its most fundamental similarity with the divine mind.

Chapter 11 *Periphyseon 5* discusses the Return of Creation to its Primordial Causes in God. What the human lost in the Fall, he argues, was human nature itself, and it is with this that it will be reunited in the Return. He presents the five stages of the Return, again taken from Maximus, and the three "aspects" of the final stage of Deification, those applying respectively to non-rational Creation, the human species as a whole, and the blessed. The chapter discusses the letter that Eriugena enclosed with the five volumes of *Periphyseon* when he sent them to his friend Wulfad for safe keeping.

Chapter 12 *The end of the story* draws together what is known of Eriugena's life at the palace school and how his work fared after his death. In spite of the protection afforded him by the Emperor and the support of colleagues and students, the condemnations of *The Book on Predestination* in 855 and 859 set severe limits to his readership during his lifetime, while the papal condemnation of *Periphyseon* in 1225 had a similar effect throughout the Latin Church. The chapter describes how all of this changed dramatically in the twentieth century, with the result that Eriugena now has more readers than ever before.

Further Reading

The following publications may be of use to readers, particularly those who would like to read more of the texts presented above. Most of the books mentioned are readily available, except for those that are indicated as being out of print or likely be found only in academic libraries.

Martianus Capella
Stahl, Johnson & Burge (1977) is an English translation of Martianus's *De nuptiis*. To my knowledge, there is no translation of Eriugena's *Annotationes in Martianum* into a modern language other than that of Ramelli (2006) into Italian.

Gregory of Nyssa
The text of *Peri kataskeués tou Anthropou* with an English translation can be found at www.ellopos.net/elpenor/physis/. The edition of the Greek text by Laplace (1943) has a translations into French that is available at www.gregoiredenysse.com. Salmona (1982) is a translation into Italian. Meredith (1999) is a general introduction to Gregory.

The Book on Predestination
Brennan (1998) is an English translation, and Mainoldi (2003) has an Italian translation beside his edition of the Latin text.

Dionysius the Areopagite
Luibhéid (1987) is a translation of all of Dionysius's writings into English. The book also contains an introduction to Dionysius, with contributions from a number of Dionysian scholars. Rorem (2005)

is a detailed analysis of Eriugena's commentary on *The Celestial Hierarchy*.

Maximus the Confessor

Some of the *Ambigua ad Iohannem* and *Questiones ad Thalassium* are translated into English in Louth (1996) and Blowers and Wilkin (2003), and other works of Maximus are translated and commented on in Berthold, Pelikan & Dalmais (1985) and Prassas (2010). All of these books provide a good introduction to the work of Maximus.

The Writings on the Gospel of John

There are French translations in Jeauneau's earlier (1969, 1999b) editions of the two works. There is an English translation of the homily in O'Meara (1988, pp. 158–176) and Bamford (2000, pp. 69–114).

Periphyseon

The first four books of Sheldon-Williams's edition of *Periphyseon* (Sheldon-Williams 1968, 1972, 1981, Jeauneau, O'Meara and Sheldon-Williams, 1995), with an English translation on the facing page, are available from the publisher (www.dias.ie). Readers of French (with access to an academic library) will find the introductions to the five volumes of Jeauneau's edition of *Periphyseon* invaluable (Jeauneau 1996, 1997, 1999a, 2000, 2003). A complete French translation of the Jeauneau edition is available in four volumes (Bertin 1995a, 1995b, 2009a, 2009b). Uhlfelder & Potter (1976/2011) is an English translation of about half of *Periphyseon*, with summaries of the sections not translated.

Poems

Eriugena's verse (Herren, 1993) with an English translation can be obtained from the publisher (www.dias.ie).

Eriugena's Life and Work

Cappuyns (1933) is still the only full-length biography, but is long out of print. Jeauneau provides a convenient short biography of Eriugena (in French) in the introduction to his 1969 edition of the

Homily on the Prologue to John's Gospel (Jeauneau 1969, pp. 9–50). Contreni and Ó Néill, in their edition of the *Old Testament Glossaries*, give an extended account of Eriugena's life that is of special interest because of the new material it contains (1997, pp. 17–85).

General

The work of Eriugena as a whole is presented and discussed in O'Meara (1988), Moran (1989), Otten (1991), and Carabine (2000). Jeauneau (1978) contains four short essays on Eriugena (in French) that provide a compelling portrait of Eriugena's personality and his style of writing as they appear to his principal modern editor.

The most important collection of recent research on Eriugena is contained in the eleven volumes reporting the proceedings of conferences held under the auspices of the SPES (Society for the Promotion of Eriugenian Studies) from 1973 to 2014. The books will be difficult to come by unless you have access to an academic library. The volumes in the series to date are:

O'Meara, J. J., and Bieler, L. (eds.) (1973) *The Mind of Eriugena*. Dublin: Irish University Press.

Roques, R. (ed.) (1975) *Jean Scot Erigène et l'histoire de la philosophie*. Paris: CNRS.

Beierwaltes, W. (ed.) (1980) *Eriugena: Studien zu seinen Quellen*. Heidelberg: Carl Winter Universitätsverlag.

Allard, G-H. (ed.) (1986) *Jean Scot écrivain*. Montréal: Bellarmin.

Beierwaltes, W. (ed.) (1987). *Eriugena Redivivus: Zur Wirkungsgeschichte seines Denkes im Mittelalter und im Übergang zur Neuzeit*. Heidelberg: Carl Winter Universitätsverlag.

Leonardi, C., and Mesestò E. (eds.) (1989) *Giovannia Scotto nel suo tempo. L'organizzazione del sapere in età carolingia*. Spoleto: Centro Italiano di Studi sul l'Alto Medioeve.

Beierwaltes, W. (ed.) (1990). *Begriff und Metapher: Sprachform des Denkens bei Eriugena*. Heidelberg: Carl Winter Universitätsverlag.

McGinn, B., and Otten, W. (eds.) (1994) *Eriugena East and West*. Notre Dame Indiana: University of Notre Dame Press.

Van Riel, G., Steele, C., and McEvoy, J. J. (1996). *Iohannes Scottus Eriugena: The Bible and Hermeneutics*. Leuven, Belgium: Leuven University Press.

McEvoy, J., and Dunne, M. (2002) *History and Eschatology in John Scottus Eriugena and his Time*. Leuven, Belgium: Leuven University Press.

Otten, W., and Allen, M. I. (2014) *Eriugena and Creation*. Instrumenta Patristica et Mediaevalia 68. Turnhout: Brepols.

References

Aquinas, Thomas *Commentarium super Epistolam ad Hebraeos.* Navarra: Universidad de Navarra.
At www.corpusthomisticum.org/icorpus.html.

Barbet, J.(ed.) (1975) *Johannis Scotti Eriugenae Expositiones in Ierarchiam Caelestem. CCCM* 31. Turnhout: Brepols.

Beierwaltes, W. (ed.) (1987) *Eriugena Redivivus: Zur Wirkungsgeschichte seines Denkens im Mittelalter und im Übergang zur Neuzeit.* Heidelberg: Carl Winter.

Berthold, G. C., Pelikan, J. & Dalmais, I. (eds.) (1985) *Maximus Confessor: Selected Writings.* New York: Paulist Press.

Bertin, F. (1995a, 1995b, 2009a, 2009b) *De la division de la nature: Periphyseon* Livres 1–5. Paris: Presses Universitaires de France

Blowers, P. M., & Wilkin, R. L. (ed.) (2003) *On the Cosmic Mystery of Jesus Christ: Selected Writings from St Maximus the Confessor.* New York: St Vladimir's Seminary Press.

Bradshaw, D. (2004). *Aristotle East and West.* Cambridge: Cambridge University Press.

Brennan, M. (1986) Materials for the biography of Johannes Scottus Eriugena. *Studi Medievali* 3a (27), 413–460.

——. (1998) *Treatise on Divine Predestination.* Notre Dame, Indiana: University of Notre Dame Press.

Byron, M. *Historicizing Modernism: Ezra Pound's Eriugena.* London: Bloomsbury 2014

Cappuyns, M. (1933) *Jean Scot Érigène: Sa vie, son oeuvre, sa pensée.* Paris: Desclée de Brouwer.

——. (ed.) (1965) Le *De Imagine* de Grégoire de Nysse traduit par Jean Scot Erigène. *Recherches de théologie ancienne et médiévale* 32, 205–262. Also at *Oxford Text Archive* http://ota.ahds.ac.uk. Text 0582.

Carabine, D. (2000) *John Scottus Eriugena*. Oxford University Press.

Contreni, J. & Ó Néill, P. (1997) *Glossae Divinae Historiae: The Biblical Glosses of John Scottus Eriugena*. Firenze: SISMEL Edizioni di Galluzzo.

Dronke, P. (1984) Theologia veluti quaedam poetria: quelques observations sur la fonction des images poétique chez Jean Scot. In Dronke, P. *The Medieval Poet and his World* (pp. 39–54). Roma: Edizioni di Storia et Letteratura.

Dutton, P. E. (2002). Eriugena's workshop: the making of the Periphyseon in Reims 875. In McEvoy, J. and Dunne, M. (eds) *History and Eschatology in John Scottus Eriugena and his Time.* Leuven: Leuven University Press.

Flanagan, D. & Flanagan L. (1994) *Irish Place Names*. Dublin: Gill & Macmillan.

Flower, R. (1966) *The Irish Tradition*. Oxford: Clarendon Press.

Gersh, S. & Moran, D. (eds) (2006) *Eriugena, Berkeley, and the Idealist Tradition*. Indiana: University of Notre Dame Press.

Giet, S. (ed.) (1968) *Basile de Césarée: Homélies sur l'Hexaéméron*. Paris: CERF.

Guillaumin, J.-Y. & Hamman, A.-G. (1982) *Gregoire de Nysse: La creation de l'homme.* Paris: Desclée De Brouwer.

Heil, G. (1970) *Denys l'Aréopagite: La hiérarchie céleste*. Paris: CERF.

Herren, M. W. (ed.) (1993) *Iohannis Scotti Eriugenae Carmina*. Dublin: Institute of Advanced Studies.

Jeauneau, É. (ed.) (1969) *Jean Scot: Homélie sur le Prologue de Jean*. Paris: CERF.

———. (ed.) (1978a) *Commentaire Érigénien sur Martianus Capella*. In É. Jeauneau *Quatre Thèmes Érigéniens* (pp. 91–166). Montréal: l'Institut d'Études Médiévales Albert-le-Grand.

———. (1978b) *Quatre Thèmes Érigéniens*. Montréal: l'Institut d'Études Médiévales Albert-le-Grand.

———. (1979) Jean Scot Érigène et le Grec. *Archivum Latinitatis Medii Aevi (ALMA) Bulletin du Cange* 41, 5–50. Also at http://hdl.handle.net/2042/3309

———. (ed.) (1996, 1997, 1999a, 2000, 2003) *Ioannes Scottus Eriugena: Periphyseon. CCCM* 161–165. Turnhout: Brepols.

REFERENCES

——. (ed.) (2008) Iohannis Scotti seu Eriugenae, *Homilia super 'In principio erat verbum'* et *Commentarius in Evangelium Iohannis. CCCM* 166. Turnhout: Brepols.

Jeauneau, É. & Dutton, P. E. (1996) *The Autograph of Eriugena.* Turnhout: Brepols.

Jeauneau, É., O'Meara, J. J., & Sheldon-Williams, I. P. (eds.) (1995) *Iohannis Scotti Eriugenae Periphyseon (De Divisione Naturae): Liber Quartus.* Dublin: Institute of Advanced Studies.

Kirk, G. S. (2010) *Heraclitus: The Cosmic Fragments.* Cambridge: Cambridge University Press.

Kneale, W. & Kneale, M. (1962) *The Development of Logic.* Oxford: Clarendon Press.

Laga, C., & Steele, C. (eds.) (1980, 1990) *Maximi Confessoris Quaestiones ad Thalassium una cum Latina interpretatione Iohannis Scotti Eriugenae iuxta posita. CCSG* 7, 22. Turnhout: Brepols.

Langer, S. (1953) *Feeling and Form: A Theory of Art.* London: Routledge & Kegan Paul.

Laplace, J. (1943) *La création de l'homme.* Sources Chrétienns 6. Paris: CERF. Also at www.gregoiredenysse.com

Louth, A. (ed.) (1996) *Maximus the Confessor.* Oxford: Routledge.

Luibhéid, C., & Rorem, P. (1987) *Pseudo-Dionysius: The Complete Works.* New York: Paulist Press.

Lutz, C. E. (ed.) (1939) *Iohannis Scotti annotationes in Marcianum.* Cambridge, Mass.: The Mediaeval Academy of America.

Mac Aogáin, E. (2009) *Iohannes ó Éirinn agus Máistrí na Gréige.* Dublin: Coiscéim.

Madec, G. (ed.) (1986) Jean Scot et ses auteurs. In Allard, G.-H. (Ed.) *Jean Scot écrivain.* Montréal: Bellarmin

Mainoldi, E. S. (ed.) (2003a) *De praedestinatione liber: Dialettica e teologia all'apogeo della rinascenza carolingia.* Fierenze: Edizioni del Galluzzo.

Mainoldi, E. (2003b) Le fonti del *De praedestinatione liber* di Giovanni Scoto Eriugena. *Studi medievali* 45(2), 651–697.

Malherbe, A. J. & Ferguson, E. (2006) *Gregory of Nyssa: The Life of Moses.* San Francisco: Harper Collins.

McGinn, B., and Otten, W. (eds.) (1994) *Eriugena East and West.* Notre Dame Indiana: University of Notre Dame Press

Meredith, A. (1999) *Gregory of Nyssa.* London: Routledge.

Meyendorff, J. (1994) Remarks on eastern patristic thought in John
Scottus Eriugena. In McGinn, B. and Otten, W. (eds.) *Eriugena:
East and West* (pp. 51–68). Notre Dame: University of Notre Dame
Press.

Moran, D. (1989) *The Philosophy of John Scottus Eriugena: A Study of
Idealism in the Middle Ages*. Cambridge: Cambridge University Press.

Muhr, K. (1999). Water imagery in early Irish. *Celtica 23*, 193–210.

O'Meara, D. J. (1987) Eriugena and Aquinas on the Beatific Vision.
In W. Beierwaltes (ed.) *Eriugena Redivivus* (pp. 224–236). Heidelberg:
Karl Winter

O'Meara, J. J. (1988) *Eriugena*. Oxford: Clarendon Press.

Otten, W. (1991) *The Anthropology of Johannes Scottus Eriugena*. Leiden:
Brill.

Petroff, V. V. (2002) *Theoriae* of the Return in John Scottus. In J.
McEvoy and M. Dunne (eds.) *History and Eschatology in John Scottus
Eriugena and his Time*. Leuven: Leuven University Press.

Prassas, D. D. (2010) *St. Maximus the Confessor: Questions and Doubts*.
DeKalb, Ill: Northern Illinois University Press.

Ramelli, I. (2006) *Tutti i Commenti a Marziano Capella*. Milano:
Bompiani.

Rorem, P. (2005) *Eriugena's Commentary on the Dionysian Celestial
Hierarchy*. Toronto: Pontifical Institute of Mediaeval Studies.

Russell, N. (2004) *The Doctrine of Deification in the Greek Patristic Tradition*.
Oxford: Oxford University Press.

Ryan, J. J. (1931) *Irish Monasticism: Origins and Early Development*.
Dublin: Talbot Press.

Salmona, B. (2000) *Gregorio di Nissa: L'Uomo*. Roma: Città Nuova.

Sheldon-Williams, I. P. (1967) The Greek Christian Platonist
tradition from the Cappadocians to Maximus and Eriugena. In H.
A. Armstrong (ed.) *The Cambridge History of Later Greek and Early
Medieval Philosophy*. Cambridge: Cambridge University Press.

——. (ed.) (1968, 1972, 1981) *Iohannis Scotti Eriugenae Periphyseon (De
Divisione Naturae): Liber Primus, Secundus, Tertius*. Dublin: Institute of
Advanced Studies.

Stein, B. E. & Meredith, M. A. (1993) *The Merging of the Senses*.
Cambridge, Mass.: MIT Press

REFERENCES

Uhlfelder, M. L. & Potter, J. A. (1976) *Periphyseon: On the Division of Nature*. Indianapolis: Bobbs-Merrill.

Willis, J. (ed.) (1983) *De nuptiis Philologiae et Mercurii*. Leipzig: Teubner.

Wolters, C. (ed.) (1961) *The Cloud of Unknowing*. Harmondsworth, UK: Penguin Books.

Subject Index

Ambrose 196

Anastasius the Librarian 79n, 80

Aquinas, Thomas 114, 210

Aristotle 25, 46, 94, 98; Categories 121, 132; *energeia* 210

Athens 25, 61, 63

Augustine 41–2, 47–8, 54–6, 59, 136–9, 143, 195, 210

Basil of Caesarea 19, 25, 137, 154–5, 163

Bede, Venerable 23

Boethius 22–3, 42, 57

Charlemagne 61

Charles the Bald, Emperor, King 1, 41, 43–5, 79, 132, 205–7

deification (*theósis*) 22–3, 29, 32, 35–40, 52–7, 63–4, 72, 78, *84–91*, 92–6, 107–9, 129, 135, 140, 142–3, 150, 152, 158, 166, 168, 171, 179, 182, 186, 192, 195–9, as predestination 47–52

Denys, St. 79n

Dionysius the Areopagite 15, 43, 49, 56–7, *61–81*, 83, 95–6, 103, 112, 114, 119, 124–6, 147–8, 151–2, 170, 177–9, 183, 189, 206–8.

Eastern and Western Christianity 47–52, 55–8, 143–7, 152–5, 208–12

elements (fire, air, water, earth) 4–11, 44, 49–52, 75–7, 104–5, 128–30, 134–5, 145–6, 163, fire 4, 47–9, 75–8, 145–6, fire and air 8–11,

13–14, water and earth 155–60, fire and deification 49–52

emotion, feeling 6–8, 14, 84–7, 181–3, and reason 16–17, 36–8

Eriugena; life at the palace 203–8, handwriting 204; name 84, Old Irish glossaries 205; translator 80–1, 98

Filioque controversy 143–47

Florus of Lyon 206

Gale, Thomas. 115n, 208

good and evil 16, 35–7; tree of 181–3 primacy of goodness 152; evil as a "mixture" of intellect and emotion 14–5, 18, 36–8, 85–6

Gottschalk of Orbais 41–2, 55, 60

grace and nature 41, 50–5, 72–3, 189

Gregory Nazianzen 25, 95

Gregory of Nyssa 13–19, *25–40*, 43, 47, 50, 52–3, 56–7, 68, 78, 83–5, 93–4, 98, 116, 120, 130, 132, 134, 137, 139–43, 152, 155–9, 161, 166, 170, 172, 177–83, 188, 190, 208–9, on the *microcosm* 171–5; on the souls of animals 162–4

Heraclitus 28

Hincmar Archbishop of Reims 41–3, 58, 60,

Honorius III, Pope 207

human (species) 31–6, 91–4, *166–84*, definition of 168–71, 175–9, as microcosm 107–9, 171–5. Return of 38–40, 185–95

226

Author Index